THE
FAIR
TRADE
HAND
BOOK

THE FAIR TRADE HAND BOOK

BUILDING A BETTER WORLD, TOGETHER

EDITED BY
Gavin Fridell
Zack Gross
Sean McHugh

FERNWOOD PUBLISHING
HALIFAX & WINNIPEG

Editing: Erik Johnson & Brenda Conroy
Text design: Brenda Conroy
Cover design: Evan Marnoch
Printed and bound in Canada

Published by Fernwood Publishing
32 Oceanvista Lane, Black Point, Nova Scotia, B0J 1B0
and 748 Broadway Avenue, Winnipeg, Manitoba, R3G 0X3
www.fernwoodpublishing.ca

Fernwood Publishing Company Limited gratefully acknowledges the financial support of the Government of Canada, the Canada Council for the Arts, the Manitoba Department of Culture, Heritage and Tourism under the Manitoba Publishers Marketing Assistance Program and the Province of Manitoba, through the Book Publishing Tax Credit, for our publishing program. We are pleased to work in partnership with the Province of Nova Scotia to develop and promote our creative industries for the benefit of all Nova Scotians.

Library and Archives Canada Cataloguing in Publication

Title: The fair trade handbook : building a better world, together / edited by Gavin Fridell, Zack Gross, Sean McHugh.
Names: Fridell, Gavin, editor. | Gross, Zack, editor. | McHugh, Sean (Fair trade expert), editor.
Description: Includes bibliographical references and index.
Identifiers: Canadiana (print) 20210258306 | Canadiana (ebook) 20210259396 | ISBN 9781773634883 (softcover) | ISBN 9781773635088 (EPUB) | ISBN 9781773635095 (PDF)
Subjects: LCSH: International trade—Moral and ethical aspects. | LCSH: Social responsibility of business. | LCSH: Competition, Unfair.
Classification: LCC HF1379 .F35 2021 | DDC 382/.3—dc23

Contents

Part Two: Fair Trade in Action / 73

*To all those working to create a fairer
and more sustainable world*

Foreword

Common Goals, Shared Ideals

On September 25, 2015, the world came together to adopt the most ambitious development strategy in our history, the UN's Sustainable Development Goals. These seventeen goals provide ideals to work toward, but more than that, they provide light in what can sometimes be a dark and gloomy world. More than the goals themselves, two key pillars emerge to me: 1) that no one should and can be left behind, and 2) that none of us can stand on the sidelines, that each and every one of us must contribute and be part of the solution.

There is no question that the world faces an array of challenges. Our history shows us that change comes slowly and not always easily. How then do we not only make the case for change, but also realize that change and finally begin addressing the world's problems, from inequality and poverty to climate change, decreasing diversity and racial injustice.

I believe it starts with finding ideals that each of us can agree on — ideals that cut across age, race, religion and political outlook; ideals that centre on building a happy, healthy, balanced world, where everyone has access to the basic wants and needs of life; ideals that bring our life on Earth into balance with the planet itself. One of those ideals is fair trade.

From these ideals come goals, or a common agenda for governments, business, public institutions and individuals to work toward. To achieve those goals, we must focus on our commonalities and accept that each of us is different. Being different is not only okay; it is what makes life on Earth so interesting.

This book explores many of these ideals and goals, while providing insight into how we got here. Most importantly, however, the book dives into ideas that can start addressing the many challenges our world faces. The challenges, as always, are daunting, but the momentum, energy and knowledge of fair traders and our allies are equally powerful and, in my view, up to the task. It is time to build and rebuild, renew and refresh, and push forward to a fair world for all.

— Sean McHugh

Acknowledgements

At a breakout session of the CFTN (Canadian Fair Trade Network) National Fair Trade Conference in Ottawa in 2019, Zack said "We need to write a book!" Little did we know how serious he was. And so began this endeavour!

The Fair Trade Handbook is not just the dream or work of three people but has had input from countless others – our team of authors, illustrators, photographers, editors, designers, fair trade activists and producers – all those who made our book better and also make the world a better place.

We thank our families, colleagues and friends for supporting us in this effort, and in the future not only using and promoting the information and ideas in the Handbook but in continuing the quest to sustain, grow and improve fair trade.

Gavin: Very special thanks, beyond words, are owed to Kate Ervine, Sasha Fridell-Ervine and Sebastian Fridell-Ervine for all that they do.

Sean: Thanks to my partner, Marianne Pemberton, for her unwavering support, and to our daughter Chloe, who we welcomed into our family midway through writing.

Zack: Heartfelt thanks to Jennifer Thompson for almost half a century of sharing our quest for social change. We hope our children, their partners and our grandchildren will benefit from these efforts, and we acknowledge gratefully where they have continued to carry the torch.

Special appreciation to Erik Johnson, for his discerning eye for grammar and consistency, whose careful copyediting work made the book that much better. And we thank Errol Sharpe, Beverley Rach, Anumeha Gokhale, Deb Mathers, Brenda Conroy and everyone at Fernwood Publishing for embracing us and our idea and making the book a reality.

This research was undertaken, in part, thanks to funding from the Canada Research Chairs Program and Saint Mary's University. Big thanks to the Canadian Fair Trade Network, our board of directors, advisory council members, funders and supporters, for the flexibility to put time into this book.

We accept all questions, critical thoughts and praise at <http://www.cftn.ca/fair-trade-handbook>.

Contributors

HAROON AKRAM-LODHI teaches agrarian political economy. He is a professor of economics and international development studies at Trent University and is also editor-in-chief of the *Canadian Journal of Development Studies*.

BILL BARRETT is a worker-owner of Planet Bean, a Fairtrade Certified and organic coffee roastery which he founded in 1997. Over the years, he has developed and facilitated hundreds of educational programs for students at all stages of education, worked extensively with unions and nongovernmental organizations, produced several independent films and travelled extensively around the globe. He has been on the board of Fairtrade Canada since 2016 and is its current chair.

ERIN BIRD is an engineer by day for the City of Calgary but her second "job" and passion is to lead the campaign for Calgary to become a Fair Trade Town. Erin is a member of Engineers Without Borders and an executive board member of the Canadian Fair Trade Network. Erin's other hobbies are cooking with Fairtrade ingredients, dancing in Fairtrade banana costumes, reading while drinking Fairtrade tea and relaxing with family and friends.

JENNIE COLEMAN has been owner/president of Equifruit since 2013. She combines a lengthy career in business with longstanding social justice roots, set during two years' volunteer work in Namibia in the mid-90s. She is a former co-chair of the Fairtrade Canada board of directors and loves fair trade for its pragmatic approach to international development. She loves Equifruit for... the fruit (yum!), the farmers and the fact that something as simple as eating a fair trade banana can have such a positive impact on someone's life.

SERGI CORBALÁN is the executive director of the Fair Trade Advocacy Office, a joint fair trade movement initiative based in Brussels. Sergi studied law and international politics and has 20 years of experience in public policy advocacy at the EU and international levels.

SUJATA DEY is the former trade campaigner at the Council of Canadians and an economics student. Dey has 20 years of experience in NGO work, writes for the *Huffington Post* on trade and regularly comments on trade agreements.

KATE ERVINE is an associate professor in the International Development Studies Program at Saint Mary's University and a faculty associate with Saint Mary's School of the Environment. Her research focuses on the global political economy of climate change mitigation, carbon trading and offsetting, carbon finance and global climate justice. She is the author of *Carbon*, published in 2018 with Polity Press.

GAVIN FRIDELL is a professor and Canada Research Chair in International Development Studies at Saint Mary's University and a member of the Royal Society of Canada's College of New Scholars. He has researched widely on trade justice and his publications include *Coffee* (Polity Press: 2014), *Alternative Trade: Legacies for the Future* (Fernwood: 2013) and *Fair Trade Coffee: The Prospects and Pitfalls of Market-Driven Social Justice* (University of Toronto Press: 2007). He and a member of the Advisory Board of the Canadian Fair Trade Network and is currently conducting research on global trade agreements and trade justice.

MARA FRIDELL is an assistant professor in the Department of Sociology at the University of Manitoba. She researches in the areas of political economy and social reproduction. Along with Mark Hudson and Ian Hudson, she has co-authored several peer reviewed articles on fair trade as well as the book *Fair Trade, Sustainability and Social Change.*

MONIKA FIRL has worked in the Cooperative Coffees Montreal office since 2002 as green coffee buyer, producer relations manager and, now, as director of sustainability. Prior to this, she lived and worked in Central America and Mexico for nearly a decade, promoting locally based development projects focused on alternative technology, farmer-to-farmer learning, best organic practices and alternative markets. This cumulative experience has fueled her keen interest in the symbiotic role of healthy soil, carbon sequestration and climate change mitigation. Monika holds a master's degree in journalism as well as a bachelor's in international relations and German.

ZACK GROSS recently retired as coordinator of Fair Trade Manitoba, based at the Manitoba Council for International Cooperation in Winnipeg.

He continues in fair trade as a member of the CFTN's Advisory Council, as a board member at Fairtrade Canada and as chair of the board of the Marquis Project in Brandon. He also sits on the board of his local food bank in Gimli, MB. Zack is also a former president of the CFTN board and a recipient of Fairtrade Canada's Lifetime Achievement Award. Zack facilitates online courses in the International Development Studies Diploma program at UBC and writes a regular "Small World" Op. Ed. column in the *Brandon Sun*.

MADISON HOPPER has been both a researcher and practitioner of fair trade for over six years as the executive director of Fair Trade Toronto (a civil society organization), on the board of Fairtrade Canada and as a marketing co-coordinator with Equifruit, a fair trade fruit importer.

IAN HUDSON is a professor in the Department of Economics at the University of Manitoba. He researches in the areas of political economy and ethical consumption. Along with Mark Hudson and Mara Fridell, he has co-authored several peer reviewed articles on fair trade as well as the book *Fair Trade, Sustainability and Social Change*.

MARK HUDSON is an associate professor in the Department of Sociology, and the coordinator of the Global Political Economy Program at the University of Manitoba. His research is focused on the ways in which capitalism structures socioecological relations. In addition to his research on fair trade and ethical consumerism with Ian Hudson and Mara Fridell, he is currently researching the political economy of fossil fuels and climate change.

NADIA IBRAHIM is the former coordinator of the Trade Justice Network and worked as a researcher on a variety of topics, including the impacts of trade agreements on gender equality, public services, the environment and food and agriculture systems. She now works as a staff representative at a national labour union. Nadia holds a master's degree in political economy from Carleton University and a bachelor's in global political economy from the University of Manitoa.

NELL JEDRZEJCZYK is studying resource and environmental management for her bachelor of environment at Simon Fraser University. Nell's start in fair trade came through coordinating SFU's student-led Fair Trade Ambassador Program, where she supported the university's continued efforts to educate and empower students and have a positive impact on the world through its purchasing. In her position as national programs coordinator with the Canadian Fair Trade Network, Nell is building on her efforts and experience at SFU by supporting other Canadian campuses in their development of similar programs.

ELENA LUNDER is a project advisor at the Fair Trade Advocacy Office, a joint fair trade movement initiative based in Brussels. Elena studied European studies and international human rights law, and, in her work, she focuses on strong human rights and environmental due diligence as part of public policy.

LAURA MACDONALD is a professor in the Department of Political Science and the Institute of Political Economy at Carleton University. She has published numerous articles in journals and edited collections on such issues as the role of NGOs in development, global civil society, social policies and citizenship struggles in Latin America, Canadian development assistance, Canada-Latin American relations and the political impact of the North American Free Trade Agreement (NAFTA). Her recent work looks at transnational activism in North America around labour rights, migration and human rights in Mexico, and policies to reduce crime and violence in Mexico City.

MARK MARSOLAIS-NAHWEGAHBOW is Ojibwe and a band member of Whitefish River First Nation, located on Birch Island, Ontario, in the District of Manitoulin Island and is the founder of the Innovative First Nations social enterprise, Birch Bark Coffee Company. He is on a mission to change Indigenous lives across Canada by providing and installing free certified water purification systems to every Indigenous home suffering under boil-water advisories.

SEAN MCHUGH is the founder and executive director of the Canadian Fair Trade Network (CFTN). Sean's passion for sustainability, grew out of international travel (2004–2009) and time spent working in Kenya. After helping to organize fair trade cities and campuses across the country, in 2011 Sean founded the CFTN and has overseen the planning of numerous programs, seven national conferences and the organization's bi-annual publication *Fair Trade Magazine*. Sean represents Canada on the International Fair Trade Towns Committee.

NELSON CAMILO MELO MAYA is a small producer of high quality and certified organic coffee in Cauca, Colombia, with his own brand, Nelson Melo, in the US market. He is the chair and legal representative of the Organic Producers Association of Cauca (ORGANICA). He has been member of the board of the Latin American and Caribbean Network of Fair Trade Small Producers and Workers (CLAC) and worked for CLAC as a strengthening official. He has worked as general secretary of the Colombian Initiative of Small Fair Trade Producers. He was vice-chair of the Small Producers' Symbol (SPP) and was elected its chair in June 2018.

SARAH NIMAN is a freelance writer and an articling student who lives and works on the unceded Algonquin Anishinaabe territory also known as Ottawa. She has a bachelor of journalism from Carelton University, and a juris doctor in common law from the University of Ottawa, with an option in Aboriginal law and Indigenous legal traditions.

ROXANA OLIVERA is a Toronto-based investigative journalist. Her reporting has appeared in the CBC, *Media, Huffington Post, The Walrus, El País, New Internationalist, Revista Ideele, Broadview,* and the *United Church Observer.* She won the journalist-in-residence fellowship from Osgoode Hall Law School (2017–2019) and awards from the New York Festival's International Radio Program Awards and the Associated Church Press in Chicago. She was a recipient of the prestigious Al Neuharth Innovation in Investigative Journalism Award (2015) for her joint work effort with the International Consortium of Investigative Journalism on a global investigation into forced evictions financed by the World Bank. Her work is informed with a passion for the rule of law, human rights and social justice, and it has been published in English, Spanish and German.

JOEY PITOELLO is a worker-member and general manager of Just Us! Coffee Roasters Co-op and a small-scale organic farmer in Hortonville, Nova Scotia. A worker-owned co-operative for over 25 years, Just Us! is inspired by the potential solutions that democratic business and supply chains offer the solidarity economy.

JERÓNIMO PRUIJN has a master's degree in anthropology. Originally from Holland, he has lived for over 30 years in Mexico. He began his work with fair trade in the late 1980s as a volunteer in the first fair trade label, Max Havelaar Netherlands. He has worked for organizations, networks and companies of organizations of small producers. He has served as executive director of the Café La Selva coffee chain, the Network Against Extreme Poverty, Fair Trade Mexico, and was the Mexican coordinator of Small Producers of Fair Trade and the Latin American and Caribbean coordinator of the Latin American and Caribbean Network of Fair Trade Small Producers and Workers (CLAC), AGROMERCADOS and SERJUSTO. He represented CLAC in the Fairtrade International Standards Committee from 2007 to 2013. Since 2009 he has served as executive director of SPP Global, an intercontinental network of organizations of small organic producers.

DARRYL REED is professor in the Faculty of Management at the University of British Columbia, Okanagan Campus, after having taught at York University for many years. His research interests include development, co-operatives studies, fair trade and business ethics. He serves as the president of the Green Campus Co-operative, a fair trade garment company.

CURT SHOULTZ has been an artist and educator in Brandon, Manitoba, since 1982. In addition to thousands of freelance art jobs for people and businesses in western Manitoba, Curt worked for DC comics as an inker. Following his muse, Curt has created a number of stories and paintings on the theme of fairness. He is the director of the Centre for Teaching, Learning and Technology at Brandon University.

ÉRIC ST-PIERRE is a photojournalist and the publisher of "Fair Trade: A Human Journey," a collection of 350 photographs and stories, taken in 15 countries throughout Asia, Africa and Latin America, covering 14 different product sectors.

JENNIFER WILLIAMS has, for over 20 years, been focused on how business can be an instrument to create a kind, just and sustainable world. Jennifer worked in microcredit in Northern Ghana and with women entrepreneurs in Ottawa, and she was instrumental in the growth of a worker-owned business that pioneered fair trade in Canada. Jennifer is a trusted advisor to companies that have sustainability in their DNA and co-owns an organic and local home delivery business that is focused on sustainability. Her four children keep her focused on why creating a more sustainable future is so important.

MARTIN VAN DEN BORRE has spent 20 years working as a cooperative developer, serving on several boards and national work groups and promoting the social and solidarity economy in Cuba and the world. He proudly acts as ambassador for the SPP Global cooperative, which unites over 300,000 small organized farmers. He was a worker-owner of La Siembra Cooperative, the North American pioneer of fair trade cocoa and sugar. He currently works as a consultant with various social economy organizations and is building a small coffee roasting workshop on his farm in western Québec.

*Juan Gonzalez rakes coffee drying in the sun on the large "patio" at the
Cooperative Montes de Oro in Costa Rica. As members of coocafe, they export
some of the finest Fairtrade-certified coffee in the world.
Source: Éric St-Pierre*

1

Why Write a Book on Fair Trade?

THE BOOK
By Zack Gross

At some point in our lives, we humans — possibly sensing that the end is near or maybe just not able to stand the clutter any longer — decide to downsize. In the households of anyone with an academic or social justice bent, there is bound to be a lot of clutter, and much of it is books and magazines. In a token show of at least trying to downsize, you might donate several boxes of books to a local thrift shop or fundraising book sale.

How we choose the books to get rid of is based on what value they now have in our lives. So, on the chopping block you might find the less memorable murder mysteries and spy thrillers, fantasy novels and certain books of which, somehow, we find ourselves owning two or even three copies. What an activist might keep are those Saul Alinsky books about community organizing, the large collection of thoroughly depressing volumes on genocide, poverty and environmental destruction, and some favourite fiction too! The books we keep are those that continue to have meaning for us, even though some might have been purchased many long years ago.

That is our hope for this book on fair trade[1] — that you, the reader, will read it, use it as a tool for global and local social change, buy more copies of it and hand them around (for sure!) and still think it has something special to say and is worth keeping when you decide to downsize sometime down the line. Well, you've accomplished the first part — you now own the book! The rest is laid out before you.

The idea for *The Fair Trade Handbook* came out of a conversation at a Canadian fair trade conference in Ottawa in 2019, where people's enthusiasm to find the "next big thing" to tell our story came together. The idea to have chapters dedicated to different commodities, different cross-cutting topics, different geographic regions and different forms of advocacy is an indication of the breadth of fair trade. And the commitment to take a critical — not just a promotional — view of fair trade is an indication of the integrity and transparency of the writer-practitioners involved. The effort to include authors from across Canada and from around the world, from diverse backgrounds and experiences, to look for creative ways to express ourselves (like a graphic novel chapter) — and to have editors from the East Coast, the West Coast and the Prairie Middle — is an indication that fair trade isn't something only relevant to one group, one city or one point of view.

A few times in any career, one will find real community. One significant community experience for the three of us has been among fair traders. It has been a great learning and building experience working with a multisector group of advocates, coming from NGOs, business, government, unions, academia, schools and faith-based groups. This is also reflected in the people who have written the book you are holding.

The Fair Trade Handbook is a how-to book. It is also a what-is book, a how-did-it-get-that-way book and a what-should-we-do-about-it book. We hope that you will see many ways in which you can use this volume as a tool to educate about and advocate for fair trade, and as a vehicle to promote concrete, positive social change in your community and around the world. Read the book and tell others about it. Seek out what the various authors are up to and support their work, whether you buy their coffee or chocolate, volunteer for their organizations or just follow them on social media. Put a copy of the book in your local public, high school or college library. Tell your local bookstores about it. Write a book review for your local media. Invite an author to speak at a local event. Suggest the book — or send a copy — to local politicians, relevant business owners, teachers and professors. Give the book out as a prize at appropriate events.

We need a relentless, respectful, results-oriented personal and public effort to transform our world in small ways and in large, with a view to fair trade principles and practices. We need to care about producers and take action with them. Many struggle at the bottom of economic and social indices while providing us with food, clothing and other commodities. We also need to stand with those unique businesses who bring fair trade products to our shelves. These businesses choose ethics over profit, even when they are struggling to get by. This book shares their stories and those of their allies and partners, and it outlines what we can and must do in solidarity with them.

THE CONTEXT

By Gavin Fridell

We would not need fair trade, of course, if the global economy was not so uneven. Capitalism has often been compared to Prometheus, a Titan who, in ancient Greek mythology, forged humanity out of clay and gave it fire. For his efforts, Prometheus was condemned by Zeus to eternal torment for defying the gods.

Prometheus is often seen as a symbol of human ambition, science and technological domination, as well as its unintended and tragic consequences. Under capitalism, the global market creates unprecedented wealth alongside unprecedented inequality. It spurs continual technological revolution alongside rampant, unchecked climate change that threatens the basis of human existence.

There is no shortage of evidence of these Promethean results. Global inequality is at shocking levels. According to Oxfam International, in 2019, the world's richest 1 percent had more than twice as much a wealth as 6.9 billion people, while almost half of the world lived on less than $5.50 a day. These inequalities are intensified by climate change, which, despite dire warnings, continues unabated, with global carbon emissions far higher than they need to be to meet internationally-agreed upon targets. In a 2019 report entitled *Climate Change and Poverty*, the UN Special Rapporteur on Extreme Poverty and Human Rights declared: "Perversely, the richest, who have the greatest capacity to adapt and are responsible for and have benefitted from the vast majority of greenhouse gas emissions, will be the best placed to cope with climate change, while the poorest, who have contributed the least to emissions and have the least capacity to react, will be the most harmed."

These trends have only been deepened by the global COVID-19 pandemic, which has caused millions of deaths while sparking economic chaos and mass unemployment. The poor have been the hardest hit, in particular women workers, who today dominate some of the most market-exposed, low-waged global industries. The garment industry, for instance, has reeled from a massive drop in clothing orders, threatening the livelihoods of millions of women workers, at the same time as they are being exposed to greater demands for unpaid care work and an escalation of domestic violence.

Many of the world's richest billionaires became even richer during the pandemic, especially those connected to ecommerce and digital technology. The richest person in the world, Jeff Bezos, founder and CEO of Amazon, increased his personal wealth by *tens of billions* of dollars during the pandemic alone, launching his total wealth to an unprecedented $196 billion by April 2021 — well beyond the total income of Ukraine and its 42 million people.

Few groups experience this inequality so deeply as the world's small farmers and rural workers. They regularly contend not only with low prices and low incomes, but intense volatility to the cyclical crashes, unpredictable price swings and climate vulnerability spurred by global markets. A sudden collapse in prices, which transnational corporations can absorb and even profit from, can be devastating to smallholders and workers, especially in countries that lack viable social safety nets. Changing rainfall patterns, warming weather and an outbreak of crop infestation can wreck the annual harvest, causing bankruptcies and migration for millions, while large-scale landholders often possess the money and resources to ride out the downturn, adopting new technologies to increase production down the line.

Sadly, very little has been done to address the global inequality gap, especially in the food industry, where matters have only worsened over the past 30 years. A 2018 report by Oxfam International, *Ripe for Change: Ending Human Suffering in Supermarket Supply Chains*, tracked the flow of money along global food supply chains and determined that, from 1995 to 2011, the share of the consumer price that went to farmers *dropped* by 13.1 percent while the share going to supermarkets *increased* by 11.5 percent.

For most rural producers, whether rice farmers in Thailand or grape farm workers in South Africa, this translates into earnings well below an estimated "living income." Kenyan coffee farmers, for instance, earned only 53 percent of a living income in 2017. Oxfam estimates that this gap could easily be closed by adding 2 percent to the final consumer price. This means that a $2.00 cup of coffee only needs to cost $2.04 to provide a living income, as long as that extra 4 cents makes its way to the farmer who grows the coffee.

Covering this 4-cent gap is both simple to achieve (given the vast wealth produced by the Promethean economy) and extremely difficult to attain (given the vast power imbalances produced by the same economy).

Understanding, challenging and changing a global trading system that can produce such unjust outcomes lies at the heart of fair trade and its call for global solidarity. On one hand, fair traders call on all of us to recognize and change the simple injustices embedded in our everyday consumption habits. On the other, they insist we appreciate the limits of the current global order and join in the movement to demand real changes that place fair trade, social justice and ecological sustainability at the centre of a vision for a new trading system.

THE NUTS AND BOLTS
By Sean McHugh

In March 2012, Randy Hooper, owner and managing director of Discovery Organics, a leading importer of fair trade organic fruits and vegetables, took Dave Wilson (produce manager at Choices Markets) and me to Peru, for a whirlwind, five-day trip. We zigzagged the north of the country, visiting avocado, mango and banana farmers and their associations. It's possible that I learned more about agriculture, export, business, markets, development and fair trade in those five days than I did through my time in university, my many years roaming around the world with a backpack on, my two years working in Kenya and my many years volunteering within the fair trade movement. Many years on, and many trips later, that first trip to visit with fair trade farmers left its mark.

While I largely understood the basics of business, markets, international trade and fair trade, that trip drove home what it all really means on the ground. I was astounded by human resilience, by community and by the warmth shown to complete strangers. I was inspired by those standing up to fight for something better, to fight for their families and communities, and to try to build something better. I was also shocked by the adversity that many of them faced, and quite frankly I felt disappointed by the global system that we have put in place, a system that exploits with almost no repercussions.

One story that stuck with me that really drove it home was from an association of mango farmers that had sold its harvest to a large corporate buyer, where 50 percent was paid up front, and the remaining 50 percent was to be paid upon delivery. However, when the delivery was completed, the remaining payment never came, and there was little to nothing that they could do about it. The worst part: that same buyer came back the next year and did the same thing again. For a community of farmers in rural Peru that relies upon income generated at harvest to sustain itself for the year, these incidents were devastating.

This is one story amongst thousands. It and stories like it are what led to the idea of fair trade. The idea that you know not only who you buy from but build a partnership and even a relationship with them. The idea that a fair price is paid, on time and in full. In many ways, it is not a revolutionary idea. It is simply basic decency and respect. It is disappointing that we need to talk about, never mind advocate for, such things, but this is the world we find ourselves in. Many of our global issues have long, deep roots, many of which will be explored in section one of this book.

The idea of fair trade is therefore not a new one; it has a long history dating back to the trade of handicrafts and organizations like Ten Thousand Villages in the 1940s. It has roots in "trade not aid," as advocates pushed to move us beyond "business as usual" and development as a token way to support "growth" to changing how we trade, do business and support each other in the 1960s and '70s. Alternative trade organizations emerged in the 1980s, bringing together buyers in consuming countries with farmers and co-ops in producing ones. Eventually, efforts were undertaken to label products that were bought and sold differently in the late 1980s and '90s.

The fair trade movement today spans much of the world, includes many products, thousands of co-ops, millions of farmers and workers, and thousands of companies. The movement's success has and continues to be built upon the fact that it is cross-sectional. It has been driven by advocates, business owners and institutional and government leaders, and it brings together several sectors.

In Canada and around the world, advocates have played a key role in educating the public and helping to build the market for fair trade products. There have been various campaigning efforts over the years, with several programs anchoring the movement. Fair Trade Town designations (first established in the United Kingdom in 2001), gave way to Fair Trade–designated campuses, schools, events, workplaces and faith groups, with Canada's first Fair Trade Town designated in 2007, and the first Fair Trade Campus designated in 2011. As of April 2021, there have been 364 designations, all of which impact policy and purchasing, and broader consumer awareness and engagement, helping to shift consumer expectations about the products they buy and the companies they buy from. The Canadian Fair Trade Network (CFTN) was founded in 2011 to bring these building blocks together, create community and strengthen the movement. Eight national conferences have brought people together in the name of building something better, supporting better business practices, improving international trade and ensuring that everyone, near and far, up and down the supply chain, is able to live a life of respect, of dignity, of purpose.

The fair trade movement has come a long way in a relatively short period of time, and while there is lots to do, there is lots to be proud of. This book explores much of it. Our hope as editors is that you, the reader, walks away feeling inspired and ready to jump in.

Note

1. Fair trade is a term that refers to trade conducted fairly, where social and environmental standards are put in place for producers and a fair price is paid. It also refers to a way to do business and a social movement. "Fairtrade" (no space) refers specifically to the Fairtrade International system and its standards and the certification it carries out through its various member organizations, such as Fairtrade Canada.

2

A Lively Bean that Brightens Lives

This is based upon people met and stories told to Bill Barrett over more than two decades of partnership with the Oromia Coffee Farmers Co-operative Union (OCFCU).

Drawing, lettering and photo editing by Curt Shoultz, who also helped with story organization.

The goats are giddy tonight.

Kaldi takes the cherries to the Imam and tells of the bush and his dancing goats.

After much thought, and a taste of the sweet cherries, they conclude the bush and the dancing are **not** linked.

The Imam asks Kaldi to throw those left into the fire...they watch as the cherries **sizzle** away.

The little green seeds in the cherries become a deep brown. They smell **inviting**.

Their fire gazing is broken by-- *POP!*

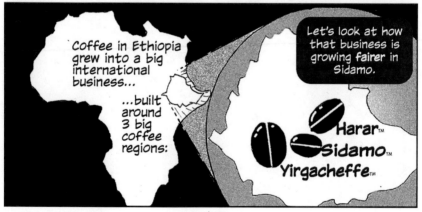

1974: After 6 decades of ruling **Ethiopia,** Emperor Haile Selassie was unceremoniously (and fatally) removed.

Then a committee of military leaders, the Derg, created a **more brutal** authoritarian regime.

Among their many victims were farmers who were **forced** into state run "co-operatives" that had none of the principles of normal co-ops like democracy, self-determination and autonomy.

One of the farmers who lived through those **nightmare** times was Tassew.

hello

After the Derg was overthrown, some positive changes began to happen in Ethiopia.

Twenty or so years ago, a government man named Tadesse first came to us in his borrowed truck, talking of forming a co-operative...

...we thought he was **crazy.**

But Tadesse told us he had learned that co-ops should be run by **farmers,** not the Derg. Finally, we agreed and formed a village co-op. At that time the price we got for our coffee was low.

Our co-op sold directly- **NO middle men,** so we made more money. Our co-op joined other village co-ops that Tadesse had formed into a union of co-ops. Then we learned about "Fairtrade"...

Tadesse had begun to sell the Oromia Coffee Farmers Co-operative Union's coffee through **Certified Fairtrade** channels. This way brought us a better price.

We also get a higher price for "Certified Organic" coffee.

A Fairtrade premium ensured that co-ops could better their villages and we can improve the quality of coffee we grow.

The first use of our Premium was to dig a borehole so our village would have **clean** water. Then we built a coffee mill.

Organic is **easy.** Our land is precious. We have never used chemicals. I use a machete to cut the weeds so they join the soil to feed the trees.

We have learned some new things about growing coffee, but mostly we follow the way of our grandfathers.

Long before the sun rises and brings the heat of the day to her village, Almaz and her sisters have been preparing the household for the day. Chores include gathering wood for the cooking fire, collecting water directly from the stream and sweeping the floor of the living space.

Fifteen year old Almaz is one of the elder daughters in a family of 13. Her mother is not well, and her father has disappeared, so it is up to her and her sisters to manage the home economy.

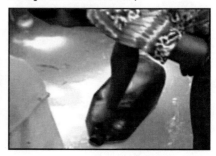

Normally Almaz would be preparing herself and siblings for school, but today is a holiday and she has heard via the village rumour mill that her home will have a visitor today.

Tadesse is bringing someone from Canada to try her family's coffee (more on Tadesse later).

Almaz welcomes the guests to the family home. It has a reed wall that separates the kitchen area from the living space.

Coffee is very important for Ethiopians. We usually prepare it three times a day. -fwoof- Each time we roast the coffee **fresh.**

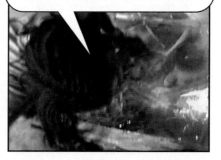

This coffee is from **our forest farm.** We leave the coffee cherry on the beans as they dry. I have removed the cherry and washed the beans. Now I roast them.

I have to keep moving the beans around the pan so they don't burn. Roasting is a combination of time and temperature.

Because the coffee is dried with the cherry on, the flavour is very **sweet** -- like berries.

As the coffee roasts, I put our special coffee pot, a **"jebena"** on to boil.

I have to get the **perfect** grind to make the coffee taste beautiful.

the grounds

I test the temperature that it is perfect for brewing, then I add the coffee grounds.

A taste test to ensure this coffee really **impresses** our guests.

As Almaz has been roasting the coffee in the kitchen, many villagers have **filled up** the other half of her home attracted by the aroma of roasting and hoping to join in. Coffee is served in tiny cups, with no need for added sugar or milk.

Please, tradition says you **must** drink 3 cups.

Enjoying coffee together is the way for villagers to get caught up on local gossip, national politics and to curiously grill the strange visitor from Canada ...
for whom this coffee has proven to be exceptionally **tasty.**

Coffee is so entwined into Ethiopian life that there is a prayer that goes with the shared celebration.

Let your family live and your house stay in peace, let your children grow well, and let God give you the grace He has accorded to coffee.

Emnet is excited to help carry the coffee her parents have picked today to the mill. Her family's farm is up the mountain from the village so she meets her family by the roadside after school.

Because coffee cherries ripen at different times, each tree must be visited **every** day.

Only the **reddest** cherries are harvested.

We take our baskets to the co-op mill at the top of the hill at the edge of our village.

Our coffee is weighed by a co-op member, who records the weight.

The co-op rep then **pays** our family "cash on delivery."

The cherries are then dumped into a large hopper.

Once other villagers have brought their coffee to the mill and the hopper is full, they start the mill.

An auger turns the coffee and it makes its way through the mill with water. Two beans are separated from each cherry.

The beans rub against each other, washing and removing any cherry bits. The cherries will become compost.

The beans are carried by water and gravity down through tubes into canals that zig zag down the hill.

The beans rest for the night in a pool of water.

The next day the beans are spread over many raised screens to dry under the warm sun.

Women from the village take turns shifting and agitating the beans so they dry evenly.

We get paid **two more times** for our beans!

Again, when the harvest is over, our coffee is evaluated. The co-op union pays us then.

... and then a **third** payment comes later as a dividend during the lean months.

Our family gets a **better** price for our coffee because of Fairtrade.

I am Tadesse, the "crazy man in the borrowed truck" pushing coffee farming co-ops back in the 1990's.

In the beginning, we had to rent processing facilities. When the women sorted the coffee, they had to sit on the floor in a poorly lit and dusty shed.

We decided to build our own facilities, but could not find financing. We created our own farmer co-op bank. We raised capital from our co-ops and some support from overseas.

The women who do the final hand sort now work in a well-lit, ventilated space.
The entire process is Certified Organic, even the warehouse. All of this has improved our coffee quality.

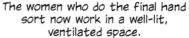

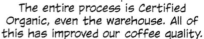

We built a state of the art coffee processing facility with machines that sort based on size, weight and colour. There are buses for the workers, a cafeteria, nurse and offices.

The co-op bank has enabled us to **grow**. We can pay farmers cash on delivery. Village co-ops can get loans to make improvements. We have built schools, health posts, dry latrines, roads and bridges. More than 87 villages now have clean water. More than 250,000 here benefit from a better price.

We started selling Fairtrade around 2000, have made great strides, but there's lots of room for growth in Fairtrade.

Tadesse

When I organized the co-operative union in 1999 there were 34 village based co-ops. I have since retired. Now there are over 400 village co-ops involved.

It has been a remarkable journey working with farmers and our committed Fairtrade coffee friends in Canada and around the world.

To think I had to borrow a truck for my first visit to farmers!

Support from Fairtrade enabled our farmers' dreams to come **true**.

I have been able to finish high school and in a year will start to learn **agronomy** in college.

Emnet

Two Canadian Fairtrade Coffee co-ops, **Planet Bean** and **Just Us!** paid four years of fees, so now I am a **nurse!**

Almaz

My new home has **solid** walls and a steel roof.

My kids have all gone to school and we drink **clean** water.

Tassew

I **Never** ever fell asleep tending my goats again.

Kaldi

Part One

Fair Trade in an Unfair World

Sugar first brings to mind sweetness, but its history does not resonate with fairness. Its close ties with the slave trade, ecological damage and health concerns give sugar a rather bitter taste. Even in fair trade, sugar is often a mere ingredient, neither promoted nor put forward. Source: Éric St-Pierre

3

Colonialism

How Unfair Trade Changed the World

A. Haroon Akram-Lodhi

On August 3, 1492, Christopher Columbus set sail from Andalusia, steering west and eventually making landfall in what is now the Bahamas on October 12. On July 8, 1497, Vasco da Gama left Lisbon, sailed around Africa and arrived at the Malabar Coast on May 20, 1498, at a location that today lies in the Indian state of Kerala. These voyages laid the foundation for the expansion of Europe beyond its boundaries, to the Americas, Africa and Asia. The voyages laid the foundation for the establishment of a global trading system. And they laid the foundation for the world we know today; when Angola, Mozambique and Zimbabwe were liberated in the 1970s, colonialism had, for almost five centuries, shaped the lives and livelihoods of most of humanity. For some, such as those in West Papua, it still does.

Although Henry Bernstein defines colonialism broadly as the political control of peoples and territories by foreign states, the principal motivation for it has always been economic. The following four principles basic to early colonialism shaped the economic future of their world and ours:

- the peoples indigenous to colonized lands were "infidels" to be enslaved;
- the "infidels" had no claim over their territories because these were gifts from God for believers;
- because such territories were empty of believers, they were in principle empty and could be seized, enclosed and bestowed upon Christians as property (the basis for the doctrine of *terra nullius*, which means "nobody's land"); and
- the goods and property of non-Christian peoples and territories that were confiscated by believers could be transported to Europe for use and profit.

Dividing Up the World for the Economic Gain of a Few

From its very beginnings, colonialism pursued the political control of resources for economic gain. John II, the king of Portugal for fourteen years prior to Vasco da Gama's departure, and the Catholic monarchs Queen Isabella of Castile and King Ferdinand of Aragon, who ruled Spain when Columbus started his fateful voyage, had agreed in 1494 to divide the world beyond Europe between them in order to build up their royal treasuries and pay off debts owed to Italian financiers. Pope Nicholas V had legitimized this half a century earlier, when he issued a papal bull stating that not only was the seizure of the lands and goods of non-Christian peoples and territories by the Iberian nobility permissible in the eyes of the Church, but also that non-Christian "infidels" in those territories should be consigned to perpetual servitude. So, hard-wired into colonialism from its inception was the principle and justification that trade should be driven by the (supposed) inequalities between peoples.

Since the 1500s, then, the messianic zeal that underwrote colonial expansion promoted a form of commercial "trade" whose origin lay in larcenous theft.

TYPES OF COLONIALISM

The history of colonialism may be divided into two distinct periods. The first, which dates from the early 1500s through to the early 1800s, was dominated by commercial interests. Merchant companies such as the Hudson's Bay Company, the Royal African Company and, most famously, the East India Company and the Dutch East India Company collectively created the first truly global economy. Small groups of wealthy partners who came together to form the first joint-stock limited liability companies were given royal charters by European sovereigns granting them exclusive trading rights into and out of different parts of the world in exchange for tax payments into the national treasury. To take advantage of these monopolistic privileges, the companies constructed trading networks by establishing sea-lane-based garrisons controlled by company-backed private militias and armies throughout their geographical sphere of influence. The companies used pillage, forced expropriation and swindles to establish control over territories that they came to administer for the private benefit of the partners and their senior employees. So, in early colonialism, the boundaries between private business interests and public administrative functions overlapped, as the merchant companies became, in effect, profit-driven "company-states" that, far from promoting any type of "free" trade, organized international trade to their advantage. But as merchant companies encroached upon the domains of other companies, they came into armed conflict with each other over the control of territory. This led European states to get more directly involved militarily and politically.

The merchant companies of early colonialism were historically unprecedented in their size and power. In the 1670s the Dutch East India Company was the richest firm in the history of the world, with over 150 merchant ships, 40 warships, 50,000 employees and a private army of 10,000 soldiers. For its shareholders, it was immensely profitable, paying a dividend of 40 percent on their original investment. A hundred years later the Dutch East India Company had been displaced by the East India Company. Headquartered in a London office so small that it had only five windows and with only thirty-five permanent employees, the company accounted for half of the world's trade, particularly in basic commodities such as cotton, silk, indigo dye, salt, spices, saltpetre, tea and opium, with its monopolistic rigged control of global trade supported by a private army that at its height had more than 200,000 troops.

In the 1800s European states came to assume direct control of colonial territories, and not just because of company conflicts. The activities of the merchant companies, and particularly the East India Company, produced a series of scandals that highlighted the degeneracy of the companies' agents in their pursuit of profit, and in 1857 East India Company soldiers in India rebelled. Ultimately, though, the reason European states supplanted their companies was because the interests of their elites had changed. By the late 1700s Britain was in the throes of an industrial revolution and incipient capitalists wanted both cheap supplies of raw materials for their factories and markets for their manufactured products. States established in colonial territories by metropolitan Britain and France during the 1800s were designed to administer colonies in order to meet these needs. In so doing, colonial states provided the means to complete the industrial revolution. But in order to meet the needs of the metropole, power, trade and investment took place on the basis of terms and conditions that put the colonies at an even more significant disadvantage than had been the case during the heyday of the monopolistic trading companies. As a result, the economic benefits to the colonizer from colonialism increased when compared to the earlier colonial period.

There were three different types of colonial states. In the first, colonists occupied no more than a minute fraction of the population. India is the example: In the 1920s only 200,000 people out of a total population of 300 million came from Britain, and half of these were soldiers. In the second, colonists remained a small minority of the population but were nonetheless significant. Haiti is the example: In the late 1700s, 10 percent of the total population were from France. The third type are those countries that received significant numbers of settlers into the colony; the United States, Canada, South Africa and Algeria are examples. In some of these colonies, settlers became a significant minority, while in others they became the majority. Each of the three types of colonial state required different forms of administration to perpetuate imperial rule.

MECHANISMS OF COLONIAL RESOURCE EXTRACTION

Five mechanisms of colonial disadvantage allowed colonizers to extract resources from the colonies. These mechanisms shaped the evolution of world trade and the development of the global economy, up to and including contemporary globalization. Together, they were a disaster for the contemporary Global South and a boon for what are now the wealthiest countries.

Violence

Colonialism was founded on the violent military control of colonies, the forced displacement of peoples and the extermination of local populations. This is most starkly illustrated by the genocide of Indigenous populations in the Americas. Some estimates place the Indigenous population in Mexico in 1520 at between 15 and 20 million; by 1600 it was less than 2 million. In Canada and the United States, Indigenous populations at time of first contact with Europeans in 1607 have been estimated at between 5 and 10 million; by 1900 they were only 500,000. As Jared Diamond put it, Indigenous deaths were caused by the "guns, germs and steel" the colonizers brought to the Americas. To these deaths can be added the tens of millions who died from the famines engineered to ensure that colonial traders, company agents and the colonial state could continue to profit from colonialism. Hosea Jaffe estimated that between 1500 and 1900, some 500 million people died as a consequence of European colonialism. Colonial domination was built upon violence because it was the systematic use of violence that ultimately allowed small numbers of colonizers to control huge swathes of territory and the resources in the colonial territories. The violence of colonialism in turn shaped the economic development of the colonies, in that ports, roads and railways were established to facilitate the forced extraction of resources through trade rigged by merchant companies and colonial states.

Property

The violent extirpation and forced dispossession of local populations allowed colonizers to claim exclusive possession of what they deemed to be "private" property. First and foremost among these were the people who were enslaved to work in the depopulated territories enclosed by colonists. The so-called "triangular trade" saw enslaved people transported from West Africa to colonies in the Western Hemisphere; sugar, tobacco and cotton transported from the Western Hemisphere to Britain; and textiles,

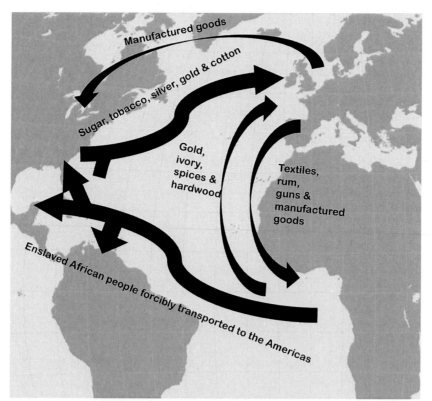

The Triangular Trade, 1500s to 1800s. Source: Gavin Fridell

rum and other manufactures transported from Britain to West Africa. It has been estimated that as a result of the triangular trade between 1500 and 1800, some 15 million people were enslaved and forcibly transported out of Africa, of whom one-fifth died in the crossing of the middle passage and one-fifth died within a year of landing in the Americas.

Slavery brutally extracted the labour power of enslaved people for profit by producing commodities that had been scarce and expensive — in the first instance, sugar, cotton and tobacco — so cheaply that they could eventually be used in large-scale manufacturing. But enslaved people were not the only form of "property" that colonists enclosed in colonies. In the Americas, Africa and Asia vast landed estates established new forms of privilege, as did the establishment of businesses by colonizers in the colonies. So colonialism rewarded elites, who often lived primarily in the metropolitan heartlands of Britain and France, with significant stocks of foreign assets. As French economist Thomas Piketty put it in his book *Capital and Ideology,* the control of property by the metropole in their colonies meant that "the rest of the world laboured to increase the consumption and standard of living of the colonial powers even as the rest of the world became indebted to the colonial powers."

Labour
Colonialism relied on cheap, productive labour, much of it by enslaved people who lived at near-subsistence levels. In the aftermath of slavery in the late 1800s, many of the available productive workers were indentured. These supposedly "free" workers lacked any kind of employment alternatives so they entered into prolonged debt bondage or highly restrictive contracts that paid either a subsistence wage or a miserly pittance on top of subsistence. The situation was not any better for productive waged workers, who were paid subsistence wages on the plantations, in the mines and in the factories of the colonizers. Altogether, colonialism imposed new and different ways of mobilizing and organizing labour in the export-oriented colonies — what Henry Bernstein calls new types of colonial labour regimes.

Colonial labour regimes worsened global human inequality in two ways. First, they depressed payments to workers in the colonies, enabling the production of comparatively and historically cheap products that nonetheless were highly profitable for the companies of the metropolitan colonizers. This sustained rising profits and the emergence of great fortunes in commerce, industry and finance in the metropole. Second, when enslaved peoples were freed, enslavers were fully compensated for their loss of "property" based upon the "market value" of the enslaved people at the time. In the case of Haiti, this compensation was paid by the newly independent country to the French elite, lumbering Haiti with a fiscal debt that shaped the continuing underdevelopment of the country into the twentieth century. In the case of Britain, this compensation was paid by lower- and middle-class taxpayers in Britain over a very long period of time, transferring money to those who had already benefited from enslavement for decades.

Trade

Mercantilism holds that favourable trade balances generated by merchant companies were a source of national wealth that should be encouraged by means of restricting the competition faced by the merchant companies. To that end, the companies that shaped mercantilism operated a "buy low, sell high" strategy. In many instances, of course, this strategy did not involve any type of exchange but rather the straightforward theft of products that could be sold in Europe. In other instances, products were bought for amounts that were derisory compared to their market price in Europe. During its heyday, mercantilist colonialism was able to construct a global trading system that was highly asymmetrical: monopolistic companies were able to extract undervalued tropical resources from colonized places, which in terms of both value and volume generated significant profits for corporate shareholders and company agents. Later, this allowed workers in urban factories in rapidly industrializing Europe to be cheaply fed, which also increased profits by reducing the need to pay adequate wages.

The role of the colonies as a market for the products of metropolitan industry became increasingly important over the late 1800s. But while colonialists spoke of "free trade," it was not; the markets of colonies were kept open to manufactured imports from the metropole while the market of the metropole used a proliferation of trade barriers to remain heavily protected from manufactured imports. This allowed metropolitan manufacturers to simultaneously sell their products into the colonies and avoid competition; the manufacturers were rewarded with the profits on which further fortunes were made.

Tax

The costs of running colonial states were not paid by the colonizers but were rather paid by the colonies themselves. In practice this meant that all expenditures by the colonial state had to be financed out of locally generated tax revenues and that the colonial state could not run a budgetary deficit. However, the expenditure side of the budgetary ledger for colonial states was different. For a start, colonial states had to pay administrators stationed in the colony from the metropole, who were far better paid than civil servants in the metropole itself. Expenditure also had to pay for the infrastructure and security services required by the colonizer to not only maintain their rule but also extend it; in most instances the costs attached to garrisoning colonies was very high.

In light of these requirements, it is not surprising that taxes in colonies were not only highly regressive but were in fact higher than tax levels in the metropole. Most popular were head taxes, in which each subject of the colonial state had to make a flat-rate tax payment. For colonial subjects engaged in peasant farming, taxation meant that they needed money, and such money had to be made by selling their farm produce. As a result, tax demands resulted in the forced commercialization of legions of farmers in highly unequal markets controlled by companies owned by colonizers; peasant farmers became adversely incorporated into these markets, which undervalued their products. When subjects were unable to find the money to finance the tax demands placed upon them, they would be expected to provide unpaid labour for the colonial state. Tax systems thus served to undervalue both labour and the products of labour in the colonies to the benefit of the colonizer.

THE VALUE OF THE COLONIES TO THE COLONIZERS

It is impossible to assess the monetary benefit of colonialism for the metropolitan colonizers. Various efforts at doing so have been attempted but can only act as a guide to the magnitude of the value of the resources extracted to the metropole.

The benefits of slavery to the colonial powers were enormous. Thomas Piketty suggests that between 1750 and 1780, 70 percent of Haiti's output was pure profit for French enslavers. Robin Blackburn (2011) has estimated that British trade profits from slavery in 1770 could have financed almost 8 percent of total investment in the United Kingdom. Jason Hickel (2017)has estimated the value of the labour of enslaved people in the United States at US$97 trillion. According to Piketty, the costs of compensating enslavers for the emancipation of the enslaved in France and in Britain amounted to around 2 percent of all national income in 1825. In Britain, payments were made to 4,000 slaveholders and were not completed until 2015. Haiti paid 5 percent of its national income to compensate French enslavers every year between 1849 and 1915 and did not liquidate its "debt" until the 1950s.

Beyond compensation to enslavers, there is the issue of the total value of the flows from the colonies to the colonizer. Utsa Patnaik (2006) has estimated that colonial transfers to the United Kingdom as a share of United Kingdom savings was over 62 percent in 1770 and almost 66 percent in 1821; in other words, the bulk of savings to finance investment within the United Kingdom came from the colonies. Michael Edelstein has calculated that investment within the United Kingdom, in the form of gross fixed capital formation, was 57 percent financed by the empire in 1870 and 91 percent financed by the empire in 1910. More generally, Piketty has estimated the value of financial profits from the colonies to French national income at between 4 and 7 percent between 1760 and 1790 and between 5 and 8 percent between 1890 and 1914. This in turn effected the stocks of wealth held as direct investment by metropolitan elites in firms, shares, private bonds and government bonds in the colonies. Piketty finds that in Paris in 1912, 20 percent of all wealth was held in foreign assets, of which between a quarter and a third were held in the colonies, and that a similar pattern was evident in the United Kingdom.

Colonialism was little more than a global confidence game that was carried out by the colonizer's superior military force to seize control of the world's resources. Then, under the guise of "trade," a set of monopolistic privileges and practices, racialized discrimination and social hierarchies, forced labour and taxes, and violence was rigged by the winners, who set the rules so that they could continue to win. The production, trade and investment flows of colonialism became the basis of the emergence of an international division of labour and a global world economy. The sums involved were vast: Utsa Patnaik has calculated that Britain drained a nearly US$45 trillion from India between 1765 and 1938, an amount equal to 17 times the United Kingdom's current annual gross domestic product. It was crucial to the success of the Industrial Revolution, particularly in Britain and France, as it produced the resources necessary to finance productivity-enhancing technological change. The effects were so profound that the winner's descendants continue to win today. Colonialism is the basis of our unequal world.

Recommended Resources

Bernstein, H. 2000. "Colonialism, Capitalism, Development." In T. Allen and A. Thomas (eds.), *Poverty and Development into the 21st Century*. Oxford: Oxford University Press.

Chakrabarti, S., and U. Patnaik (eds.). 2018. *Agrarian and Other Histories: Essays for Binay Bhushan Chaudhuri*. Delhi: Tulika Books.

Cope, Z. 2019. *The Wealth of (Some) Nations: Imperialism and the Mechanics of Value Transfer*. London: Pluto Press.

Piketty, T. 2020. *Capital and Ideology*. Harvard, MA: Belknap Press.

4

Trade Is Not Gender Neutral

Laura Macdonald and Nadia Ibrahim

International trade organizations and agreements often seem far removed from the day-to-day concerns of individuals. Yet trade affects every aspect of our lives, from what we eat to what jobs we perform, what clothes we wear and what services we have available to us. Globalization has been linked with a rapid and massive increase in the flow of goods, services and investment across borders. While the expansion of international trade linkages has been associated with economic growth, the benefits of that growth have been unevenly distributed. One aspect of that inequality is related to the uneven ways in which women and men are incorporated into the global economy. Feminist academics and activists, such as those involved in the International Gender and Trade Network (IGTN), have insisted that trade, including fair trade, is not gender neutral and that it is essential to recognize the gendered nature of the international economy in order to develop trade policies and practices that benefit everyone. In particular, they highlight how unequal gender relations underpin the expansion of trade and investment across borders.

In response to these growing concerns, in recent years, governments around the world have sought ways to ensure that women gain a greater share of the benefits of trade and growth, including through the inclusion of stand-alone gender chapters into free trade agreements (FTAS). Many feminists, however, have pointed out the weaknesses of such efforts and their failure to come to terms with the structural causes of gender inequalities, as well as how those inequalities intersect with other forms of inequality such as race, ethnicity, class, age, ability, sexual orientation and others. In what follows, we provide an overview of how international trade affects relations between men and women, what initiatives have been adopted to address gender inequalities in trade policy and what a feminist international trade policy might look like, based on demands that have been made by feminist activists around the world.

WHAT DOES GENDER HAVE TO DO WITH INTERNATIONAL TRADE?

Trade liberalization is one component of neoliberalism, a school of thought that became predominant in the global economy in the 1980s. Neoliberals advocate for policies that dramatically reduce the role of the state in the economy. These policies include cutbacks in state spending, privatization, deregulation and free trade. Proponents of neoliberalism will point out that neoliberal policies have contributed to an increase in women's participation in the paid labour force. However, neoliberal policies have led to the prevalence of low-wage and precarious jobs; the internationalization of reproductive and care work (with immigrants and racialized workers providing the bulk of the low-wage labour force in such fields as childcare, health care and elder care); the feminization of poverty; and the intensification of women's workloads overall.

The United Nations Conference on Trade and Development has, in its work on its Trade and Gender Toolbox, pointed to the gender-based segregation in labour markets. In the Global South, international trade may have contributed to new employment opportunities for women, but those jobs tend to be considered low-skilled and labour-intensive. The growth of international trade and globalization has also led to the expansion of women's employment in the informal sector, which tends to include jobs with lower wages, fewer benefits and less government regulation.

Trade also frequently places women-run businesses at a disadvantage. Trade liberalization brings increased global competition, but women-run businesses face barriers to accessing the credit, technical knowledge and marketing networks that might be needed to remain competitive. These barriers are especially high for Indigenous women, women with disabilities and other marginalized groups.

In addition, globally, women continue to be responsible for most unpaid care work. Because neoliberal policies have reduced governments' ability to regulate and tax capital, while also clawing back public and social services, there has been a shift towards community-based services that rely largely on women's work. Cuts to public services, such as education and health care, have disproportionately impacted women as both service users and providers — paid and unpaid.

The gendered impacts of trade are also evident in the globalized food and agricultural system. According to a joint report by the International Agriculture and Trade Policy (IATP) and the IGTN, "A Row to Hoe: The Gender Impact of Trade Liberalization on Our Food System,

Agricultural Markets and Women's Human Rights," trade liberalization in combination with deregulation and privatization has led to the overproduction of commodities, volatile commodity prices and increased market concentration in the food and agricultural system. This shift has disproportionately impacted farmers in the Global South, particularly women producers. Women producers are responsible for the majority of the world's food production and are particularly dominant in peasant production in the Global South. However, women producers tend to have less access to land, credit, training and markets. Those who are agricultural workers are often in temporary, seasonal or informal jobs with low pay.

It is also important to examine the gender impacts of fair trade networks and certification requirements. As in most production of agricultural goods for export, women involved in fair trade production are not registered as landowners and their unpaid work is often not recognized or adequately rewarded. Women tend to perform jobs that are less well paid and protected, and they are often not able to join co-operatives, producers' organizations or unions. Nevertheless, fair trade organizations often are committed to improving the gender relations in agriculture among their members. For example, Fairtrade International requires that its members adopt the following policies: no discrimination on the basis of gender or marital status; zero tolerance of behaviour that is sexually intimidating, abusive or exploitative; no testing for pregnancy when recruiting workers; programs to support disadvantaged and minority groups, such as women; and developing a gender policy, over time.

The impact of such commitments may vary from place to place, however, and must be carefully monitored and promoted. There is inadequate research available on women' and girls' participation in fair trade and how they may be affected by fair trade policies compared to men and boys. Data from Fairtrade International shows that women represent only 22 percent of the officially registered members of Fairtrade-certified small-scale producer organizations (SPOs) worldwide. A study of women's participation in SPOs in six countries showed that women made up a minority of the membership, leadership and professional staff in all of these countries (Fairtrade International 2015). The worst situation was in India, where only 5 to 6 percent of the SPOs' members are women, and the boards of the two organizations studied contained only one woman between them. In the Dominican Republic, women make up 17 to 23 percent of the members, but only half of women members manage their farms themselves, and there are no women board members. In Mesoamerica, the fair trade organic coffee producer organizations demonstrated that many women benefit, sometimes more than men, from participation in these organizations. Women may not, however, have access to the resources required to become "farm operators," which would give them the right to participate in decision-making processes in their organizations, and women's participation in higher levels of these organizations is rare.

In sum, if trade impacts different sectors, groups and regions in different ways, the gendered impacts of trade will be variable, too. It is important to consider the context-specific impacts of trade policy and agreements.

THE MOVE TO INCORPORATE GENDER IN TRADE POLICY

The ways in which trade relations are gendered went largely unnoticed in trade policy discussions and trade negotiations for many years, even though feminist economists and activists have been raising concerns for decades. Recently, however, initiatives to address these inequities have become more widespread. The most prominent example of this shift in approach is the Buenos Aires Declaration on Trade and Women's Economic Empowerment, launched at the eleventh World Trade Organization (WTO) ministerial conference in December 2017, which has now been signed by over 120 WTO members and observers. The declaration acknowledges "the importance of incorporating a gender perspective into the promotion of inclusive economic growth, and the key role that gender-responsive policies can play in achieving sustainable socioeconomic development" and "that inclusive trade policies can contribute to advancing gender equality and women's economic empowerment, which has a positive impact on economic growth and helps to reduce poverty." Signatories committed themselves to sharing information and "best practices" to gather data on the impact of trade on men and women and to promote women's incorporation into national and international economies through such measures as tackling barriers to women-owned businesses' access to trade financing and to public procurement markets. As well, in March 2018, the vast majority of European Union members approved a motion in the EU Parliament called "Gender in EU Trade Agreements." The motion states that in future trade agreements there will be a gender equality chapter, women's rights will be included, and the economic independence of women will be supported.

As the WTO declaration shows, one common method states have

adopted to address gender discrimination in the trade arena is through programs to promote the participation of women-owned businesses in trade opportunities. For example, the International Trade Centre developed the SheTrades initiative, which aims to connect one million women entrepreneurs to the global marketplace by 2021. Canada has a similar program, Women in Trade, run by Export Development Canada (EDC), designed to help women-owned businesses to engage in trade. In 2019, EDC announced a new $50 million program to provide equity capital for women entrepreneurs. The Canadian government says such programs address the fact that even though Canadian women start businesses at a greater rate than men, women-owned business represent only 11 percent of all exporters.

Another method that has been adopted to address gender inequities in trade is the inclusion of chapters or provisions in bilateral and regional trade agreements. While many trade agreements contain some provisions related to gender, as of 2020 there exist only four FTAs that contain specific gender chapters: Chile-Uruguay, Chile-Argentina, Chile-Canada and Canada-Israel. The Canada-Chile gender chapter, for example, includes commitments to cooperate in such areas as:

- capacity building and skills enhancement at work, in business and at "senior levels in all sectors of society (including on corporate boards)"
- "improving women's access to, and participation and leadership in, science, technology and innovation, including education in science, technology, engineering, mathematics and business";
- "promoting financial inclusion and education as well as promoting access to financing and financial assistance";
- "advancing women's leadership and developing women's networks"; and
- "promoting female entrepreneurship."

Again, there is a heavy emphasis on providing greater opportunities to more elite women, such as women entrepreneurs, to access trade opportunities, with little attention devoted to less elite women.

The Canadian government has been a leader in promoting gender chapters in trade agreements and has adopted the Gender Based Analysis Plus (GBA+) approach to analysis of trade policy. The Liberal government of Justin Trudeau has adopted an "inclusive" approach to trade policy, calling for policies to ensure that the benefits that flow from trade are more shared, particularly among women, Indigenous peoples and small- and medium-sized enterprises, as well as the middle class. Canada has included gender chapters in recent trade agreements and in ongoing negotiations, for example with the South American Mercosur bloc. So far, however, the government's GBA+ analysis is not truly gender-based, since it analyzes the differential impact of trade agreements on men and women, understood as a biologically based and binary distinction, rather than as a socially constructed reality in which gender differences are often fluid rather than fixed. The inclusion of "plus" in the term GBA+ indicates that the government has adopted an "intersectional" approach, which assesses how different groups of women, men and gender-diverse individuals may experience policies, programs and initiatives depending on differences in race, ethnicity, religion, age, sexuality and disability. In practice, however, GBA+ often leaves out or downplays the impact of these other intersectional elements of discrimination such as race, class, ethnicity, age, etc.

While the gender chapters Canada has promoted may prove helpful in drawing attention to gender inequalities in trade relations and to potential ways to address them, they normally lack mechanisms for enforcement, unlike other, more conventional, aspects of trade agreements. A broad coalition of some 200 women's organizations mostly based in the Global South signed a counter-declaration to the WTO Declaration on Women and Trade. The counter-declaration calls the WTO declaration a "pink herring," "an attempt to obscure the harm WTO provisions have on women while ensuring the WTO can bring in 'new issues,' likely to deepen inequality." Critics also claim that there was not sufficient consultation with feminist organizations prior to adoption of new trade agreements and policies. And one of the main concerns of feminist critics about such initiatives is the overwhelming focus on elite women and the failure to develop concrete measures to address the differential impact of trade liberalization on marginalized women, women workers, racialized women and women in the Global South.

COVID-19 and Women in Global Supply Chains

In the contemporary global economy, trade often takes the form of cross-border exchanges within extensive networks that connect companies in different countries, all producing different parts of components of the final product. Women and girls often make up a large percentage of the

Indigenous Woman-Owned Business: Exporting Smoked Salmon

Ellen Melcosky, a member of the Esketemc First Nation, launched her business, Little Miss Chief Gourmet Products Inc., in 1995 (https://littlemisschief.com). Melcosky lives in the Westbank First Nation outside of Kelowna and is president and CEO of the company. She sells wild pacific smoked salmon, using a recipe for brining and smoking inherited from her mother and grandmother, but includes Okanagan white wine in her brining ingredients. Her products support the local economy and other Indigenous artists and businesses, and the seafood is sustainably harvested. She began the company using sockeye salmon but switched to using the wild keta salmon (chum) when sockeye stocks were revealed to be endangered. The salmon is packed in a commercial plant on Vancouver Island and is sold in cedar boxes decorated with designs by Indigenous artists that contain cards which recount native legends.

Melcosky faced many of the obstacles frequently encountered by small First Nations– and women-owned businesses. As an Indigenous woman who had been out of the labour force raising children, she had trouble getting a bank loan to start the company. The bank, she told us, basically laughed at her and told her she wouldn't be able to do anything, so she began her company with investment from her husband and some friends. She has been able, however, to access provincial and federal government support to facilitate export opportunities. In the past, she has been able to export her product to Spain, Poland, Switzerland, the Netherlands and the United States, but is not currently exporting at all. She is, however, negotiating a deal with a Japanese food company and has received assistance with translation from the Canadian government. Over the last several years, however, she has had trouble finding distributors in other countries. Since she is selling a high-end product, she faces particular barriers to entry into export markets. The COVID-19 pandemic has also created big challenges, particularly to her sales in airport gift stores and to large retail stores in Canada, which are facing bankruptcy (Interview, December 15, 2020). Her story illustrates some of the major challenges encountered by women and other marginalized groups in benefiting from export opportunities. (Photo: Stuart Bish) workforce in these networks, partly because firms find them easier to exploit than male workers. Increased global trade has led to increased exploitation of women workers in global value chains. One frequently overlooked and devastating impact of the COVID-19 crisis has been its effect on women working in global supply chains, in which low-paid jobs have been outsourced to factories and production sites in the Global South.

Approximately 190 million women around the world work in these supply chains, which have been disrupted by the COVID-19 crisis. Workplace closures or layoffs have thrust many women workers into crisis, since they struggle to make ends meet even under normal conditions. Lost jobs or reduced hours may push these women over the brink into starvation or extreme poverty.

In Bangladesh, over $2.4 billion of garment orders were cancelled or suspended by global buyers during the first four months of the COVID-19 crisis and the associated global economic crisis, and women are bearing the brunt of this calamity. Many of the jobs performed by women in the garment industry are exceptionally risky for contamination from the virus, since they are required to work in close proximity, with few safety

Workers in a Honduran garment factory.
Source: Solidarity Center/Molly McCoy

provisions. Labour activists also say employers are using COVID-19 as an excuse to target unions and purge workers seen as "undesirable."

Women workers are also at increased risk of domestic violence during the pandemic. The stress associated with the pandemic and increased economic vulnerability are widely associated with increased intimate partner violence.

HOW TO MEANINGFULLY ADDRESS GENDER IN TRADE POLICY

These varied, complex and context-specific gendered impacts of trade underscore the value of a gender-based analysis. Just as economic impact assessments have become common practice, it is crucial to apply an intersectional analysis of any trade policy or agreement prior to and after implementation. This process requires the necessary resources and information, such as dedicated funding and the availability of gender-disaggregated data. During interviews we conducted in 2018 with representatives of Canadian civil society organizations, nearly every inter-viewee pointed to the importance of gender-based analysis (Macdonald and Ibrahim 2019). The UNCTAD Trade and Gender Toolbox outlines a framework for analyzing the gendered impacts of a trade agreement.

Relatedly, gender experts, women's organizations and women and gender-diverse people themselves must be at the table. The international trade regime and negotiating processes are notoriously opaque. Meaningful consultation with experts, civil society and the public is key to any policymaking, and trade should be no exception. Another common recommendation was related to what's known as gender mainstreaming. This involves employing a gender lens throughout an entire trade policy or agreement, particularly in the area of labour, rather than stand-alone gender chapters or a singular focus on reducing export barriers for women entrepreneurs. Arguably, an intersectional analysis should be mainstreamed throughout policymaking in general.

Notably, carving out certain areas or sectors from trade agreements, such as public services, will also be important for gender equity. Negotiating exemptions from trade rules helps governments to preserve their ability to create policy or regulations in the future. Here we might think of the possibility of national programs for pharmacare or childcare in Canada, which would be especially beneficial for women, particularly women from marginalized groups.

Even if trade policy and agreements could be designed to more meaningfully contribute to gender equity, these measures alone will not even begin to address the complex and multi-dimensional forms of inequality and exploitation faced by many women. Complementary laws, policies and programs, such as ones that support care work and protect human rights, will be crucial to advancing gender equity. Furthermore, trade must not be a barrier to broader efforts to advance equity.

Recommended Resources

Fairtrade International. *Gender Equity*. <https://www.fairtrade.net/issue/gender-equality>

Oxfam Canada. *Tackling Inequalities in the Global Economy: Making Canada's Foreign Policy Work for Women.* <https://www.oxfam.ca/publication/tackling-inequalities-in-the-global-economy-making-canadas-foreign-policy-work-for-women/>.

Staveren, Irene van, Diane Elson, Caren Grown and Nilufer Cagatay (eds.). 2007. *The Feminist Economics of Trade*. London and New York: Routledge.

UNCTAD Trade and Gender Toolbox. <https://unctad.org/en/PublicationsLibrary/ditc2017d1_en.pdf>.

5

Climate Justice?

Wake Up, Canada, and Smell the Coffee!

Monika Firl

Swept up in the *tourbillon* of climate emergencies, environmental degradation and eco-system collapse around the world, it can be challenging to stay focused. We stare dumbfounded as Australia and the Amazon burn, while the Arctic is melting. We deplore enormous islands of floating plastics yet remain silent as island-nations sink under rising sea levels. We lament the incalculable species loss as planet Earth enters its sixth mass extinction yet struggle to grasp the magnitude of this biological unravelling. And now, we debate strategies to confront little-understood diseases — like COVID-19 — while continuing to push ecological, economic and social systems dangerously past the point of no return. We've built a worldview upon a foundation of unsustainable contradictions.

Living in Canada, with our vast resources, small population and relatively stable political, social and economic systems, it's all too easy to fall into complacency. We seem to take collective solace, thinking we won't be the hardest hit with climate emergencies. And yet — from coast to coast to coast — in Canada we're already suffering the consequences of our inaction. Economic costs linked to climate-related disasters in Canada have shifted dramatically. According to the Insurance Bureau of Canada, the invoice for "insurable weather events" has ballooned by more than 400 percent since the 1980s. Recovery from increasingly violent coastal storms, flash floods, deadly heatwaves and raging wildfires now costs nearly $2 billion in damages, annually (Team Green Analytics 2015).

But we're only beginning to understand the additional human and environmental costs and the potential future risks. Researchers from the UN Special Report on Climate Change say that temperature rises in the northern boreal forests are happening two to three times faster than in other parts of the country, with profound impacts on Indigenous ways of life (Rogelj et al. 2018).

The United Nations Permanent Forum on Indigenous Issues states that Indigenous peoples in many parts of the world "are among the first to face the direct consequences of climate change, due to their dependence upon, and close relationship with the environment and its resources" (United Nations Department of Economic and Social Affairs n.d.). As a result, Indigenous communities are facing increasing ecological hardships precisely at a time when the world needs to learn from Indigenous culture and their practice of living in harmony with nature to expand and flourish.

Meanwhile the Arctic tundra continues to warm. This leads to permafrost melt and accelerates the release of stored carbon and methane, a greenhouse gas 84 times more potent than carbon dioxide, into the atmosphere. The loop of rising temperatures, thawing tundra and released greenhouse gases represents a potential tipping point. According to the International Institute for Sustainable Development, if this loop is left unchecked it could create a cascading wave of additional, and potentially irreversible, negative impacts (McLaughin 2018).

"All of these impacts point to the need for enhancing Canada's mitigation efforts, while encouraging other countries to do the same," says Dr. Zafar Adeel, executive director of the Pacific Water Research Centre at Simon Fraser University, "Canada should, therefore, double up its efforts to enhance its water resources management, flood preparation, and drought preparedness"(Westcott 2018). Unfortunately, Canada's political leaders have not taken the steps necessary to truly address climate change. This might, in part, reflect widespread perception in the country that Canada is a relatively small overall contributor to global carbon dioxide emissions. But, while our total emissions might seem small, around 2 percent of the world's total emissions, the carbon footprint of individual Canadians is larger than we think.

According to the World Bank, countries in the Global South have a carbon footprint ranging between 0.1 and 2.0 metric tons of carbon dioxide per capita. In Canada, the average carbon footprint is 18.9 metric tons of carbon dioxide per capita. That's more than 150 times the average in many developing countries. Or in other words, the average Canadian emits as much carbon dioxide in just two and a half days as the average Malian or Nigerian emits in an entire year! (World Bank n.d.). Even compared to other industrialized nations, with whom we share a more comparable lifestyle, the average Canadian footprint is still more than double the G20 country average. In fact, Canada is the third worst performer in per capita

Canada's Greenhouse Gas Emissions Per Capita

PER CAPITA GREENHOUSE GAS (GHG) EMISSIONS ABOVE G20 AVERAGE

GHG emissions (incl. land use) per capita (tCO$_2$e/capita)[1]

Canada's total GHG emissions (excl. land use) increased by 19% between 1990 and 2017.

19

7.32

Canada

G20 average

Data for 2017 Sources: Enerdata, 2020; UN Department of Economic and Social Affairs Population Division, 2020

5-year trend (2012-2017)

-3.5%
Canada

-2.3%
G20 average

NOT ON TRACK FOR A 1.5°C WORLD

 Canada's fair-share range is below 332 MtCO$_2$e by 2030 and below -156 MtCO$_2$e by 2050. Under Canada's 2030 NDC target, emissions would only be limited to 526 MtCO$_2$e. Canada can achieve 1.5°C-compatibility via strong domestic emissions reductions, supplemented with contributions to global emissions reduction efforts. All figures exclude land use and are based on pre-COVID-19 projections.

Canada's 1.5°C 'fair-share' pathway (MtCO$_2$e/year)[1,2]

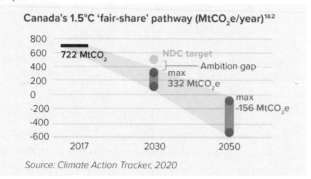

Source: Climate Action Tracker, 2020

Source: Climate Transparency (2020) Berlin, Germany, www.climate-transparency.org

emissions in the entire world, behind only Australia and the United States!

What's more, Canada's national climate mitigation and emissions reduction plan is considered by watchdog organizations such as Climate Action Network completely inadequate and unlikely to get us anywhere near the official target of net-zero emission economies by 2050. And the longer we wait to take effective measures to slow climate change, the more the burden falls on the shoulders of the most vulnerable populations, in Canada and around the world, of whom many already suffer extreme impacts from climate change, for which they share only the smallest fraction of responsibility.

As of this writing, Canada and the rest of the world has been coming to terms with physical self-distancing and economic slowdown provoked by the COVID-19 pandemic. Environmental and civil society organizations from across Canada are calling on government to prioritize the climate emergency and ecosystem health, before any post-COVID economic recovery plan is approved. This moment is an opportunity to reflect upon the lifestyle changes we've adopted to confront COVID-19 and to reassess what we've historically considered basic needs and wants versus realistic expectations looking forward into the future. The real shift will only materialize once we stop considering a climate-smart lifestyle as an option and begin to see it as a moral obligation.

A GLOBAL PATH FORWARD

The irony of this pending environmental disaster is that climate solutions already exist; we're surrounded by them! Whether it's transportation, energy generation and use, land management practices, food or clothing — a vast repertoire of climate-smart options are already available to us. But we must choose to prioritize their use and incorporate them into our day-to-day lifestyle. As individual citizens, we can mobilize our personal or professional networks to activate the change we need for a healthy environment. But we must also mobilize human and financial resources to pressure governments and major industries to invest in and to implement these solutions on a massive scale. The most important step, right now, is to move from paralysis to smart, specific actions. We must shift from the dominant *extraction mentality* to a symbiotic approach of living in harmony with nature and within the limits of our fair share of the global carbon budget. And we must immediately halt the destruction of natural landscapes.

Diverse and well-functioning ecosystems provide society with important benefits, including water and food security, climate change resiliency and disaster risk reduction. According to ongoing research at the United Nations Environment Programme, "ecosystem-based approaches to climate change adaptation and mitigation, provide significant contributions to stabilize global warming to below the target limit of 1.5°C above pre-industrial levels, while delivering multiple co-benefits for biodiversity and sustainable development" (United Nations Convention on Biological Diversity n.d.).

Below is a portrait of how one fair trade coffee importing co-operative is creating win-win-win solutions that are healthy for the planet, advantageous for the farmer and delightful for your tastebuds — while confronting the climate crisis. This example is intended to illustrate some of the challenges, solutions and alternative ways of seeing and behaving for a healthier future.

THE CARBON, CLIMATE AND COFFEE INITIATIVE

Cooperative Coffees is a green coffee importer comprised of and governed by its twenty-three coffee-roaster owner-members across Canada and the United States. Each owner-member is committed to "building and supporting 'Fair and Direct' trade relationships for the benefit of small-scale farmer families, their communities and exporting cooperatives" (Cooperative Coffees n.d.). The foundation of the enterprise is a vision to develop long-term, mutually beneficial partnerships through trade.

As a pro-active and collaborative response to climate change, in 2017 Cooperative Coffees launched the Carbon, Climate and Coffee Initiative, which encourages roasters and their importing operation to track and reduce carbon dioxide emissions; adds a $0.03 per pound "carbon-tax" on all green coffee sales; and, most importantly, channels these accumulated funds back to its producer-partners to support education and learning exchange, soil regeneration, reforestation and other field and farming innovations to support carbon sequestration and landscape recovery — in order to offset the carbon dioxide emissions a roaster is unable to eliminate.

"We're witnessing the state of the environment changing more rapidly than most climate scientists had initially envisioned," says Michael King, owner of Bean North Coffee Roasting based in Whitehorse, Yukon, and current chair of the Cooperative Coffees board of directors. "Humanity has a small window of opportunity to respond to the challenge, and I'm concerned that this window is closing fast, yet society continues forward as if everything is going just fine." "I believe it's my responsibility to try and find ways to work with the tools available and calculate a true cost of goods that includes the cost to the environment," he adds. "And we've found that rather than this being a burden, our aspiration for carbon neutrality gives us an opportunity to educate ourselves, our customers and others on our successes and ongoing challenges, and hopefully, also helps to further raise consumer expectations."

Cooperative Coffees is banking on the cumulative, positive impact that millions of organic farmers' can have on the environmental balance of the planet when they apply regenerative organic practices that actually build up the microbiological life in farmers' soils and improve carbon sequestration in their fields. This hard and innovative work should be acknowledged both intellectually and financially. Since 2020 Cooperative Coffees has been investing in the use of the Cool Farm Tool, a farmer-facing carbon footprint calculator. This tool not only quantifies the levels of carbon being sequestered in farmers' fields but also serves to validate the co-op's progress towards its own commitment to achieve net-zero carbon before 2030. Any emissions that the co-op is not yet able to reduce will be offset with direct environmental service payments to farmers, per tonne of carbon sequestered. At the end of the day, the co-op hopes this work will illustrate the positive benefits of collaboration, to connect and mobilize across the entire supply chain, and ultimately to make coffee an important piece of the climate solution puzzle.

COFFEE AS A CLIMATE SOLUTION

In a commodities world, coffee is second only to petroleum in economic value; so, you could say that coffee is actually our favourite source of "alternative energy." Between imports, roasting, store shelf and over-the-counter sales, coffee represents more than US$100 billion in annual sales and supports the livelihoods of at least 125 million people across the supply chain, including some 25 million farmers, of whom the vast majority are small-scale. Worldwide, we consume more than two billion cups of coffee every day. And like other avid consumers, I wouldn't want to wake up in a world without coffee. But unfortunately, that's exactly where we're headed.

Coffee is another delicate plant species threatened by runaway climate change. Research shows that with the current trend of carbon dioxide emissions and rising global temperatures, more than 50 percent of coffee-growing landscapes will no longer be appropriate for production within the next two decades. And with the disappearance of the coffee-growing landscapes also go the coffee-related livelihoods (Bunn et al. 2015). The irony of this situation is glaring, since coffee, when properly produced and traded, is linked to a universe of potential for providing climate solutions! In a best-case, supply-chain scenario — from the cup a barista hands you, to the fair and mutually beneficial trade relationships that encourage and support functional, farmer co-operatives — coffee can be traced all the way back to farmers, working to transform their coffee plots into productive agroforestry systems and carbon-sequestering fields of goodness.

"Our trade relationships, built upon mutual benefit, confidence and sharing, have helped build commitment and trust not only between roasters and producers, but also between roaster members themselves; growing closer and growing together has been critical to our success," King explains. "When I first got involved in coffee I had no idea the impact these relationships would have on my daily life. To remain grounded and focused on what's important in both business and daily life, I often find myself replaying situations I've experienced with farmers and friends in communities in the coffee lands." And because of these fair and direct trade relationships, co-op roaster members and staff have experienced, firsthand, the increasingly severe impacts that climate change is having on farmer communities but also the enormous potential for climate solutions.

Indeed. Travelling down this long and circuitous path throughout my career in coffee, I have witnessed incredible resiliency, creativity and innovation and have met some of the most extraordinary people. Oscar Alonzo, a small-scale, organic coffee farmer in a remote corner of Honduras, is a prime example. I met Oscar in his coffee fields with a roaster delegation to Marcala, Honduras, in 2013. My visit coincided with the peak of the coffee leaf rust crisis that was sweeping across Central America. This climate change–accentuated fungus attacks the leaves of the plant and depending on its intensity can kill a branch or the entire tree. In many regions, leaf rust had already wiped out entire fields of coffee.

According to International Coffee Organization research, coffee production and economic losses due to leaf rust were more than US$500 million during that initial harvest year alone. In panicked response, industry and national coffee boards across Latin America were spending

Oscar Alonzo in his organic coffee farm in Honduras. Source: Monika Firl

hundreds of millions of dollars to promote more persistent chemical fungicide spraying and buckling down for the "dirty-but-necessary" war against leaf rust in an attempt to save the harvest.

But here was Oscar, surrounded by his neighbours' rows of barren coffee shrubs, while his fields were virtually untouched by the fungus. Oscar was getting unbelievable yields of high quality, organic coffee from his fields, while his conventional neighbours were going bankrupt. And in the process, Oscar was proving false every assumption mainstream research and the coffee industry was making about how the leaf rust crisis must be managed. What I learned that day completely blew the intensive-chemical, or "conventional," discourse out of the water!

And interestingly enough, it wasn't that many years prior that Oscar himself was struggling to keep his coffee fields healthy and productive. But back then, he received some good, practical and timely advice from his producer co-operative, Café Orgánica Marcala. He was taught how to work in harmony with the forces of nature, to bring back the beneficial microorganisms that are part of a healthy ecosystem, regenerate his soils and effectively immunize his fields from common pests and disease.

When Oscar saw that his coffee trees were beginning to defend themselves from disease and drought and other production challenges, he worked twofold, then fourfold, then tenfold in order to accelerate the regenerative process. Examples of Oscar's field practices include increasing the quantities of organic matter; strengthening the quality of his compost with locally produced, beneficial bacteria and fungi; spraying a liquid form of this compost to cover vulnerable leaf surfaces; and mulching with water-logged coconut husks to support soil life with stable humidity. He had reverted to a simple, yet intensive, regenerative organic regime to strengthen the natural, immune system protecting his fields.

If we were to compare these two approaches, intensive-chemical versus regenerative-organic agriculture to our own personal health, it would be the difference between taking antibiotics every time you get a runny nose, as opposed to eating a truly nutritious and balanced diet, exercising your muscles, reducing stress and drinking plenty of water. The first destroys your natural immune system, while the second builds it up.

What I learned from Oscar that afternoon literally turned my world upside down. Standing there in the middle of his fields, I grabbed a fistful of soil teeming with life and listened to him share his secrets. It sent my mind reeling in a high-speed rewind of everything I thought I understood about organic agriculture and realistic production potential in coffee. Suddenly all the pieces were fitting together but to create a very different story. Seeing Oscar's fields functioning as a natural, living-system moved me from perceiving the world from a perspective of increasing "nutrient scarcity" to one of incredible and regenerative "nutrient abundance." And above all, it underscored the absolute necessity of keeping farmers at the centre of research, innovation and the co-creation of climate solutions.

There are many examples of small-scale coffee farmers like Oscar Alonso already showing us a path forward towards climate solutions. But they are rarely offered the platform to champion their cause or showcase their results. Formal acknowledgement of their know-how and fair financial rewards for their efforts are sorely lacking — when in fact, the hard work provided by these farmers results in so much more for us and the planet than just harvesting coffee for our breakfast tables.

This "bigger picture" is a mind-shift that we urgently need to understand and latch onto. And fortunately, the roaster-members of Cooperative Coffees have quickly and enthusiastically gotten on board. Laughing Whale Coffee, founded in Lunenburg, Nova Scotia, in 2003, is a good example. As roaster-owners, Deborah and Steve Zubalik say that one of their earliest goals was to make Laughing Whale the "greenest" coffee roaster in Atlantic Canada. Between their investments in energy efficient roasting equipment; their staunch commitment to composting, recycling and reuse to avoid as much waste as possible; and the company's longstanding support of local farmers and farmers' markets, they've definitely strived to achieve that goal.

"We want to act responsibly to address our own carbon load, and by doing so influence other people and businesses to undertake actions of their own," Zubalik explains. "The fact that our coffee is organic and Fairtrade-certified means that we tend to attract customers who are already more environmentally and socially conscious than the norm. That said, the speed and magnitude of the change so urgently needed does not seem to be registering with the general population. As we (as a society) have been able in 2020 to mobilize quickly and massively around the COVID-19 pandemic, and to demand an end to racial and human rights abuses around the world, so too we must mobilize to avoid the even more devastating and all-encompassing outcomes that would result from runaway climate change."

We live in a critical era for the very survival of our species and for so many species surrounding us, and at this particular juncture in history, we cannot afford to underestimate the impact of our choices. Remember those two billion cups of coffee per day? We can leverage change through our purchasing power. It starts by asking ourselves, where does this product come from? How has it been produced? Was it grown under a life-giving or a life-destroying process? What if we bought and used a single, durable cup rather than hundreds of disposables a year? By purchasing not only the product itself, but also the production system behind it, consumers can drive change! But we need to look beyond just recycling our paper cups and train our eyes to see the bigger picture.

If the estimated 10 million hectares of coffee worldwide were produced under regenerative, organic agroforestry systems, we would avoid massive amounts of carbon dioxide emissions and the air, soil and water pollution that comes from the production and use of intensive chemicals. And simultaneously, we could accelerate carbon sequestration with potentially hundreds of millions of cubic tons of stable carbon held in organic soils and biomass. Collectively, we can create the market-pull for carbon-sequestering coffee, grown in lush, diversified forest systems that are good for people and for the planet. And if we can bring this all together, it will only make our cup of coffee taste that much more delicious.

Demand transparency, economic justice and climate-change solutions in your daily cup, and together, we could be creating a new dawn for one of the most influential industries on the planet. And after our cup of coffee — let's do the same thing with everything else that we consume!

Recommended Resources

Climate Transparency. 2020. *The Climate Transparency Report*. Berlin, Germany <www.climate-transparency.org>.
Intergovernmental Science-Policy Platform on Biodiversity and Ecosystem

Services. N.d. *Global Assessment Report on Biodiversity and Ecosystem Services.* <https://www.ipbes.net/global-assessment>.

McLaughin, David. 2018. *What the UN Panel's Special Climate Change Report Means for Canada.* October 19. International Institute for Sustainable Development. <https://www.iisd.org/articles/ipcc-canada>.

Project Drawdown. 2020. *Drawdown 2020: The World's Leading Resource for Climate Solutions.* <https://www.drawdown.org/>.

Rodale Institute. 2014. *Regenerative Organic Agriculture and Climate Change. A Down-to-Earth Solution to Global Warming.* <https://rodaleinstitute.org/wp-content/uploads/rodale-white-paper.pdf>

6

From (Invisible) Coffee Farmer to Undocumented Construction Worker

The Life and Death of Álvaro Vargas Fonseca

Roxana Olivera

On March 20, 2008, after a 6-hour flight and 17-hour layover in Miami, the body of Álvaro Vargas Fonseca arrived from Toronto to the Juan Santamaría Airport in San José, Costa Rica. From there, it was driven by his younger brother Rodrigo for six hours along narrow, winding roads, crossing the Cerro de la Muerte, to bring him home for burial at his hometown of San Vito de Coto Brus.

But the ordeal was far from over. The hermetically sealed metal casket that held Álvaro's body would not fit in the grave slot the family had purchased. As the priest and family members watched and waited in dismay, Rodrigo rushed out of town to find a funeral home to buy a wooden coffin to hold his brother's remains. Dressed in a white shirt and a black suit, Álvaro was, at last, buried after a Good Friday prayer. Twenty-three days earlier, Álvaro, then 38, had died at a Toronto construction site while working as an undocumented labourer.

Born and bred in the fields of Coto Brus, Álvaro — the second of eight children — was the eldest son of a coffee farmer who taught him to work hard and earn an honest living. From childhood, while in school, he had also worked on the family farm, picking coffee cherries from arabica trees and packing jute bags full of coffee for shipment. He loved spending his days at the family farm.

"Álvaro would often wander across the coffee field, his dog Bobby trotting at his side, where he would grab a handful of coffee cherries, admire their bright, deep red colour, and then boast about their high quality," recalled Álvaro's mother, Rosa María Fonseca. "This, of course, was music to his father's ears." Her face lights up at the memory as she brews coffee, pouring hot water over a Costa Rican *chorreador*, a sock-like coffee filter.

Álvaro was convinced that his future belonged in coffee production.

A photo of Álvaro Vargas Fonseca, held up by his mother, Rosa María Fonseca Godines. Source: Rosa María Fonseca Godines

THE INTERNATIONAL COFFEE AGREEMENTS

Beginning in 1963, the International Coffee Agreement (ICA) had provided some protection to small independent coffee farmers like Álvaro. The provisions of the agreement sustained price stability by assigning countries export quotas to prevent oversupply. In Costa Rica, the quota system had worked extremely well by minimizing extreme price swings. But in 1989, several countries, led by the United States, abandoned their support for the quotas. The Costa Rican government was persuaded to actively endorse the abandonment of the very quota system that for years had provided higher and stable prices for coffee farmers across the country.

With the end of the agreement, prices crashed, causing widespread despair in the world's coffee growing communities. And as the old quota system crumbled, so too did Álvaro's lifelong dream. In Costa Rica, renowned as one of the most successful coffee-producing countries in the world, the small- and medium-sized independent farmers who had traditionally played a key role in national coffee production panicked. Wages plummeted and unemployment soared. Farming families struggled to survive. This was particularly true for the Coto Brus region, one of the areas worst hit by the crisis. The fall in prices was so dramatic that many of the coffee growers ended up switching from coffee to subsistence crops such as corn and beans. Others abandoned their farms altogether to travel to the United States — the world's largest consumer of coffee — in search of work.

Through acquaintances, Álvaro heard rumours about job opportunities in the United States. Several producers from Coto Brus and surrounding regions were preparing to head north — under the guidance of a so-called *coyote*, a migrant smuggler. Álvaro decided to go with them. His plan was to work there temporarily, just until the economic situation improved back home. So, in November 1990, Álvaro joined other farmers on a harrowing, nearly 3,000-mile journey — by bus, by freight train and by foot — to cross the Rio Grande from Mexico into the United States. Shouldering a small black backpack, he carried a few precious items with him. Among them was his prized Sony portable cassette player. Along the way, the 20-year-old would make daily audio recordings of his journey, sending the cassettes back to his family. As she received them, Rosa María prayed incessantly for her son's safety.

Relieved at having arrived unharmed in the United States, Álvaro made his way to New Jersey, where he landed a job as a dishwasher at an Italian restaurant. He often picked up extra shifts, sending most of his wages home. In New Jersey, though, Álvaro was unimaginably lonely. His job was monotonous and exhausting; sometimes he worked over 60 hours per week, leaving little time for sleep and relaxation. He didn't speak English. He had no friends. He missed his mother's cooking. After a long day of non-stop hustling in the restaurant's kitchen, he would yearn to be back at the farm with his family in San Vito.

Álvaro had a reputation for looking out for others. In January 1992, a little over a year into his stay in the United States, he saved a child from a fire in the three-storey building where he lived. Álvaro had just returned home from a late shift when he heard his landlord's frantic calls for help. Her four-year-old daughter, Mary, was fast asleep in her bedroom, trapped by the flames. Without stopping to think, Álvaro made his way to the child, grabbed her and carried her in his arms through the smoke-filled hallway down the stairs to safety. A clipping in a local newspaper, the *Daily Record,* captured the act, but the hero himself was nowhere to be found. As an undocumented worker, Álvaro did not want to attract attention. He had to remain invisible.

Half a world away in the coffee fields of Álvaro's dreams, his father, Evelio, worked tirelessly to keep the family farm alive, without much luck.

Coffee production was still in turmoil — so much so that three years into the crisis, Costa Rica joined other countries to demand the return of price regulation. Coffee cultivators like Evelio were, at that point, confronting a significant drop in their farm income, finding it impossible to cover their living expenses. Evelio was embarrassed to rely on Álvaro's help to meet his family's basic needs.

But Evelio wasn't alone. Coffee farmers throughout Costa Rica couldn't weather the crisis. Lack of international regulation combined with booming production globally generated oversupply in coffee that kept prices low. While depressed prices demoralized coffee producers in Costa Rica and the world over, multinational companies, which dominated — and continue to dominate — the world coffee market (today, just two companies, Nestlé and Jacobs Douwe Egberts [JDE], control nearly 20 percent of the world's coffee market, according to the 2018 Coffee Barometer), effectively controlling the price of coffee, actively encouraging increased supply as they reeled in substantial profits.

After a four-year collapse, coffee prices began to recover in 1994. Álvaro was thrilled, certain that the crisis was finally coming to an end. Encouraged by the modest rise in prices in global markets, he couldn't wait to set foot on his beloved coffee fields and reunite with his family. In December of that year, he grabbed his few belongings, threw them into his backpack, and returned to Costa Rica just before Christmas. In San Vito, his family was elated to have him back home. Álvaro resumed his work at the family farm and took an additional part-time job as a taxi driver to help pay the family debts — and get them a few long-promised gifts. He bought his mother her first electric refrigerator, and for his youngest sister, Heylin, her first bicycle. For three consecutive years after his return from the United States, Álvaro worked around the clock. But despite his hard work and hope for a better future, the outlook for the family farm was grim.

As it turned out, the recovery in global bean prices did not last long. In 1997, another crisis began to brew. This time, coffee prices would drop to as low as 45 cents per pound — from roughly 96 cents in 1994, forcing many farmers out of business. Coffee farmers and rural workers were becoming even poorer. For its part, Álvaro's family began to drastically cut back on food consumption, but even then they were barely scraping by. If that were not enough, Evelio was diagnosed with stomach cancer. These were already difficult and uncertain times for independent farmers like Álvaro, and Evelio's poor health only intensified troubles for the family farm.

Álvaro felt mounting pressure to leave again. As he prepared to head off to the United States, he made a final visit to the fields. The coffee berries were at their prime; they had never looked so beautiful, recalls Rosa María, and it pained Álvaro to leave them to spoil on the tree. Still, in November 1998, he travelled alongside roughly 100 desperate coffee growers on the treacherous journey to the United States in search of work. Tragically, many of them died or went missing along the way, and Álvaro was one of the few from his group who actually made it. Once in New Jersey, Álvaro was able to get his old dishwasher job back and was eventually promoted to busboy. As before, he frequently worked extra hours and sent most of his meagre earnings to his family.

In San Vito, meanwhile, the coffee drama continued unabated. But after spending just one year in the United States, Álvaro returned to Costa Rica, earlier than planned, unable to stop worrying about his father's deteriorating health. As soon as he got back, Álvaro made for the coffee fields to try to resurrect the farm and keep it in the family. He also resumed his part-time job as a taxi driver. But he felt helpless. He could hardly afford to pay the bills. His siblings couldn't find work. Some good news came in the form of Evelio's recovery from cancer after a successful surgery. Nevertheless, Álvaro didn't want his father working in the fields anymore.

On the coffee front, things kept getting worse. Prices plunged 50 percent from 1998 through 2001, when prices reached an all-time low — the lowest they had been in half a century. Farmers couldn't cope with the low and unpredictable prices. Despair and uncertainty overwhelmed the coffee-growing regions of Costa Rica. Once again, waves of farmers left their plots of land and took off to try their luck in the United States in order to support their families.

THE MISSING FARMERS

Alberto Fonseca Vargas (not related to Álvaro), then 32, was among those who migrated from the Coto Brus coffee-growing region. On July 17, 2001, he boarded flight number 386 on the now-defunct Mexicana Airlines destined for Mexico City, as arranged by a smuggler, to then cross the Arizona desert into the United States. Alberto, along with some dozen farmers who had embarked on the same perilous multi-day journey with him, was never heard from again. Yet even now, Alberto's mother, Margarita Vargas Uleta, is clinging to the hope that her son will one day find his way home.

In southern Arizona, there is a stretch of desert known as the "corridor of death." There, the remains of more than 3,000 people have been found over the course of the past two decades — and more than 10,000 remains have been recovered across the entire US-Mexico border over the same period. Dr. Bruce Anderson is very familiar with these cases. As a forensic anthropologist at the Pima County Office of the Medical Examiner, his hands have touched the bodies of more than 2,000 people found in the desert, and he has determined how those people died. In 2000, the Pima County Office of the Medical Examiner began to track the deaths of suspected undocumented border crossers. Since then, it has received the recovered remains of as many as 3,081 migrants, but only 1,970 of them have actually been identified. Of those, four were recorded as Costa Ricans, but the vast majority came from Mexico. The rest were from Central and South America, as well as the Caribbean. Dr. Anderson suspects that the missing Costa Rican coffee farmers — Alberto included — may be among those yet to be identified.

When found, many of the bodies are in an advanced state of decomposition. But their remains often carry with them a few precious belongings that hint at their identities. A rosary, love letters, faded photographs of loved ones. A scrap of paper with an address written on it, along with two words: *"mi mamá."*

Rumours of these migrant deaths eventually made their way back to Costa Rica and throughout Latin America. But the dangers did not deter desperate people from trying to reach what was, to them, the land of opportunity. Indeed, several coffee farmers from Santa Teresa de Cajón took off for New Jersey, where some of them were to be employed at Donald Trump's Bedminster golf course, even though they were undocumented.

Álvaro, however, was conflicted. In the face of the continuing coffee crisis, his life — along with those of so many other farmers — was in utter disarray. As it became apparent that the coffee farm could no longer sustain the family, his siblings gave up on production on the farm, taking up odd jobs here and there. To make matters worse, Evelio's recovery was halted by a new diagnosis of colon cancer.

It was a difficult reality for Álvaro to accept, but his previous trip to the United States, during which his companions had vanished en route, had left him traumatized. He had spent countless nights awake, thinking about them. He was afraid to embark on yet another dangerous trip north to the United States and risk the same fate, but with his father ill again, staying in San Vito was no longer an option. So, this time he struck out for Canada, a much safer — and more welcoming — destination, or so he thought.

On March 12, 2004, Álvaro flew on TACA Airlines, via El Salvador and Cuba, to land at Pearson International Airport. He arrived in Canada filled with hope. In his pockets, he carried his passport, along with $1,250. He gained entry to the country as a visitor — at the time, Costa Ricans did not require visas. He arrived just in time for Toronto's construction boom. Not long after, Álvaro found a job as a house framer. He knew nothing about the construction trade, but he was a fast learner. He was reliable and meticulous, and he had a sharp eye for detail. At the time, construction-related jobs were in high demand, with many undocumented migrants filling in the labour void. At various construction sites around Toronto and Mississauga, Álvaro worked long shifts, often seven days a week. He wasn't always paid on time and sometimes his employer didn't pay him what was owed, noted his landlord Cristina Carballo. But he never complained. Without legal status, Álvaro couldn't afford to. As in the United States, he had to remain invisible in Canada.

"Undocumented workers' lack of authorized immigration status is a barrier to voicing complaints in general, and especially, in the context of employment and conditions at work," said Amar Bhatia, associate professor of law at Osgoode Hall Law School, at York University in Toronto. "As with migrant workers who have valid work permits tied to one employer, they fear that a complaint could lead to reprisals from their employers or recruiters and that discovery of their lack of status could lead to detention and deportation by government agents."

Still, Álvaro thought himself lucky. He was in good health. He had a steady job and a roof over his head, renting a basement room in Toronto's west end. But after almost four years in Canada, he was making plans to return to Costa Rica. He told his mother that he would be home within weeks, as soon as he finished his contract. "Have a nice *chorreada* ready for me when I get home!" he said during their last telephone conversation.

On the morning of February 25, 2008, Álvaro and his supervisor, Jimmy, were heading to work at a Mattamy Homes construction project located at 7273 St. Barbara Boulevard in Mississauga, Ontario. On their way, they made their usual stop at Tim Horton's. At 7:00 a.m., Álvaro was already doing carpentry work on the second floor of the unfinished house. By 9:35 a.m., he was pronounced dead at Credit Valley Hospital.

THE "COFFEE ROLLERCOASTER"

Álvaro's story is part and parcel of a much broader story, one about the coffee crisis and involuntary migration — not to mention systemic discrimination. The story of his invisible life and death tells the hidden story behind the coffee trade and the farmers who are caught in the middle.

Álvaro's migration dates closely follow the ebbs and flows of coffee prices in the world market. He first left for the United States when prices were collapsing in the early 1990s, and he returned home when they were recovering. He went back to the United States in 1998, at which point coffee prices had completely collapsed. Then, prices stayed low, not recovering until 2007 — the second major coffee crisis was still ongoing when he came to Canada in 2004. And when he died in 2008, prices were just recovering. In a strange twist of fate, Álvaro died as an invisible undocumented worker in Canada — a country where, among adults aged 18 to79, coffee is the most consumed beverage, even more so than water. Yet few Canadian coffee lovers know about the farmers that cultivate, harvest, dry and roast the beans used to brew the drink they enjoy every morning.

If one ever needed an example of how an individual life can be driven by economic forces beyond their control, this would be it. Álvaro's life in many ways reflects what Gavin Fridell (2014) has called the "coffee rollercoaster." The wild and unpredictable swings of the coffee market was one of the determining factors of Álvaro's life, even when he was not growing it. From the time of his death, the details of what happened to Álvaro become muddy and difficult to navigate. He died in full view of his co-workers, but his family never received official records of how the event unfolded. They have never even received formal notification of his death, instead getting the news of his passing through his landlord Cristina's brother. They don't know if he died of a heart attack, electrocution or even whether he was shot. More than a dozen years after her son's death, Rosa María says she doesn't want to die without knowing what truly happened to him. In a desperate attempt to obtain long-overdue answers, she sent a letter to Prime Minister Justin Trudeau and opposition leaders.

Dear Prime Minister Trudeau

My name is Rosa María Fonseca Godines, mother of Álvaro Vargas Fonseca, who perished near Toronto, Canada, on February 25, 2008, at his workplace. Since that date, I have been unable to obtain information about the exact circumstances of my son's death. Twelve years of lies and deceits have gone by concerning his death. During all this time we have experienced this terrible pain together as a family.

Canada is considered to be one of the more just countries in the world. After the downing of the Ukrainian plane in Iran, we listened very carefully to your statements as they were broadcast in our country. You stated that "The families of the victims and all Canadians want answers. I want answers. That means closure, transparency, accountability and justice." And that your government will not rest until you got that.

Given your willingness to seek answers and resolve the cases of these victims, I would be grateful if you could do the same to resolve my son's matter, and request, with the same determination, composure and transparency, accountability from all those who over these twelve years have been dodging responsibility. This is what we have been waiting for in a harrowing silence, which keeps on extending indefinitely, in order to be able to heal one day our wounds.

You are seeking justice for something that took place in Iran. We seek the same response from your country. We are still waiting for an official answer from a Canadian official. We are still waiting for the money supposedly gathered to cover the family expenses as well as the funds from an account which was supposedly opened at the Portuguese Canadian Credit Union, according to the *Globe and Mail,* in support of Álvaro's children. But, above all, we are waiting for all the details which have been blocked or redacted by the Ontario Ministry of Labour, the Construction Local Union LiUNA Local 183, the Credit Valley Hospital, the ambulance service, the 911 call centre, the funeral home and autopsy to exactly clarify how Álvaro died and who should be held responsible for it.

Attached please find the link to the *Globe and Mail* article (httpc://www.theglobeandmail.com/news/national/an-8000-bill-to-pay-before-he-rests-in-peace/article668462/) and a copy of the article telling Álvaro's story, which appeared in the March 2020 issue of *Broadview* (https://broadview.org/alvaro-vargas-fonseca/).

Yours sincerely,

Rosa María Fonseca Godines

Álvaro's mother writes, "Given your willingness to seek answers [to the January 8, 2020, downing of the Ukrainian plane in Iran] and resolve the cases of these victims, I would be grateful if you could do the same to resolve my son's matter, and request, with the same determination, composure and transparency, accountability from all those who over these twelve years have been dodging responsibility. This is what we have been waiting for in a harrowing silence, which keeps on extending indefinitely, in order to be able to heal one day our wounds."

Note

A version of this article first appeared in *Broadview Magazine* in February 2020, where the author details Álvaro's time in Canada, what is known of his tragic death, and the family's quest for justice and closure after his passing (available online: https://broaview.org/alvaro-vargas-fonseca/).

Recommended Resources

Bhatia, A. 2012. "'In a Settled Country, Everyone Must Eat': Four Questions About Transnational Private Regulation, Migration, and Migrant Work." *German Law Journal*, 13, 12 (Winter).

Fridell, Gavin. 2014. *Coffee*. Cambridge: Polity Press.

Humane Borders. N.d. *Migrant Death Mapping*. <humaneborders.org/migrant-death-mapping.html>.

Olivera, Roxana. 2020. "The Life and Death of an Undocumented Construction Worker." *Broadview*, March.

Ramsaroop, Chris. 2016. "The Case of Unemployment Insurance Benefits for Migrant Agricultural Workers in Canada." In Aziz Choudry and Adrian A. Smith (eds.), *Unfree Labour? Struggles of Migrant and Immigrant Workers in Canada*. Oakland: PM Press.

7

Putting Southern Farmers First

Journeys to Decolonization

Nelson Melo Maya and Joey Pittoello

The small producers' fight for fair trade and the struggle to make their collective voice heard have been ongoing for centuries, including within the fair trade system itself. For example, while Fairtrade International was founded in 1997, producer networks did not become members until 2012, and producers were not given equal voice on the board until 2013. The long history of paternalistic behaviours toward small producers in the Global South cannot be undone with words or policy changes alone. Real change must come from shifting power from those who have historically held it, and continue to do so, to those who have been, and remain, oppressed. This chapter explores how to bring about these shifts through a conversation between Nelson Melo Maya (ORGANICA, Colombia) and Joey Pittoello (Just Us! Coffee Roasters Co-op, Canada).

Nelson Melo Maya is a small-scale farmer from Cauca, Colombia. He grows certified organic coffee and represents ORGANICA, a small coffee producer association of 100 members, formed 20 years ago. Nelson has been a vocal advocate for small producers through several roles within the Latin American and Caribbean Network of Fair Trade Small Producers and Workers (CLAC); the Colombian Initiative of Small Producers of Fair Trade Solidarity; and Simbolo de Pequeños Productores Global (SPP), a network of small producers, buyers and value chain representatives. SPP is the only 100 percent small producer owned fair trade initiative in the world.

Joey Pittoello is a small-scale ecological farmer and worker-member of Just Us! Coffee Roasters Co-op. Joey has been responsible for producer relations since 2015 and currently serves as general manager. He represents North American buyers as a board member of SPP.

Nelson Melo Maya and Joey Pittoello sample SPP coffee in Cauca, Colombia in June of 2018. Source: Janice Chipman

JOEY PITTOELLO: In 1995, Just Us! chose to sell organic, fair trade products and organize as a worker co-op to effect positive social change and better understand the democratic decision-making structures that small producers often use in the Global South. Does ORGANICA feel similarly about the business of coffee and positive social changes?

NELSON MELO MAYA: The solidarity economy is the same anywhere in the world, and structures like co-operatives or simpler democratic structures such as producer associations, like ORGANICA, have similar identities in their economic, social, cultural and environmental objectives. That said, the conditions for members are not necessarily the same. For example, although our organizations' philosophies may be similar, *our* situation entails more urgent basic needs and limitations; one often feels that because of these conditions we are taken advantage of by many companies, including those that work within fair trade and the solidarity economy.

When we created ORGANICA, we wanted to be able to work together and live from the fruit of our work. First, we understood that we wanted to conserve the soil, water and environment for future generations. Second, we did not want to depend on external resources such as grants and philanthropy. Third, we wanted to differentiate ourselves in those markets that recognize our efforts and the resulting quality. This allows us to live with more dignity. Our work and organization have been effective in achieving a better quality of life for our families and our communities. We have managed to achieve above-average sustainability indicators within our department of Cauca.

JP: Your comment that the solidarity economy has similar objectives, but very different situations in the South and North is often on my mind. Our co-op wants fair trade to be fairer than our current economic system. We want to be part of a solution that builds capacity so that producers earn a fair wage. We do not want to feel guilty about how we earn our income, and we want to create a product where our customers don't feel guilty either. Fair trade certification ensures that coffee producer organizations receive a minimum price, plus a premium for organic practices, plus another premium to invest in the communities. Does all of that help producers' situations? Most of us in Canada cannot know the farmers that grow our coffee. We want to trust that the company or the logo on the products are ensuring that farmers are making a fair wage. Can we trust that?

NMM: Everyone involved in fair trade does not think alike. Your philosophy is the ideal, because in our opinion, this is how the current economic system should be. However, it is not like this. This is why authentic fair trade is so important. Across the world, in a culture of consumerism, we are so busy. Certifications and logos have become one more service provided to those who live in consumer countries to easily identify ethical products, when it was supposed to be our means of speaking the truth and defending true fair trade. What a disappointment it is when we see logos and certifications that do not guarantee anything. We see products on the market with "ethical" certifications being sold at prices that will never provide a small producer with a dignified living. Buyers often use these certifications as a mere brand differentiator, without any true commitment to the values.

So today we find ourselves fighting two battles: one against global trade practices and the other defending the authentic principles of fair trade and truly fair prices. The small producers of ORGANICA believe that we work within those principles because we have trade allies like you with whom we work transparently and fairly. That is why we support the movement being led by the SPP network. That way, more organizations, companies and consumers can be sure that we are succeeding in our businesses and contributing positively to our communities and the planet.

JP: When I first started this work in fair trade, I did not realize producers might feel like they are providing me, as a consumer, with yet another service by ensuring organic and fair trade certifications are in place. Naively, I thought producers were eager to be part of a community of sustainability-minded people. I can see now that this likely perpetuates the injustice that producers feel. The power dynamic continues to be in favour of the consumers who are predominantly from the Global North.

NMM: I do not know if the power dynamic is truly in favour of the consumers in the North or instead, the good intentions of these consumers are taken advantage of through their trust in brands and certifications. The power dynamic is in favour of large companies, but now we sometimes see co-operatives and fair traders in the North using their position to impose their will on small producers. It worries small producers when we see how the rules of the game are changed in favour of large companies. For example, in the free market, minimum prices are not allowed because of anti-trust laws that were created to protect consumers from high costs, but the fair trade minimum prices, other than SPP's, are often not fair. They were set a long time ago. When we tell potential buyers about our costs, they say the market is not ready to cover them and that consumers are unable to pay that much. This is how the industry takes advantage of naive consumers and the small suppliers of raw materials.

It is even sadder that nobody pays attention to our cries when we make these complaints within the industry. It is comforting that the SPP network of small producer organizations, with the participation of Northern organizations like yours and many others, are working hard to consider the well-being of everyone and the planet. That is reason enough to continue telling the truth.

JP: Our small co-op pays, on average, more than the SPP minimum price and has policies that limit the highest wages to three times the lowest wage and that ensure 10 percent of any annual surplus is shared with producer-partners to support capacity-building projects. Why large companies can't pay more for their coffee is a mystery to me. Our coffee is a premium product at the grocery store, but it is competitively priced within its category. That said, how could certifications better serve producers, Nelson? Certifications are a way to ensure that a certain set of standards is met so that the customers know what they are buying. I suppose governments, fair traders and other ethically minded people have decided that the best substitute for trust is independent certification schemes. If some companies abuse this system, it loses its meaning and becomes an expensive means of monitoring organic and fair trade practices (for which producers pay a substantial part). What can be done? From the perspective of a small producer, what would you propose?

NMM: We proposed it 15 years ago! We created a logo and an independent certification system that is the intercontinental network of small ecological producers: SPP. We created the SPP for that purpose, but we are working against global commercial power and national policies that make it difficult to reach consumers with our message. What we need now is to communicate the benefits we seek for all — including our planet — and take care to not be corrupted by these bad practices along the way.

JP: As I've spent more time with producers in their communities, I've realized the relationship between fair traders and producers can often be demeaning or create unhealthy relationships of dependency. Small producers are proud and capable, but their circumstances are different, and their means are modest compared to ours. I often see a paternalistic attitude among those of us in the North, an attitude that suggests we know best. I even see it in the various fair trade and ethical standards that are increasingly complex and expensive for small producers to implement. Conversations like this one help me understand some of the nuances and privileged blind spots. How is another certification going to be the solution to this issue of power dynamics in the marketplace?

NMM: For us, fair trade is simply a means, not an end. Some certifications seek to control everything, and producers are considered beneficiaries: Those are paternalistic schemes. In SPP we are not beneficiaries; we are protagonists of our own development. This is a huge difference. We must demonstrate our agency and promote relationships that truly generate sustainable development for us and that generate awareness of our existence and objectives for everyone in the value chain. The standards that exist in some certifications come from distrust. The standards of the SPP were built from trust. We started with the essence of who we are: families of small producers where love, trust, respect and equality are innate; where quality is integral; and where the values of fair trade were born.

Humanity needs to rethink many of its forms of coexistence. Today we are dominated by commercialism. The current priority is power, which is achieved with money no matter what or who is harmed along the way. They measure our work using the units of efficiency and competitiveness. That must change. We must act in ways that always seek balance. That is why the SPP small producers are telling the truth about what is happening. Our intention is not to hurt anyone, but we must generate awareness that many companies are not acting responsibly. Responsible consumers are lied to. We want those consumers to join our network. We can all grow, have power and feel good in this network of like-minded organizations and individuals. We will lead through example. That is the right way.

JP: Telling the truth is a very powerful statement, Nelson. Frankly, your last response makes me think of the power dynamics we see in North America concerning race. You don't know what you don't know. For example, I'm white. As a result, I am privileged in ways that Black, Indigenous and People of Colour are not. Until I was able to recognize and fully acknowledge that privilege, I thought that I could be neutral about racism. It comes down to the question of being fair or being equitable. To many white people, to be fair means to treat everyone equally and to be neutral or objective. But I must acknowledge that non-white people need more than neutral treatment to achieve equity. White people in a sense need to give more power to non-white people than we might think is fair. The same can be said of our colonial relationships with small producers in the South.

How do you see the imbalance of power between a small producer like yourself and a buyer play out? What would force the power to shift from the buyer to the producer in a more balanced way?

NMM: When a buyer and a producer come together to work, it is often because the buyer has found a quality product that they need. From there, an inequality often occurs because that relationship continues under rules and not under joint dreams. Ethical standards are often governed by pre-established parameters that are not updated in the current context and formulated from a position of distrust. Essentially, small, organic producers are being forced to pay for the damage and irresponsible behaviour of chemical agriculture and unethical global trade culture. The payment comes in the form of costly tasks and high inspection costs — and we are not the ones that caused the imbalances to occur in the first place. In fact, we are already paying disproportionally as destructive weather patterns, brought about by climate change, bring flooding, drought and erosion to our communities.

Consumers mistrust producers. As a result, many of the fair trade and organic regulations are not aimed at the producers' dreams of a dignified life; a price for their harvest that allows them to take care of their family and their crop; the conservation of their land; or community building. A permanent, joint responsibility between the producer and the buyer would be ideal because we would both grow. But often, when the producer states that the sale prices offered for their crop does not cover production costs, the buyer responds by saying the market cannot pay them more; competition is too tough; the consumer does not have time to think about the producer when they go to the supermarket; or other similar arguments.

The voice of the buyer and the producer at the fair trade table must be different because they are different identities, but they must be aligned with the same objectives and purposes for joint growth. And of course, the needs of the least powerful must be addressed as a priority. Before anything else, producers must have a voice at the fair trade table, but even today that is not yet fully realized. Having a voice does not simply mean hearing our voices say words — but working together to achieve it.

We need to reinvent fair trade. We must accept the great life lessons resulting from our mismanagement of the planet and abuse of power. Isn't this a fitting time to do it? If we unite conscious producers, consumers and buyers and jointly work on a proposal for systemic change, we will achieve a fair trade that is truly fair and the balance that we so badly need.

JP: It's interesting that you say the voice of the buyer and producer must be different because they are different identities. Perhaps there is an idealism within fair trade that we are all one voice and should be able to share the fair trade table together. Power dynamics and the culture of the global marketplace seem to make sharing impossible. Instead, producers are required to assimilate and learn the language of the Global North. Even in fair trade, we are forced to focus on the market as the common language between buyers and producers. It's the language of buying and selling and presumed acceptance of the "truth" of the global marketplace: efficiency, efficacy, productivity, measurability and quality.

But you're saying that producers want to speak a different language focused on balance, human relationships and relationships with our environment. Again, I see the same challenges within the anti-racism conversation in North America as it relates to assimilation. Assimilation only exists when one cultural norm is taken as the "standard" or "right" way of doing things, and, to belong or be accepted, other cultural groups with different norms must assimilate. But unequal power dynamics are the reason that assimilation exists. I suppose small producers would like an organization that speaks the language of small producers and doesn't allow unfair compromises to dilute their goals and vision as a unified group. Does this make sense?

NMM: Indeed, fair trade has been selling the idealistic image that we are all one voice, and we all sit nicely at the table together. But there is a deeply rooted dynamic within the relationship between small producers and buyers of power and dependency. It seriously affects the agency of small producers, and within SPP we feel the need to take steps away from that relationship and find our own power. We need to be a single voice that states the need for equality and balance. It sometimes feels risky, and we must always be assessing the price we pay for taking these steps.

Focusing on the market is fine — because we need to develop fair trade markets — but not without considering the true principles and values of fair trade. Each voice speaks of their own interests while ignoring the realities of small producers. Even worse is when we hear those voices telling us we must be more competitive and efficient and that our small production systems must disappear. It is the same global discourse that aims to soothe the consumer's consciousness by promoting the mistaken idea that fairness should not be too expensive.

The small producers of SPP do not want a different language; we want the truth of fair trade to be spoken. Fair trade is selling an idealistic image because the global trade system has ultimate control. Capital is the one in charge. That is why we have organized into SPP. The language of fair trade is part of our own identity and was born of who we are and what we do every day.

Buyers need to understand and demonstrate their co-responsibility with small producers, and SPP is only interested in connecting with buyers who understand that. With those buyers within our network, we can make consumers aware of the reality of small producers; by uniting everyone in the chain in this common understanding, we can be stronger.

JP: Nelson, would you say that all small producer co-ops and associations feel the same way about balance, relationships between people of the Global South and Global North, the goals of fair trade and the global marketplace? Our small worker co-op has relationships with several different producer organizations in different parts of the world. All are democratic organizations. Some of them want to talk about these issues and others do not. Do all these small producers agree on how to best forward the needs and desires of small producers? Moreover, how do large organizations maintain and preserve the authenticity of human relationships at a global scale? Is it even possible?

NMM: Yes, I think it is the dream of all small producers to have a healthy planet of which we all take care, where our work is recognized so that our families have a dignified life. A world where power relations between buyers, consumers and producers are balanced. A world where governments make favourable decisions for the most vulnerable. May all families on the planet benefit! How very dreamy this must sound in the face of a totally different reality, but who does not want us all to live better?

Just because the SPP is a democratically structured organization does not mean that we cannot make mistakes in our decisions or differ in our opinions. Unfortunately, we have disagreements on how we achieve our needs in the world, but that is part of the process of discovering our agency. We have always been orphans in the global market. SPP gives us a unified front from which we fight. It allows us the dignity of becoming protagonists in our own development and not mere beneficiaries of a system that does not allow us to be what we are.

Many producers who work independently from producer-owned organizations often receive biased information on the reality of the world and live dissatisfied with what they have. On the other hand, many producers' organizations are too afraid to lose their current share of the "better than conventional trade" market to fight for the prices they truly need to satisfy the needs of their members. We want all of them to understand that only together, with their support, can we achieve our goals. If we work hard to grow the reach of the SPP network, we will involve more small producers organized into more commercial alliances and more consumers. I think it is possible, but only if we trade the Global North's mantra of efficiency and productivity for that of balance and respect for people and our planet.

Recommended Resource
Símbolo de Pequeños Productores/Small Producers's Symbol. <www. spp.coop>

Part Two

Fair Trade in Action

The same day they are picked, flowers leave the Nevado Ecuador facilities for Quito airport, ready to be shipped to Europe or North America. Approximately 224 million roses are sold each year for Valentine's Day only! Source: Éric St-Pierre

8

A Brief History of Fair Trade

From Charity to Autonomy and Justice

Darryl Reed

In 1988, an organization of small producers in Mexico, the Union of Indigenous Communities of the Isthmus Region (commonly known by its Spanish acronym, UCIRI), joined with a Dutch non-governmental organization, Solidaridad, to establish the first non-state regulatory body with the mission of supporting small producers. Underlying this joint act of political autonomy, which many see as inaugurating the fair trade movement, was the producer organization's previous history with Northern NGOs in the alternative trade movement. The producers saw these two initiatives as complementary components in a locally driven development strategy. While solidarity-based relationships with alternative trade organizations (ATOs) provided a wider range of benefits and facilitated greater economic autonomy, fair trade policies were intended to ensure more just economic relationships with corporate buyers who bought most of their produce. Small producers, however, would encounter difficulties trying to combine these two strategies of alternative trade and fair trade. One major problem was with Northern NGOs, specifically with the new certifying bodies that excluded small producers from their decision-making structures. This chapter examines the complex relationships between small producer organizations and Northern NGOs. It concludes with a brief account of the causes of the mission drift within the certifying bodies that restricted the ability of producer associations to exercise political and economic autonomy in pursuit of their development aspirations.

CHARITY TRADE, HUMANITARIAN AID AND DIGNITY

Many Northern NGOs trace the roots of fair trade back to the 1950s and 1960s. During this period various religious-based NGOs started working with small producers in different contexts (e.g., as refugees displaced by conflict, as victims of natural disasters, as communities suffering from abject poverty). While the focus of their work was primarily humanitarian, some of these aid organizations began importing goods, mostly handicrafts, produced by members of these vulnerable groups. The NGOs provided little training and resources to the producers to develop as commercial enterprises, while the artisanal goods they produced could not be sold in conventional commercial outlets. As a result, sales depended upon the willingness of church members to support vulnerable groups. This original form of direct trade has been referred to by some as charity trade. This latter term is a bit ironic, as the intent of those involved was to enable these vulnerable groups to maintain a sense of dignity, by allowing them to see themselves as more than the objects of charity.

INTERNATIONAL TRADE, STATE AUTONOMY AND NGO ADVOCACY

By the mid-1970s and early 1980s, as Northern NGOs' awareness of the economic and political roots of poverty and humanitarian crises grew, much of their work shifted from humanitarian aid to development programs and advocacy. Regarding the latter, NGOs supported greater autonomy for Southern states, both collectively and individually, and actively advocated for policy initiatives that they designed to promote more just economic and social outcomes. Supporting Southern states was important because, in the absence of democratically controlled international legislative and judicial institutions, these states were forced to negotiate on unequal terms with much more powerful Northern states.

Organizing collectively through the Group of 77, Southern states initiated a series of proposals to adopt/adapt international agreements to ensure greater economic autonomy and more just trade relations. Northern NGOs saw an important role for themselves in advocating for such initiatives, especially with their home governments. Among the collective initiatives supported by Northern NGOs were the Trade, Not Aid campaign (premised on analyses that Northern aid programs largely benefitted donor countries), the work of the UN Commission on Transnational Corporations and efforts associated with the Report of the World Commission on Environment and Development (the Brundtland Report).

Southern states also sought to exercise their autonomy individually by adopting state-led development strategies, in contrast to more market-led approaches. Three models were most prominent:

- state-led capitalist industrialization (e.g., in East Asia, India, Brazil), with strong state support for large, mostly family-owned, national corporations;
- state-led development (e.g., Cuba), featuring centralized planning, extensive ownership or control over productive assets and relatively generous social programs; and
- "third way" approaches (e.g., Chile, Tanzania, Jamaica, Nicaragua), which allowed for state ownership in some key sectors (finance, infrastructure and natural resources) and some intervention in markets (e.g., through agricultural marketing boards), while emphasizing greater economic opportunity for "popular classes" (small producers, workers, chronically under- and unemployed) in the form of land reform, reforms to co-operative and labour legislation, stronger social programs, etc.

Northern NGOs tended to advocate most strongly for governments adopting "third way" approaches.

With the economic liberalization of the late 1980s and early 1990s, efforts by Southern states to assert their autonomy, both collectively and individually, largely dissipated. Attempts to hold multinational corporations (MNCs) more accountable through hard regulation and more equitable trade agreements had been derailed, while the Southern states' ability to effectively promote greater economic opportunities and autonomy for vulnerable groups, including small producers, waned, with the elimination of trade quotas, the dismantling of agricultural marketing boards, etc.

ALTERNATIVE TRADE, SOLIDARITY AND ECONOMIC AUTONOMY

As Northern NGOs increased their development programing in the 1970s, much of their activity was directed towards agriculture, where they focused both on organizational and technical capacity building. With the failure of Southern states to promote more just trade relations and their decreasing ability to support small producers, by the mid 1980s Northern NGOs began to perceive an increased need for facilitating market access for small producers.

The resulting practice of "alternative trade" that emerged would include several key features:

- solidarity-based commercial relations between producer organizations and ATOs dedicated to supporting small producer organizations;
- a commitment to improving the productive and organizational capacities of small producers; and
- an increase in alternative retail capacity dedicated to make purchasing more convenient for supporters (with "world shops" in Europe numbering in the thousands by the mid-1980s).

For small producer organizations, like UCIRI, the initial allure of alternative trade relations was higher prices, generated by eliminating local intermediaries and creating more direct trade relations. In addition, however, ATOs were able to provide resources (e.g., training, finance, market knowledge, etc.) which had the potential for significantly increasing their organizational, productive and commercial capacity. Such increased capacities could facilitate producers' abilities to improve product quality, to process and export their own products, to better access higher paying (fair trade, organic, gourmet) markets and even to diversify their product offerings. To the extent that these capacities were realized, they increased the economic autonomy of producers and their ability to pursue their own development visions.

The ability of ATOs to facilitate greater economic autonomy among producers was hampered, however, by two factors. First, ATOs were themselves underfunded and understaffed and, therefore, had limited capacity for collaboration and coordination. As a result, the movement only had the expertise and resources to provide capacity building and alternative markets for an extremely small percentage of small producers. Second, the movement did not directly address the unfair trade relationships, dominated by oligopolistic MNCs, under which small producers had to conduct most of their business. It was this latter situation of unjust trade relations that sparked a novel response by UCIRI and Solidarity.

FAIR TRADE, CERTIFICATION AND ECONOMIC JUSTICE
In 1988 UCIRI and Solidaridad established the Max Havelaar certification scheme, which was designed to induce corporate buyers to act more fairly with small coffee producers. As a form of social or non-state regulation, certification programs seek to induce more responsible corporate behaviour by leveraging support from ethical consumers or citizen consumers,

rather than relying upon laws or policies enforced by the state (e.g., state marketing boards, international trade agreements).

The most distinctive feature of fair trade certification, vis-à-vis other schemes, is that it required buyers to source exclusively from democratically organized small producers. It also established standards for fairness in the relationship between small producers and (corporate) buyers, including the payment of a guaranteed minimum price and a social premium (to support community projects, organizational development, etc.). Other practices were encouraged, such as long-term contracts and advance payments.

Establishing a certification scheme was an important act of (collective) political autonomy by small producers (and their allies) in the face of regulatory inaction by states. Strategically, fair trade was important because it provided a necessary second front in the efforts of small producers to implement a local or endogenous development strategy based on community discourse and values and reflecting relationships of social and economic solidarity. Alternative trade relationships directly supported the capacity building and economic autonomy needed to implement such a strategy. Fair trade, however, was necessary as a complementary strategy to address the dependence of small producers on corporate buyers. By limiting unfair competitive advantages of corporate actors, fair trade enabled small producers to ensure basic subsistence for their members, while they developed their capacities to compete in high quality (organic, gourmet) markets and established more supportive commercial relationships with ATOs.

As a strategy, certification initially seemed to be highly successful. In its first year of operation, Max Havelaar captured 1.8 percent of the Dutch coffee market. UCIRI, as a co-founder of the first certification scheme, was initially the biggest beneficiary of fair trade. While fair trade did not significantly change most aspects of their relationships with corporate buyers, it did provide them with higher prices, which they were able to invest in capacity building and various regional development activities. The latter included, among others, social infrastructure (schools, clinics), physical infrastructure (e.g., roads, a bus company), the opening up of a domestic market for their coffee and moving into non-agricultural products (to help generate local employment). Thus, an increase in economic justice (in the form of higher prices from corporate buyers) indirectly facilitated the economic autonomy of UCIRI (complementing the direct efforts of ATOs) and their ability to implement a development strategy based upon the vision and values of their indigenous communities.

While UCIRI and other producers enjoyed the surprisingly rapid success of Max Havlaar, they and their allies understood that it would not be easy to induce the participation of all or even most corporate actors. The largest Dutch coffee company, after initially agreeing to participate, pulled out of the initiative before its launch and, shortly thereafter, organized a competing industry-led scheme. This foreshadowed the type of resistance from industry that would emerge for fair trade across a range of product sectors in the coming years. It was not only industry initiatives, however, that would emerge as new competitors to Max Havelaar.

THE TAKEOVER OF CERTIFICATION BY NORTHERN NGOS

Max Havelaar's success in the Netherlands did not go unnoticed. Although initially reluctant to expand into other countries, as it saw itself as a local initiative, Max Havelaar began to support the establishment of new national organizations (e.g., in Belgium and France) in 1991. However, it encouraged these organizations to set their own standards and procedures.

In the meantime, the founding of Max Havelaar induced the formation of two new certification bodies. The first of these was developed by the European Fair Trade Association (EFTA), a new organization of ATOs formed in 1991. EFTA proposed an international certifying body comprising national members (which would have NGOs and other ATOs as their members). The new international certification organization was to develop common standards for use by the national bodies for the certification of a range of products. In 1992, EFTA and another partner founded TransFair International, and in the same year TransFair Germany became its first national member. Subsequent national "franchises" were quickly added in Europe and then in Japan, Canada and the United States. At the same time, a group of NGOs in the United Kingdom was forming its own national certification body, the Fairtrade Foundation, with its own standards and monitoring and enforcement practices. It launched its first certified product in 1994.

This rapid expansion of new labelling bodies provided a great spur to fair trade sales. It also created some significant problems for small producers. First, the use of different standards and monitoring/enforcement procedures led to increased costs (and confusion), as producer organizations had to use different packaging, were subject to multiple inspections, etc. Second, the decision by TransFair to certify products from privately owned estates in some product categories (e.g., tea), introduced direct competition between small producers and estates within the fair trade label. Small producers saw this both as unfair competition (due to the lower cost structures of private estates) and duplicitous on the part of the certifying body (as it focused its marketing on small producers, but did not provide consumers a way to ensure that the products there were buying were produced by small producers). Third, small producers had been excluded from representation in the governance of these new organizations.

Over the next few years, national members of the three certifying bodies would engage in negotiations to form a single organization, a process in which small producers had voice but no vote. By 1997 fourteen national initiatives had agreed to form the Fairtrade Labelling Organizations International (FLO). The formation of the new international umbrella organization went some way toward solving the concern of small producers regarding competing standards by creating one common set of norms. Still, there were concerns about the fairness of the new standards, as producers thought that they were based upon an inadequate understanding of their reality and the full costs being imposed upon them. The agreement regarding the new organization also failed to address small producer concerns about the certification of privately owned estates, as the use of estate production was not only reaffirmed, but over time was extended to almost all new product categories. Finally, ignoring the calls from small producers to be included in decision making, the national initiatives decided that they would be the sole members and owners of FLO and that they alone would have voting rights.

The resulting exclusion from shared political autonomy within FLO meant that small producers could not effectively raise two other major issues of concern. One entailed the rules for licensees within fair trade. Key issues here were whether buyers should have to make minimum purchases (e.g., a certain percentage of their total sales) and whether standards should be graduated (to force buyers to increase their commitment over time). A second issue was whether licensees with a stronger commitment to fair trade (e.g., the 100 percenters that purchased only certified products) should receive special benefits (e.g., lower fees, special recognition, etc.).

The exclusion of small producers from sharing in political autonomy within FLO adversely affected economic justice within the system in three primary ways. First, the resulting failure of FLO to establish minimum prices for all products (and to regularly update them) meant that FLO was not effectively addressing a key feature of the oligopolistic power of corporations. Second, inadequate monitoring and enforcement enabled corporations to shift costs onto small producers. Third, estate production constituted unfair competition within the Fairtrade label itself, as small producers had to compete with estates that had lower cost structures. What made this competition especially unfair was the unwillingness of FLO to be transparent and let consumers know how their products were being produced.

Their lack of political autonomy within FLO also had adverse impacts on the economic autonomy of small producers, as Fairtrade regulations inhibited the ability of consumers and ATOs to support them. Several mechanisms are involved:

- oligopolistic practices by MNCs that have tended to squeeze the products of ATOs off of supermarket shelves;
- MNCs regularly buying out more successful "mission-driven" competitors;
- unfair competition as corporate competitors enjoy cost advantages by sourcing from large estates;
- the unchecked lack of transparency in corporate practices (e.g., misleading consumers about product certification); and

UCIRI's main warehouse in Lachiviza, Mexico.
Source: Francisco VanderHoff Boersma.

- the lack of disclosure requirements by FLO (e.g., not requiring buyers to disclose what percentage of fair trade sales constitute of their total sales).

PRODUCER EFFORTS TO RECLAIM AUTONOMY

In an effort to (re)claim their autonomy within the fair trade movement, small producers pursued three strategies. The first entailed developing strong institutional relationships between small producer organizations. This was done along both geographic lines and product lines. UCIRI initially spearheaded these efforts by supporting the formation and development of other producer associations in Mexico and starting a national network. Following this example, producer organizations across Latin America and the Caribbean formed their own organizations and developed international connections. Such activity eventually resulted in the founding in 2004 of the Coordinating Body of the Latin American and Caribbean Network of Fair Trade Small Producers and Workers (CLAC). During the same period, producer organizations also started organizing around product lines, first in coffee and honey and later in other products.

The strengthening of small producer organizations through national and international networks was important for two primary reasons. First, interacting as small producers, they did not experience the same power differentials among themselves as existed in their relationships with Northern NGOs. In this space, they could learn from each other, share resources and strategize as to how they could best promote their common interests and vision for fair trade. Secondly, stronger internal organization enabled producers to better leverage their collective economic weight and other resources in bargaining with other actors, most notably the national initiatives in FLO.

The second strategy was oriented towards (re)claiming autonomy within FLO through promoting more inclusive democratic structures. It primarily consisted of attacking the FLO regulations that excluded small producers by marshalling the support of fair trade activists, consumers, ATOs and even sympathizers within some of the (smaller) national labelling associations. Establishing CLAC as an international producer organization was an important step in this struggle for political autonomy within the FLO system, as it enabled Latin America and the Caribbean small producers to speak with one voice and more effectively mobilize resources and supporters.

Progress in attaining a more equitable role in decision making would be slow and somewhat frustrating for producers as FLO initially made only minor concessions. These started by FLO offering a single board seat to producers and increasing the number slowly over time. In 2012, however, FLO (now Fairtrade International) announced that "producer organizations" would become equal members and co-owners of the organization and would have an equal share of voting rights.

While this development represented a major victory, small producers did not experience it as constituting full equality and truly shared political autonomy for two main reasons. First, the national labelling bodies kept some key powers for themselves, such as the right to name the chair of the board. More importantly, however, for small producers, the claim for equal participation was vitiated by an earlier problematic initiative by FLO. Specifically, after Latin American and Caribbean small producers organized CLAC in 2003, FLO pre-emptively initiated the organization of producer networks in Asian and Africa to ensure that they would include estate owners as well as small producer associations and co-operatives. CLAC members viewed this as a somewhat cynical move on the part of FLO to ensure that small producers could not effectively organize (alone) on a worldwide basis.

The third strategy small producers adopted to exert their autonomy entailed establishing their own standards for fair trade. In 1999 Mexican producers took the first step in this direction by founding the first national labelling body in a Southern country, Comerico Justo Mexico (CJM). Two significant features distinguished CJM from the national members of FLO. First, only small producers could be certified suppliers. Second, traders and processors (especially larger corporate actors) were held to higher standards that restricted the role of intermediaries, promoted more processing (value-added) by small producers and required increased purchases over time. Due to these more stringent norms, CJM was never recognized as a full member of FLO.

These standards and the conception of fair trade that they embodied, were not only shared by Mexican producers. A few years later, CLAC established the Small Producers Symbol, which closely reflected the vision and principles of CJM. This new symbol had two strategic goals. First, it was an attempt by small producers in the South to assert their right to establish standards for fair trade in their own countries. Second, it was an effort to pressure FLO to adopt more progressive standards, standards that would both contribute to their economic autonomy and hold corporations to fairer practices vis-à-vis small producers. The establishment of the Small Producers Symbol created huge tensions between Fairtrade International and CLAC, with the former threatening to sue. As a result, small producer organizations had to set up independent organizations to promote the new label. The Small Producers Symbol continues to be a major source of tension.

CONCLUSION

The question that remains to be answered is why the fair trade movement, initiated as it was by and for small producers with the help of NGOs, underwent an apparent mission drift, involving a series of decisions that undermined the ability of small producers to simultaneously pursue increased economic autonomy while inducing more just trade relationships with corporate buyers. Four factors are most important in accounting for this state of affairs. First, although UCIRI initiated the first fair trade certification body, it took time for small producers to organize nationally or internationally. Before this occurred, individual producer organizations were engaging in partnerships with Northern NGOs characterized by significant power differentials. Thus, when new certification initiatives did not include producers in the decision-making structures, individual small producer organizations were neither in a position to contest such decisions nor to refuse to participate. Second, Northern NGOs produced a range of (largely pragmatic) arguments to justify the exclusion of small producers (e.g., they lacked requisite competencies, it would be too costly and/or bothersome for them, it would put them in a conflict of interest, etc.). For their part, small producers rejected these arguments, starting with the problematic (and paternalistic, if not neo-colonial) presupposition that Southern actors needed to be empowered by Northern actors before they could participate, rather than the assumption that, for reasons of justice and efficacy, small producers were essential partners in any such endeavour. Third, as FLO and the national initiatives grew, they increasingly recruited corporate professionals with specialized knowledge but limited or no experience in fair trade and little commitment to fair trade values. Fourth, addressing institutional interests (e.g., paying the bills, career aspirations of executives, competition with rival initiatives) became more of a priority. These interests were best served by strategies (e.g., estate production, rapid growth, lower standards) that aligned more with the interests of (potential) corporate licensees rather than those of small producers.

One interesting question that cannot be answered, unfortunately, is how fair trade would have developed if small producers had been fully integrated into the system as equal partners from the beginning. Another question — whether small producers can still reclaim their autonomy within the fair trade system and alter the established path dependency — remains open.

Recommended Resources

Anderson, Matthew. 2015. *A History of Fair Trade in Contemporary Britain: From Civil Society Campaigns to Corporate Compliance.* Basingstoke, UK: Palgrave Macmillan.

Bennett, Elizabeth. 2012. "A Short History of Fairtrade Certification Governance." In Janet Dine and Brigitte Granville (eds.), *The Processes and Practices of Fair Trade: Trust, Ethics and Governance.* London and NY: Routledge.

Coscione, Marco. 2014. *In Defense of Small Producers: The Story of* CLAC. Halifax, Winnipeg: Fernwood Publishing.

Jaffee, Daniel. 2012. "Weak Coffee: Certification and Co-Optation in the Fair Trade Movement." *Social Problems,* 59, 1.

Renard, Marie-Christine. 2010. "In the Name of Conservation: CAFE Practices and Fair Trade in Mexico." *Journal of Business Ethics,* 92, 2.

Smith, Alastair, and Francisco VanderHoff Boersma. 2013. "Comercio Justo Mexico: Potential Lessons for Fairtrade?" In Darryl Reed, Peter Utting and Ananya Mukherjee (eds.), *Business Regulation and Non-State Actors: Whose Standards? Whose Development?* London and NY: Routledge.

9

The Roots of Fair Trade and SPP

My Experiences Alongside Small Producers

Jerónimo Pruijn

"Half-heartedness leads to nothing. Half-good is not good. Half-true is untrue." — Multatuli, *Max Havelaar*, 1860

PROLOGUE

I was born and lived for the first 17-odd years of my life, during the 1960s and 1970s, in the Dutch countryside, near the land where Vincent van Gogh was born. There, I was fortunate to have as neighbours a traditional peasant family with a very small farm, which produced a variety of products, mainly eggs, milk, potatoes and various vegetables. Tasks were still largely performed manually. Wout and Anna Van den Aker and their children, Sjaan and Chiel, worked the land with a plow and horse. Whenever the horse got nervous, Wout, like a snake charmer, always knew how to tame it. My brothers and I spent many hours on that farm — wearing traditional dark blue overalls and the now unusual wooden swedes included — with the intention of both playing and helping with milking, collecting eggs, feeding animals, gathering straw or anything else. There we learned the value of hard work and peasant culture, which was strongly discriminated against and already in the process of extermination in Holland at that time. Peasant culture is attached to nature and the disciplined art of turning that nature into food for the entire population. It is a culture that's constantly exposed to inclement weather, harsh markets and government policies.

A PERSONAL PERSPECTIVE ON FAIR TRADE

While various forms of alternative trade, managed by charitable organizations, existed prior to the 1980s, the idea of "fair trade" as a model for tapping into, appropriating and reorienting conventional markets toward fairer trade practices on a larger scale came into its own in the late 1980s as a response to the strong need of tens of thousands of small producer families who were not able to make a dignified living from the sale of products they grew, such as coffee, in countries with high poverty rates. In the course of fair trade's more than 30-year existence, there have been many successes and, at the same time, changes concerning its practice and interpretation.

I want to share some of my experiences in the fair trade movement, from the origins of what is now the Fairtrade label to the creation and consolidation of the Small Producers Symbol (SPP). Of the 31 years I have been involved in fair trade, I have worked the last 30 directly for small

Wout van den Aker on the farm, Vught, Netherlands, ca. 1966.
Source: Archives of Chiel van den Aker

producers' organizations and their projects. The perspective and expectations of small producers regarding fair trade are key to understanding the
origins of this movement, and, at the same time, they help communicate
SPP's *raison d'être*. What I am going to narrate here is a personal perspective; it is not the official perspective of SPP Global, the organization for
which I have been working for over ten years.

THE EARLY DAYS OF FAIR TRADE

In 1988, the first fair trade guarantee label, Max Havelaar,[1] was launched
in Holland, from a collaboration between the Union of Indigenous
Communities of the Isthmus Region (UCIRI), a co-operative of small coffee
producers from the south of the Mexican state of Oaxaca, and Solidarity, a
Dutch inter-church foundation for cooperation. The main reason for this
initiative, as recounted in the book *Fair Trade* by Frans van der Hoff and
Nico Roozen,[2] was the fact that coffee producers had to live on less than a
dollar a day, in poverty, despite their hard work to produce the beans for
the most appreciated beverage in the world. The Max Havelaar guarantee
label was aimed at ensuring that the coffee from these producers could be
sold on a large scale, in collaboration with many coffee brands, through
mass distribution channels in Holland and other countries, guaranteeing
a minimum price and, therefore, a dignified income. It was devised as an
economically sustainable solution to the issue of peasant labour exploitation caused by the "normal" functioning of the market.

For the Max Havelaar model to work it was important to ensure that
big volumes of coffee and other products could reach consumers' tables.
As said, at that time, alternative trade markets already existed, such as
the so-called Third World Shops (later renamed World Shops), where
products were sold mainly handicrafts but also some food items, such
as coffee, tea and sugar, from "developing" countries. The volumes that
these stores moved were, however, very small. For a small producers'
organization like UCIRI, the economic impact of selling something like
100 bags of green, unroasted coffee a year at good prices would have
been negligible, considering that it needed to place perhaps 20,000 bags
produced by its members.

Max Havelaar quickly managed to involve several small- and medium-
sized coffee roasting companies and thus achieved a rapid and growing
presence in Dutch supermarkets and soon, in supermarkets in countries
such as Germany, Switzerland, France, Austria, Belgium, Denmark,

Canada, the United States, etc., in alliance with the equivalent labels of those countries. More and more small coffee producers' organizations were able to increase their participation in this market under guaranteed prices. They achieved better incomes for their members and increased their commercial and management capacities and socio-economic impact.

MOVING TO THE OTHER SIDE

In 1981, I went to study social anthropology in Mexico City for a year. "You're going beyond abroad," neighbour Wout had told me. In the years that followed, I again spent long periods of time in different parts of Mexico. Some time before obtaining my degree as an anthropologist in Utrecht, Holland, and at the intervention of Mexican friends, I got to work as a volunteer for the Max Havelaar Foundation in Holland between 1989 and 1990. In 1990, I served as interpreter and guide for Arturo Jiménez, coffee producer and president of the Union de Ejidos de la Selva, Chiapas, Mexico. Arturo had arrived in the Netherlands from Mexico together with Isaías Martínez Morales and Francisco van der Hoff, both founding members of UCIRI, to celebrate Max Havelaar's first producers' assembly and promote this innovative initiative.

At this assembly, representatives of coffee producers from different countries in Latin America and Africa celebrated the first and encouraging successes of the Max Havelaar guarantee label. It was an excellent opportunity for these representatives, from different countries and continents, to meet and share their experiences and dreams, an experience that laid the foundations for the creation of international networks of fair trade producers. At this time, in the early 90s, the producers' assembly within the Max Havelaar network was considered the highest authority of certified fair trade, and producers took it as truly theirs, even though it was an informal body.

It was thanks to my friendship with Arturo Jiménez that in April 1991 I got to work for the Union de Ejidos de la Selva, or La Selva (The Jungle, in Spanish) in the municipality of Las Margaritas, Selva Region, Chiapas State, Mexico. This working relationship lasted until 1999.

LA SELVA, CHIAPAS

La Selva had just experienced a long unification process resulting in the formation of the Union of Ejidos in 1986. They had been fighting in the first place for the recovery of *ejidos,* or collective land titles, to which they had the right, as stated in the post-revolutionary agrarian reform originally proclaimed in 1911, but these were never conceded. Many members of the organization had been *peones acasillados* (housed workers), that is, semi-enslaved workers from the large coffee and cattle farms in the region.

When I arrived in Las Margaritas in April 1991, La Selva had achieved the right and ability to export directly and had recently accomplished certification of its organic production and became a member of the Max Havelaar system. The organization had also participated in the process of acquisition and subsequent administration of an abandoned coffee processing plant, together with other producer organizations.

Toward its communities, the La Selva team did a hard job to train members for organic production and for coffee quality control. The process of becoming independent from large and small *coyotes* — wild dogs or intermediaries with abusive practices — in the region and selling directly in the organic and fair trade market required greater quality control. Obtaining timely loans was one of the great objectives at that time for La Selva and other co-operatives, to be able to face the *coyotes* in the region and meet the needs of producers. Commercial or government banks did not grant loans to co-operatives or applied excessively high interest rates. Pre-financing offered by fair trade clients opened the door to obtaining more accessible loans and the ability to give a first payment to the producer right when they delivered their coffee.

However, the co-operative, counting more than 1,000 members, had many other concerns. In the communities, there was flagrant malnutrition and lack of access to health, education and communication infrastructure. The mere transport from communities to the municipal centre, via dirt roads or trails, was very difficult and expensive. On one occasion, a baby died in his mother's arms because they did not make it to a medical facility. The diverse needs, both commercial and socio-economic, made it necessary for producers to also mobilize themselves periodically to participate in social protests organized by the national union of coffee producers (CNOC) and peasant-movements in general.

The co-operative entrusted me to work in community development to advance the resolution of diverse basic needs. This work resulted mainly in the creation of various groups of peasant women committed to improving the nutrition of their families by growing vegetables and making bread and other foods. Subsequently, the co-operative undertook a host of other projects, for example, the creation of the chain of coffee shops and coffee outlets Café La Selva, where I was entrusted to collaborate, based in Mexico City. This generated added value for the coffee producers, which was at times better than that obtained through fair trade exports.

THE IMPORTANCE OF FAIR TRADE

During my years working for La Selva I had the opportunity to accompany producers representing the organization in different meetings and visits to clients related to fair trade, alongside other small producers' organizations in the region and other countries. It was a time when the Max Havelaar system[3] had a simple Producers' Register and a monitoring and follow-up system to promote and encourage producer organizations. There was no fair trade certification system in place until the creation of FLOCERT several years later, in 2003.

Producers felt that, with this fair trade system, they had really managed to respond to the interests of organized small producers. Although the daily tasks to achieve work progress in the co-operative and its communities were in no way dominated by the issue of fair trade, and the objective of placing all the coffee in those privileged markets was far from reached, participation in the fair trade market had allowed the co-operative to enter a more stable phase of consolidation in terms of management capacities and results. Having guaranteed prices for a good part of the production and having access to financing became an engine for the development processes.

FAIR TRADE WITHIN A PRODUCER COUNTRY

In the late 1990s, when I was ready to return to my homeland, this time with the family that I had formed in Mexico, I was invited to work on the idea of creating a Mexican fair trade label, the first of its kind in a producer country. For small producers' organizations and civil society organizations involved in strengthening peasant organizations and popular economy in Mexico, the successes obtained in the international fair trade market were a source of inspiration for the creation of Fair Trade Mexico. How was it possible that we were exporting our products for a fair market abroad and not having a fairer market in our own country?

In the first years of this millennium, with Fair Trade Mexico we were able to introduce fair trade in the Mexican market in collaboration with the Solidarity foundation, which was the cradle of fair trade itself, and with financial support from the European Commission. As a result of this project, we also worked on the creation and consolidation of the Mexican Network of Small Fair Trade Producers, the first national network of fair trade producers linked to the Fairtrade Labelling Organizations' fair trade scheme.

THE CONSOLIDATION OF THE NETWORK OF
SMALL PRODUCERS IN LATIN AMERICA AND THE CARIBBEAN

In 2004, we promoted, via Fair Trade Mexico and the Mexican Network of Small Fair Trade Producers, the constitution of the Latin American and Caribbean Network of Small Fair Trade Producers (CLAC), a confluence of the Latin American Network of Fair Trade Coffee, the Fair Trade Banana Network and the PAUAL, the Latin American Network of Small Beekeepers.

In that constitutive assembly of CLAC — during the Fifth Regional Assembly of the Latin American Fair Trade Coffee Coordinator — a broad analysis of the exponential development process of the market and fair trade movement was made, and its conclusions emphasized the need to promote in particular "the progress of small producers in the world fair trade market."[4] In previous years, there had been some changes in the scope and the operating way of fair trade labels that were the focus of the agenda.[5] From the point of view of small producers' organizations, FLO's fair trade had changed its course and core values, since it had moved away from focusing exclusively on organized small producers' organizations. One of the central discussions of this assembly was the issue of including private plantations in the FLO fair trade system. In the case of bananas, tea and other products, private plantations belonging to large producers and small, unorganized producers contracted individually by private exporters had already been incorporated. Small producers' organizations were concerned about this situation — considering it unfair competition, for large plantations historically controlled market access and have much lower production costs — as stated in the resolutions of the assembly. The resounding opposition of the entire regional assembly of Latin America and the Caribbean to the certification of plantations of any product in the FLO system was ratified.[6]

Another central issue on the agenda of this assembly was the request to focus the mission and vision of FLO towards small producers, as narrated by its resolutions: "The mission of FLO International is to promote, by means of Fair Trade labeling, sustainable development and the

empowerment of disadvantaged small producers in developing countries."
Finally, the discussion around an eventual reduction in minimum prices
for fair trade coffee led to the following decision: "Minimum prices must
not be lowered in any case. For products having no minimum price, it is
urgent that a minimum price and the amount of the corresponding social
premium be defined."

THE CREATION OF SPP, SMALL PRODUCERS SYMBOL

Following up on these strategic agreements, CLAC agreed in 2005 to create its own label, an element of identification among small producers'
organizations. This initiative was finally presented on March 26, 2006,
in Tuxtla, Mexico, in the framework of the International Fair of Social
Tourism and Fair Trade, FITS, bearing the name Small Producers Symbol.
In the official statement of this launch we can read some phrases that
marked both SPP's origin and orientation[7]:

> We are pleased to realize that the Fair Trade Concept has begun
> to be used more and more widely, but we are concerned that the
> concept may also have increasingly light weighted and distorted
> content, so we have decided to recall the original principles that
> gave rise to the fair trade system and to fight for them…. With
> this initiative we all commit ourselves to fight for the original
> concept of fair trade, supporting each other in this effort and
> increasing our voice in the American continent and globally.
> Starting today, we have adopted the symbol of our initiative,
> which will identify all the small fair trade producers in Latin
> America and the Caribbean.

After SPP's launch, as a distinctive identifier — not yet as a label with
a certification system — CLAC decided to carry out a feasibility study
and subsequently a strategic plan for SPP's development and launch as a
guarantee label in the market. I had the pleasure of participating in this
process of collective development, between producers and buyers, which
concluded that there was enough interest among buyers and producers
for the SPP to come to life as a label in the market.

In 2010, the first version of SPP's regulatory and certification system was
approved, including the first SPP minimum sustainable prices. In the case
of coffee, these were guaranteed prices based on a study commissioned
by CLAC to define the prices necessary to cover the production costs of

most fair trade small producers' organizations.[8] SPP prices were set above the minimum prices of the FLO fair trade system at that time.

In early 2011, the first SPP products were introduced to the market in Canada, the United States, France and Mexico thanks to the collaboration of several companies in Europe and North America that applauded SPP's creation process as a guarantee label in the market. At the same time, it was decided to expand SPP's presence, from Latin America and the Caribbean exclusively to both Africa and Asia, giving the SPP a more global reach.

From this moment on, SPP developed step by step until it became what it is today, an intercontinental network of small producer families from Latin America, Africa and Asia, now independent from CLAC. With regard to the market, SPP works with companies and worker co-operatives, particularly in Canada, the United States and Western Europe, that are committed to fair trade and small producers as part of their *raison d'être*. SPP has also achieved its goal of becoming a recognized voice for small producers and the fair trade label for fair trade small organic producers par excellence.

FAIR TRADE AS EXPERIENCED BY SMALL PRODUCERS

Fair trade for small producers is a necessary and extremely powerful tool, as long as the value of the work of small producers who were in the cradle of its creation is truly recognized and defended. A true fair trade must cover, to begin with, the integral production costs borne by small organized and ecological producers as part of the principle of economic justice. The work of small, organized producers, as we saw in the example of my experiences in Chiapas, Mexico, has an important and positive effect for local communities and even generates benefits for ecosystems and economies not only at local but also at national and international levels. Consumers on the other side of the world also benefit directly from this, because small organic producers help curb climate change. Fair trade products' countries of origin also benefit since they achieve a better local economy because international migration for economic reasons is slowed down.

From my experience over these more than 30 years, fair trade inevitably is and must be based on specific objectives and values, so it cannot be an objective itself, but it is always a working tool. If for some, fair trade can be at the service of any economic model, from the perspective of organized small producers with whom I have worked, fair trade must be at the service of economic models that guarantee equality, equity, democracy, inclusion and acknowledgement of the value of any work, particularly the work of peasants, whose work has historically been devalued and discriminated against.

Today there are millions of small producer families in Latin America, Africa and Asia, but also in Europe and North America and other parts of the world, who deserve to be recognized for the value of their work, just as the Van den Aker family, my neighbours during my early life, deserved it. A well-focused fair trade has the great potential to strengthen these families of small rural producers in their decision not to let themselves go extinct and show their great value for a more balanced world. Personally, I predict a great future for this type of production and trade in the context of current climatic and health crises, which have once again shown the great contribution and great resilience of this way of producing and making business.

Notes

1   Main character in the novel *Max Havelaar* by the Dutch writer Multatuli, published in 1860, which reflects the exploitation situation in which the coffee producers of Indonesia, a former Dutch colony, lived.

2. This is an English translation of the title of the book, Roozen and van der Hoff (2001) *La aventura del comerce equitable,* J.C. Lattès: Paris.

3   In some countries the name Max Havelaar was used; others preferred Transfair. Later, they merged into the Fairtrade Labelling Organizations.

4   CLAC, Memoria V Asamblea Regional CLA, Parte 4, p. 154, 2004. <http://clac-comerciojusto.org/wp-content/uploads/2015/04/Memoria-CLA-2004-4parte.pdf>.

5   CLAC, Memoria V Asamblea Regional CLA, Parte 1, p. 1, 2004. <http://clac-comerciojusto.org/wp-content/uploads/2015/04/Memoria-CLA-2004-1parte.pdf>.

6   CLAC, Memoria V Asamblea Regional CLA, Parte 4, 2004, p.145. <http://clac-comerciojusto.org/wp-content/uploads/2015/04/Memoria-CLA-2004-4parte.pdf>.

7   CLAC, Declaración Oficial, Lanzamiento Símbolo de Pequeños Productores, 2006

8   CLAC, Estudio de Costos y Precios de Café de Comercio Justo vs Crisis Internacional, 2010. <https://comerciojusto.org/wp-content/uploads/2013/07/estudio-de-costos-y-precio-del-cafe-0000.pdf>.

Recommended Resources

Símbolo de Pequeños Productores/Small Producers's Symbol (SPP). <www.
  spp.coop>.

SPP announcements. <https://spp.coop/resources/communiques/?lang
  =en>.

SPP *Urgent Declaration and Call to Save Fair Trade.* 2017. <https://spp.
  coop/wp-content/uploads/2017/07/Declaration-Call-Fair-Trade_
  VI-GA-SPP_2017_06-29_PUBLIC.pdf>

10

The Only Banana You Should Buy

Changing Canadian Mindsets to Choose Fairtrade

Jennie Coleman and Madison Hopper

Canadians love cheap bananas, but few of us are aware that the international banana trade has a more than century-long tradition of human and environmental exploitation. At Equifruit, a small Canadian company dedicated to importing Fairtrade-certified produce, we have been unpacking this story for consumers and retailers alike and offering Fairtrade bananas as a sustainable alternative. In essence, Fairtrade banana sales in Canada are inextricably linked to changing mindsets. In this chapter, we look at the roots of cheap banana thinking and the alternative that Fairtrade provides, and we'll share success stories from a couple of retailers whose responsible procurement decisions are changing the Canadian Fairtrade landscape.

WHO IS EQUIFRUIT?

At Equifruit, we like to say that we've been "fair from the start." There's a double meaning there: for one, we put great emphasis on the first link of our supply chain, our grower partners, to ensure there's been a fair distribution of value, and for two, we want to highlight that every container of fruit we've ever imported has been certified by Fairtrade. At its core, Fairtrade is a producer movement, but one that requires dedicated business partners in the North, willing to take risks and put themselves out there to make things happen in core marketplaces. On this front, Fairtrade has many different business partners, with varying degrees of dedication, from larger retailers who sell some Fairtrade as an often small proportion of their much wider sales, to a small company like Equifruit, which is 100 percent committed to fair trade and its values.

Equifruit was founded by a mother-daughter duo from Drummondville,

Is paying more for bananas really bananas? Against this common retail assumption, Equifruit seeks to demonstrate the opposite is true.
Source: Jennie Coleman

Quebec, in 2006. It took them about eighteen months to develop their supply chain and build a market for Fairtrade, organic bananas. In produce, it is especially critical that fruit is pre-sold since inventory doesn't last more than a few days after arrival in Canada, by which time you have already paid producers and shipping — and taken on enormous risk. That first container of bananas was delivered on Boxing Day, 2007, to a Montreal distributor. The pair eventually began supply relationships with two small organic distributors in Ontario, but they never got far beyond the minimum container a week needed to keep a produce business viable.

In 2013, Equifruit changed ownership, and under this new management, our current team is driven to make Fairtrade bananas mainstream across Canada. Heavily motivated by our advocacy mission, we are the only Canadian members of the World Banana Forum and were recognized with an Excellence in Producer Partnerships Award at the 2020 Canadian Fairtrade Awards. But we also emphasize that we are a business, simply wishing to trade within the ethical framework that Fairtrade provides. We've invested heavily in our marketing and we've pitched to all major produce buyers across Canada: We aim for national distribution, high brand salience and widespread understanding of why Fairtrade matters — and we won't rest until we get there.

In our banana journey, we've come to realize that many Canadians have little understanding of where their fruit comes from, who has grown it and under what conditions. When we do advocacy work at consumer trade shows and events, we are frequently asked whether these Fairtrade bananas are "local." For most, Banana Republic is the name of a trendy clothing chain, and most assume that bananas are cheap at the grocery store because the inherent growing and shipping processes are cheap, too. In one Toronto-area grocery store, there's an enormous banner in the corner of the produce department that declares "Paying too much for bananas is bananas" — and so with messaging like that, it's no wonder that cheap banana pricing is the accepted norm.

A LITTLE BANANA HISTORY

The export banana industry got its start in the late nineteenth century, thanks to a handful of entrepreneurs whose banana ventures eventually morphed into the United Fruit Company (known today under the Chiquita brand name) and Standard Fruit Company (now known as Dole). These two multinationals grew across Central and South America through huge land deals made with often unelected, authoritarian governments, political machinations and "gunboat diplomacy," with military and financial support from the United States government, leaving human and environmental exploitation in their wake. They owned the full chain of production and made innovations in logistics to keep fruit fresh on its long voyage to grocery stores northward.

The United and Standard Fruit companies were joined by a handful of other players, and by 2002, just five companies (Chiquita, Dole, Del Monte, Fyffes and Noboa) controlled 70 percent of the global export industry. While it is estimated that the market power of these multinationals had dropped to 44 percent by 2013, it is still rare in Canada to see bananas that aren't stickered Dole, Del Monte or Chiquita. Their names continue to be the most recognizable brands in produce: Most Canadians can easily rhyme these off, but you'd be hard pressed to find someone who could name even one apple or broccoli brand.

The early banana companies poured vast funds into branding and based their marketing plan on making bananas in North America cheaper and more popular than apples. In this, they succeeded handily. To this day, bananas are the most consumed fruit in Canada, averaging 15 kg per capita, well ahead of second-place apples, which hover around 10 kg per capita, despite local production and ready availability. Pricewise, bananas average just C$1.55/kg (70 cents/lb), far below the cost of apples, which retail at approximately C$4.50/kg (C$2/lb).

THE POWER OF RETAILERS

In the last 30 years, the major banana companies have changed their business model by divesting actual land and production ownership to working instead through contract plantations in their former growing countries — a much less risky strategy that also provides a buffer from liabilities at farm level. Independent growers have gained market share, though small producers continue to struggle to access the export market directly and are often forced to sell to the big companies at often impossibly-low prices in order to make ends meet. It's an hourglass problem: Thousands of small producers are forced to sell production to a narrow bottleneck of a handful of exporting companies, providing little choice to consumers in countries like Canada. Though companies such as ours have managed to emerge, Fairtrade bananas in Canada have eked out less than 1 percent market share, and so, even though the major banana companies hold less power than a generation ago, their legacy continues through the world's fixation with low-priced bananas.

In the power shift away from the major banana companies, retailers have come away the big winners. With concentrated supermarket ownership, major players have incredible purchasing power. In recent years, the German-owned transnational discount retailer Aldi has effectively set banana pricing across Europe by declaring what price per case it would be paying for the year ahead. In autumn 2020, although production costs had increased due to necessary COVID-19 precautions, Aldi unilaterally announced it would pay US$1.25 less per case in its 2021 contracts than in 2020. Production countries contested the decision — but eventually fell into line. This included Ecuador, the world's largest banana exporter, which resisted at first but then set its official minimum price per case at lower than 2020 levels in a bid to not lose market share.

KNOWN-VALUE ITEM CONSTRAINTS

In Canada, retailers feel immense competitive pressure to keep banana prices low. For literally the last century, cheap bananas have been used as a bellwether for price perception in stores. Despite there being thousands of items in a typical grocery store, bananas are the most visible product in stores, and drawings or photos of bananas often adorn the outside of stores (No Frills, Farm Boy, Walmart). They are deemed a "known-value item" (KVI): one of those products that consumers buy on such a regular basis that they remember the price from week to week and will notice changes from one store to another. (Other KVIs include milk, ground beef, Heinz ketchup and boneless chicken breasts.)

Some KVI companies have worked to differentiate themselves in the market. A classic example are eggs: While you can still buy generic large eggs, new markets have grown for omega-3 eggs, free-run eggs or even eggs grown from hens on "comfort farms" ("Eggs coming from hens raised in furnished housing including perches and nesting areas"). Bananas, however, continue to be marketed solely on price, ignoring that there are growing segments of the buying public who are looking for more sustainable options in their produce department. We at Equifruit have wondered whether we should market Fairtrade bananas as having come from comfort farms. Would photos of Fairtrade producers sipping cocktails on posh sofas in the midst of their plantation lead us to the long sought-after tipping point in market penetration?

Pitching Fairtrade bananas is a challenge. The fruit is still the Cavendish (the leading banana type under cultivation in the world), the same variety of banana being peddled by the large banana companies — but it comes in at a higher price. Contrary to every other fresh commodity in stores, buyers at the major Canadian supermarket chains have been buying bananas from the same three suppliers for a hundred years. Relationships have developed, and a certain way of understanding banana pricing is well entrenched. The feedback we often hears is this: "We love what you're doing and what you advocate for, but our customers won't understand the reason for the price increase, and we will lose market share to our competitors."

THE MECHANICS OF FAIRTRADE

Despite these roadblocks, we persist, buoyed by the transparency of Fairtrade's standards, which in turn allow us to be transparent about the building blocks of our price. Under Fairtrade standards, both buyers and sellers must respect set rules to be able to market fruit using the Fairtrade logo. For producers, there are two standards: one for smallholder farmers[1] and the other for "hired labour," the latter of these standards applies to the way workers must be treated on larger plantations. The standards cover a large swath of sustainability (economic, environmental and social) and governance objectives. To meet these, though, producers can expect something in return from buyers, who must respect both minimum price standards and the payment of the Fairtrade Premium.[2]

Fairtrade minimum pricing is established through a collaborative process between Fairtrade International's central standards team and banana producers. (In fact, Fairtrade minimum prices are set by commodity, by country and not just for bananas.) Producers each submit their cost structure to come up with an average minimum price, called the Cost of Sustainable Production. Stakeholders in the Fairtrade system are consulted on proposed pricing, and once this is set, that Fairtrade minimum price is a floor price that cannot be touched. If market prices fall below the set minimum, buyers must respect it. When they agree to the minimum, buyers are agreeing to pay a fair price for fruit that has been produced sustainably, according to Fairtrade standards. The minimum price is not necessarily the price to be paid, but it represents a starting point for negotiations, and when market prices rise above the minimum price, producers have every right to negotiate their pricing upward.

The Fairtrade Premium is an additional amount contributed by buyers and used by small producer co-operatives or worker councils to invest in capacity building or community development projects. The premium is usually correlated to commodity weight, and in the case of bananas, it is set at US$1/standard 40 lb case. We work with two co-operatives of small producers, one in Ecuador and the other in Peru, and these partners have used the social premium for a range of projects, from building new offices and a warehouse for stuffing containers, water conservation projects in packing houses and a composting project to enrich growing soils, to contributions to two schools for disabled children, support for a shelter for child victims of sexual violence and a maternal health unit at a local community health centre. In Covid times, the Fairtrade premium has been used to provide health security measures for workers, donations of medical equipment and food aid to vulnerable people.

While the social premium gets all the best photos and great press, it is really the Fairtrade minimum price that is the bedrock of Fairtrade for small producers. With a guaranteed minimum price and long-term contracts with buyers like us, producers have income stability over the year regardless of the vagaries of the market or the pricing whims of the large players. Each of the small producers in our partner co-operatives is a small business run by a family who wishes to see their business grow.

With Fairtrade conditions locked in, they are more likely to secure loans to invest in improvements to their farms. And with income security, they know that they have the means to hire workers and pay them decent wages — and the confidence to send their own children to school. We hope that Fairtrade will make banana farming a viable career path for these children once their education is complete, so that we in Canada will continue to have delicious bananas for many years to come. (The same question applies to many, many other agricultural crops worldwide: What young, educated person would want to continue in their parents' footsteps if there isn't an economic upside? How long can we rely on exploitative production to maintain our long-term food supply?)

BUILDING MOMENTUM

In August 2020, Fairtrade Canada commissioned Leger Marketing to survey 2,000 people in Ontario and Quebec to gauge their interest in Fairtrade bananas — and the results were extremely positive. The study found that 54 percent of consumers who were educated about fair trade would choose to purchase Fairtrade bananas, but that only 29 percent of these currently had access to them. Leger also found that 19 percent of consumers are willing to switch grocery stores in order to get Fairtrade bananas — a staggeringly high number that, even if it were halved to account for good intention inflation, would point to a strong movement toward sustainable choices at the grocery store. No matter the naysayers, we forge on: Our sales have grown an average 20 percent per year over the last ten years, and we've never rolled out a program with a new customer who didn't see an increase thereafter in both sales and tonnage. While our path to growth has been driven by the hard work of small producers who deliver high quality bananas, year after year, it has also required dedicated retail allies, education and a good measure of patience.

FAIRTRADE BANANAS AS A SOURCE OF PRIDE
AND DIFFERENTIATION AT SOBEYS IN QUEBEC

Sobeys is Canada's second largest grocery store chain, and while most procurement works on a national basis, produce is bought separately for the Quebec market by a team in Montreal. This team, led by visionary produce leader Francis Bérubé, started buying our bananas through a distributor soon after imports began, and in 2014, we began a direct selling relationship with them. Around this time, they decided to make a full switch from their non-Fairtrade organic bananas to our Fairtrade organic bananas in all their Quebec banners (IGA, IGA Extra, Rachelle Bery, Marché Tradition and Bonichoix).

This responsible purchasing decision makes Sobeys the largest single seller of Fairtrade organic bananas in Canada and generates tremendous pride internally across the Quebec team. Sobeys has signs up in all their stores touting their Fairtrade commitment, and it's clear that messaging is intended as much for their store customers as it is a reinforcement of company culture. Over the first six months of 2019, Sobeys' manager of produce innovation, Guillaume Durocher, organized a series of training sessions for produce staff across the province and in French-speaking New Brunswick. Each session included an icebreaker where staff were taught about our Fairtrade bananas and then required to get up and sell the product to each other, modelling how they would talk about the bananas to customers and thereby reinforcing the information they'd learned about Fairtrade. We prepared a couple of videos to accompany these training sessions, one to explain the banana supply chain from the banana plant, packing process, shipping, ripening and then to store, and the other to present the Fairtrade Premium impact of Sobeys' ethical purchasing policy. At the end of these videos, staff were asked if they'd known that each Equifruit case they sold translated into US$1 for producers, and the sense of pride in the room was tangible. Around this same time, Sobeys' marketing team created and ran a fifteen-second television and digital ad highlighting their Fairtrade banana offering — an absolute first in Canada. They were rewarded for this with a Business Innovator Award at the Canadian Fairtrade Awards in 2020, and rightly so.

EDUCATING LONGO'S GUESTS AT POINT OF SALE

In many instances, your best chance at success is to build a relation-ship with someone who "gets you" and will champion Fairtrade in their organization. At Longo's, a family-owned grocery chain with thirty-six stores in the Greater Toronto Area, that champion has been their direc-tor of produce and floral, Mimmo Franzone. In 2017, Franzone gave us our start by switching out their former organic banana supplier to our Fairtrade product in eight of their downtown locations — and saw sales grow by 27 percent within the first two months of the launch.

More Longo's stores came on board the Fairtrade organic banana program, but in early 2020, Longo's decided to switch to Fairtrade organic in all their stores, with heavy emphasis on educating their guests on the basics of Fairtrade. Each store was outfitted with customized point-of-sale material, anchored in two key messages: "These Bananas Change Farmers Lives" and "These Bananas Build Communities." We also placed portable banana racks to build exposure at opportune spots around the store and increase their guests' repeated encounters with fair trade messaging. There were several other activations: staff training, flyer support, demos in all stores and an article in Longo's quarterly *Experience* magazine, all designed to further build Fairtrade comprehension.

A month into the new organic Fairtrade banana program, sales had increased by over 50 percent. Since bananas are highly perishable and Longo's conventional banana program was relatively untouched by the surge in organic bananas, the increase in sales stemmed from one of two things: First, Longo's acquired new organic banana customers from other grocery stores, and second, our Fairtrade messaging motivated non-buyers of bananas to become Longo's banana shoppers. In either case, we conclude that communicating on fairness in bananas closed a previous gap between Fairtrade banana availability and demand.

Fairtrade banana producer in Ecuador holds up a promotional banana as part of Equifruit's "Only Banana You Should Buy" campaign.
Source: Andree Bull/Play Studio

KEEPING AN EYE ON LONG-TERM CHANGE

In 2020, when it became clear that the year was going to play out much differently than anticipated and that no travel would be possible, we decided to launch a major rebranding project. Though we are proud of our sales growth, we recognized that we would have to capture significantly more volume for Fairtrade bananas to reach the mainstream. The new look is bold, confident, colourful, young and playful — all the while bringing customers back to the fact that Equifruit is the "Only Banana You Should Buy." This key message is supported by various ways of saying, essentially, "Farmers Gotta Get Paid."

Longo's Franzone immediately spotted the potential for this bold new approach and launched a trial of Fairtrade conventional bananas on Grocery Gateway, its online delivery business, and six of its brick-and-mortar stores. Goal for the trial? Maintaining sales and tonnage, and after three months, when this was achieved, Longo's management gathered to decide whether they'd make the full switch across their network of stores. No guests had complained about the price increase, and the quality of the fruit was excellent. "Can anyone think of a reason NOT to do this?", they asked, and finding no objections, they approved this momentous change in strategy. On May 6, 2021, Longo's became the first grocery store chain in North America to make a 100 percent commitment to Fairtrade bananas, both conventional and organic. Company president Anthony Longo was a vocal proponent of the move, which he deemed in line with both Longo's values and growers' best interests.

Though we've had to learn the value of patience in our dealings with some of the bigger Canadian players, we know that with Longo's and Sobeys making highly visible sustainable sourcing moves, our Fairtrade bananas will soon be impossible to ignore. With more Canadians seeking sustainable products and Fairtrade's transparent standards, coupled with our innovative branding and credibility in the marketplace, we have seen that price becomes secondary. The future is Fairtrade, and those Fairtrade bananas will be Equifruit.

Notes

1. The standards for Small-Scale Producer Organization and Hired Labour can be found at <https://www.fairtrade.net/standard/fairtrade-standards>.
2. Fairtrade's Price & Premiums database is available at <https://www.fairtrade.net/standard/minimum-price-info>.

Recommended Resources

Adams, Tim. 2018. "Colombia: No Guns, No Drugs, No Atrocities, No Rape, No Murder. Just Bananas." *Guardian*, 25 February. <https://www.theguardian.com/world/2018/feb/25/colombia-farmers-fairtrade-bananas-civil-war-drug-trafficking>.

Bananalink. <https://www.bananalink.org.uk/>.

Koeppel, Dan. 2008. *Banana: The Fate of the Fruit That Changed the World*. New York: Penguin Publishing.

Produce Talks. 2020. "Fairtrade Practices, Certification and Sustainability." Podcast produced by the Canadian Produce Marketing Association, 30 April. <https://podtail.com/podcast/produce-talks/fairtrade-practices-certification-and-sustainabili/>..

World Banana Forum. <http://www.fao.org/world-banana-forum/en/>.

11

Footprints for Change

An Indigenous Entrepreneur Weaves Traditional Teachings into His Fair Trade Coffee Business

Sarah Niman

Mark Marsolais-Nahwegahbow is a man with a plan. In early 2019, Mark appeared on an Ontario television news program and explained to a growing audience how his fair trade, organic, sustainably-sourced coffee sales would directly address Canada's Indigenous water crisis. For every 100 coffee bags sold in retail stores and for every 50 bags sold online to consumers, the Birch Bark Coffee company would deliver and install a certified water purification system in one Indigenous home. Mark understood he was providing concerned consumers with a socially responsible way to address the Indigenous water crisis.

Over 100 First Nation communities across Canada either cannot consume their tap water, have to boil their tap water or cannot rely on their community's water treatment facilities to be safe on a regular basis. The federal government responded to the crises with plans to eliminate boil water advisories on First Nation reserves, but Mark, who is not independently wealthy, wanted to get clean water into homes faster. He woke up a dormant idea he once briefly explored and started a fair trade coffee company. He adapted his business model to allow him to get cleaner water into Indigenous families' homes.

Mark introduced Birch Bark Coffee on radio stations, television programs and social media. On Instagram, Birch Bark Coffee counts over 3,000 followers, and growing. Mark quickly realized the value in giving consumers a way to directly impact the Indigenous drinking water crisis. "The social impact resonates with people," said Mark. "It touches their hearts. The issue with government promises to fix the water crisis is that we have a legacy of broken promises. Reconciliation is more than words spoken in promise. We need to see it in action."

Mark Marsolais-Nahwegahbow, founder of the First Nations social enterprise Birch Bark Coffee Company, promoting coffee that is "Making a Difference." Source: Mark Marsolais-Nahwegahbow

Mark knew it was important to focus on a sustainable revenue plan. "Without that element of long-term sustainability, I know that I would not be getting the kind of support from the communities," he said. "I am working to make profits, but in keeping with an Indigenous business model, I share those profits with my community. That's the kind of entrepreneur I am working to be." He named his company after birch trees because they served Indigenous peoples, settlers and voyageurs for centuries.

Mark initiated relationships with coffee roasters, farmers and distributors who aligned with his business values to bring coffee from bean to bag. He found small-scale organic coffee bean farms to source his beans, knowing he was supporting Indigenous communities in other countries. Mark tested out a few roasters before landing on one that could meet his growing company's demands and was aligned with his business values. Birch Bark Coffee beans are roasted and packaged in Mi'qmaw territory in Nova Scotia. The labels feature teachings about Indigenous peoples and traditions to educate coffee drinkers about the people with whom they share their lands. The labels are pasted onto the bags by Flower Cart employees, adults with intellectual disabilities. Mark says these steps infuse each bag with dignity and pride.

At the other end of the production chain, Mark connected with a company to produce and install water purifiers in First Nation homes. The water had to come out clean and safe to drink, and the parts had to be reliable. A local water company approached Mark and convinced him their 40-year business experience with water purification products was the path forward. Mark opted for its six-stage washable cartridge to filter out harmful chemicals, viruses, bacteria and parasites while keeping calcium and other minerals that are important for health.

It is one thing to promise water purifiers, and another to follow through. Because Mark has already begun installing water purifiers at Indigenous homes in Northern Ontario, he has developed trust. In return for his dedication to alleviate the water crisis, Indigenous people across Canada count themselves among Mark's best customers and most steadfast advocates. Unfortunately, the COVID-19 crisis temporarily disrupted his scheduled Northern visits, but he plans to resume the work as soon as the pandemic subsides.

Mark installed the first water purifiers funded by Birch Bark Coffee sales himself. He becomes emotional when he shares the stories from this trip. He said the families deeply appreciated the gift. The first installation journeys had challenges, and Mark said he initially felt discouraged because he was not meeting his own expectations. "It's one thing to get frustrated working on a project in your own home, but when a family invites you in and you know their health is on the line, installation hiccups can feel stressful," he said. Mark smiled and said he got the hang of things after navigating the installation procedure a few times. He saw the challenges through to the end and continues to help homes receive water purifiers, one by one.

When Mark launched Birch Bark Coffee, he promised to first address the water crisis in his home province, Ontario. As of autumn 2020, Birch Bark Coffee sales had translated to 15 water purifier installations, and counting.

Decolonizing Water, Drinking Coffee

Once Birch Bark Coffee's momentum began to build, Mark found it increasingly important to balance the fervour and excitement by grounding himself in his teachings. Indigenous leaders approach business not by relying solely on market reports and shareholder input, but also by seeking

Indigenous families. When children grow up learning water is a sacred medicine according to their Indigenous tradition, but cannot access safe water, their culture is at stake. Today, Indigenous communities work hard to reclaim their cultures and their traditional lands. Canada is engaged in an ongoing reconciliation process with Indigenous peoples to right historical wrongs. The federal government promised to end water advisories in First Nation communities by 2021. The David Suzuki Foundation found that the government is not on track to fulfill this promise, and the steps taken so far do not address underlying water pollution issues (Amnesty International 2017). Most water advisories occur in Ontario First Nations. Ironically, this province is also home to the Great Lakes, James Bay and several watersheds. It is also home to the Algonquin, Anishinaabe, Ojibwe, Cree and Haudenosaunee peoples.

Mark returns to his traditional Ojibwe territory regularly. When he goes home, he enjoys reuniting with family members over moose hunts, swimming in the lake during warm months and sharing stories in the colder months. He said these visits show him how honouring those who have walked before him and those who will follow in his footsteps is important to living *mino bimadiziwin*. With this responsibility weighing heavily on his mind, Mark launched a business in alignment with his Ojibwe traditions, selling a product that connects people across the globe. Birch Bark Coffee was Mark's experiment to test whether he could grow a successful business using Indigenous business principles while helping First Nations communities to access safe water.

LIGHTS, CAMERA, ACTION

Anyone who knows Mark can recognize he is a dreamer who makes good on his word. He percolates big ideas and can easily persuade those around him to join in his enthusiasm for reforming criminal justice. After working in corrections for years, Mark started IndiGenius & Associates, a firm that specializes in writing sentencing reports for Indigenous people who have been convicted of criminal offences. These reports are known as Gladue reports or Sacred Stories, and they encourage courts to include reconciliation goals in sentences. Mark also wrote and delivered one of Canada's first college-level Gladue report certification programs.

When Mark launched Birch Bark Coffee in March 2018, media outlets gave increased space to Indigenous water advocates who raised awareness about their access to safe drinking water for cooking and bathing. People across the country and the world began turning their attention toward what was quickly becoming a dark stain on Canada's reputation as an enviable place to live. Incensed Canadians had few options: They could contact elected representatives or contribute money to charities raising money to address the crisis.

Any entrepreneur whose business takes off feels the pull to measure success in dollars, but Mark knew he needed to remember the big picture. "I understood a business that helps Indigenous people access clean water needed to be grounded in a clean ecological footprint," he said. This clean ecological footprint concept grew to become Birch Bark Coffee's guiding ethos. Mark's face became animated when explaining his new business philosophy: A Footprint for Change. Birch Bark Coffee's business model would compete with other fair trade coffee companies in a competitive market. Footprint for Change is the guideline from which Birch Bark operates; it sets Mark's company apart by its multi-generational responsibility to honour the connection between humans, plants and water. Footprint for Change means balancing profits with responsibility to water, earth and future generations.

"I am very aware that as I set the groundwork for this coffee business, the young ones are watching," explained Mark. He wanted Indigenous youth who are learning their traditional, land-based knowledge to see a First Nation–owned business honour those same teachings and earn a profit in a capitalist economy.

Footprints for Change
Birch Bark Coffee's guiding principles:

- The footprints we leave planted on the ground must be good ones, as our young ones are impressionable.
- The footprints must hold faith and dreams for a better future. They must hold encouragement and family support.
- The footprints must hold medicines of Mother Earth and the knowledge to care for her, so the lands and waters may flourish.
- The footprints must have balance to ensure we are emotionally, physically, spiritually and mentally connected.
- The footprints must contain our teachings of wisdom, love, respect, humility, bravery, truth and honesty, in order that we may live a good life. On a global scale, the path we choose will make a world of difference for all our relations, waters and lands to follow.

The Seven Grandfather Teachings (wisdom, love, respect, humility, bravery, truth and honesty) guide Ojibwe people towards *mino bimaadiziwin*. The teachings are goals to strive toward and values that underpin relations between living things. Birch Bark Coffee's early successes and challenges test Mark's resolve to apply these teachings, but the high benchmark "keeps him focused," he said.

Birch Bark Coffee "is an act of self-determination." Mark explained historical policies and laws have limited Indigenous people's ability to govern themselves according to their own laws and traditions. Mark deliberately focuses on maintaining good relations because this is how he infuses his business structure with his cultural teachings. As Birch Bark Coffee grows in a competitive market, Mark knows he is decolonizing coffee for his consumers. Decolonization necessarily links to fair trade principles and practices. Where fair trade responds to paternalistic corporate conglomerates monopolizing profits at the expense of the labourers and lands worked, decolonization is alive. The fair trade ethos and certification is an important element of Birch Bark's mission. "If we took all these steps to produce and sell a coffee that helps support Canada's Indigenous communities but sourced our beans through the lowest bidder with the highest harms to farmers and harvest lands, I'd be a hypocrite," he said.

Decolonization is a path running parallel to reconciliation. Canada's various government levels have made promises to reconcile with Indigenous peoples. Decolonization is the Indigenous community's efforts to reclaim sovereignty and express its right to self-determination. Decolonization and fair trade mirror each other's goal to shift autonomy from the hierarchy back into the people's hands. Mark said he found it a natural fit to seek organic, fair trade and SPP certification for his coffees. (SPP is the Spanish acronym *simbolo de pequeños productores*, an alliance among small producers). Mark sources his Fairtrade-certified coffee through Just Us! Coffee Roasters Co-operative in Nova Scotia, who get the product through co-ops in Latin America using the SPP label.

"This was really my way to get my foot in the door," said Mark. He explained that today's consumers are driving the coffee market to include these certifications in coffee products. What distinguishes Birch Bark Coffee in the Canadian market? For one, Birch Bark Coffee is owned and operated by a First Nation entrepreneur. Second, the business is rooted in Indigenous business principles and traditional teachings. Third, Birch

Bark Coffee is not just a way to support an Indigenous business but also a mechanism to install water purifiers in Indigenous homes.

RIPPLE EFFECT

Birch Bark Coffee's early success instills Mark with great pride, but he acknowledges the work will continue to outpace him. Progress can sometimes feel slow. He is often managing Birch Bark Coffee's day-to-day operations on his own. He said water purifiers line his office shelves waiting for him to arrange transport to homes in northern Ontario. Pandemic-related production and border delays mean he cannot deliver water purifiers as fast as he would like. No matter how many coffee bags he sells, many more families need water purifiers.

When one person stands up against injustice and offers to help, others are drawn to the light in the darkness. As Birch Bark Coffee's mission spreads, Indigenous people without access to water continue to ask Mark for help. "They want to know when I can help them, how soon," he said. "It's heartbreaking to tell them I can't — yet." He understands he can help one home at a time, and he is one person. Constant water crisis–related issues compel Mark to keep going when the mountain seems too high. The water issues are urgent. This urgency makes him wonder why those who promised to help aren't working faster with the resources they have.

Mark is happy to appear at speaking engagements and is often invited to explain how he integrates Indigenous business philosophies with traditional business practices. These gatherings help refuel his passion for social advocacy. Mark's social outreach also introduces him to new ways he can make an impact without spreading himself too thin. For example, Mark expanded Birch Bark Coffee's social impact to honour Two-Spirit people. Two-Spirit people carry both male and female spirits and are revered for their roles as visionaries, healers, medicine people and caregivers. They also face discriminatory barriers. For every Birch Bark Coffee bag sold, the company donates $1 to a trust fund supporting Two-Spirit educational initiatives.

Birch Bark Coffee's impact can be measured beyond its profit margin. Applying an Indigenous business lens, Mark works to ensure everyone who contacts him feels seen and heard. He regularly checks in with himself to make sure he is applying his Seven Grandfather Teachings. He promotes his Footprint for Change philosophy and is challenged to see it differently each time he explains it to a new audience.

Fair trade coffee is one step towards living in greater harmony with Mother Earth. Birch Bark Coffee sales also seek to decolonize coffee sales, undoing harmful colonial policies one cup of coffee at a time.

Recommended Resources

Gilio-Whitaker, Dina. 2019. *As Long as Grass Grows: The Indigenous Fight for Environmental Justice, from Colonization to Standing Rock.* Boston, MA: Beacon Press.

Phare, Merrell-Ann S. 2009. *Denying the Source.* Surrey, BC; Custer, WA: Rocky Mountain Books.

Ruffo, Armand Garnet. 2019. *Treaty #.* Hamilton, ON: Wolsak & Wynn Publications.

Talaga, Tanya. 2017. *Seven Fallen Feathers: Racism, Death, and Hard Truths in a Northern City.* Toronto: House of Anansi Press.

12

Sweet!

How Fair Trade Powers the Sugar Revolution

Martin Van den Borre

On a beautiful day in October 2016, the sun is slowly setting on the small Paraguayan community of Arroyos and Esteros. After a long day of work and meetings with sugar farmers, my colleague, Josiane Paquette, and I are enjoying a late afternoon boat ride on the Manduvira River. We are guided by Andrès Gonzales, the general manager of Manduvira Cooperative, and his brother Francisco, who is also part of a workforce of more than 400 workers in peak season. As the boat moves away from the shore, Andrès points to a small and scrubby looking tree in the middle of a bay, half submerged in the high waters and says with a smile: "You see that tree over there? It's called the *manduvira* tree.[1] It inspired the name of our co-operative, because just like our co-op it can survive anything."

Josiane and I are both visiting Paraguay for the first time, but over the years we have spent quite a bit of time with Andrès and other members of Manduvira. During that period Andrès Gonzales served as director on the Fairtrade Canada board and so he is a regular visitor to Canada. On his many trips north, he never missed a chance to stop by the La Siembra office so we could work on our various projects together. He has stayed at our homes, sometimes weeks at a time, sharing our daily lives and participating in family and community gatherings, going to concerts, agricultural fairs and a few fishing trips in western Quebec. He particularly liked to visit small Canadian organic and biodynamic farmers to learn and share perspectives on the world. Over the years we have become more than partners. We have become close friends.

So, this is an emotionally exciting trip for Josiane and me. Our co-op has been working with this group of more than 1,300 families since 2002, and we are still trying to understand where these small Paraguayan farmers found the determination to face the brutal Paraguayan sugar oligarchy and become one of the first producer groups in the world to own and operate a world-class sugar mill with the capacity to produce 20,000 metric tons of sugar annually.

Because of this accomplishment and its constant social innovations, Manduvira Cooperative has become one of the poster children of the fair trade movement and one of the most obvious examples of its transformative power. The co-op's financial results speak eloquently of its success: Between 2002 and 2018 the overall assets of the co-op grew from a little more than $8,000 to over $16 million, multiplying by more than 200 times. Ask anyone at Manduvira how this is possible, and, ignoring their own sacrifices, genius and hard work, they immediately point to fair trade and to the strong relationships they have developed with the world's leading fair trade organizations, like Just Us!, Equal Exchange, Equita, Pronatec AG, IDEAS, Gepa, Traid Aid, Ethiquable, Oxfam Belgium, La Siembra and many others. The reason? These long-term committed relationships were fundamental to its success, not only because they paid better prices and offered fair trade premiums, but also because their long-term commitments, an important and essential principle of fair trade, introduced a new variable to the equation — something that small Paraguayan sugar cane farmers could count on for the first time in their history: the possibility to plan long term. It also gave the management and elected representatives of the co-operative something just as important to guide their planning: reliable information on the market and on the preoccupations and aspirations of consumer-citizens. Information that they could act on. They realized, for the first time, they were not alone with their dreams — they had found an echo to their vision and it gave them the courage to leapfrog into an amazing journey that would lead them to build the most ecological sugar mill in Paraguay and become the largest investor and employer in their region, creating hundreds of well paid jobs and bringing tens of millions of dollars in investments into this once impoverished town. The collateral impact of their development as a co-op led to the emergence of an ecosystem of small hotels and restaurants to accommodate the growing number of visitors, students, outside contractors and travellers coming from all corners of the world to witness and study the co-op's transformation.

To understand how positively disruptive this was, one first needs to look at the sugar industry's complex structure, in which the farmer has been, with a few rare exceptions, the servile supplier — if not a slave or a bonded laborer — of an industry dominated by large corporations, and to a certain extent by other co-operatives that serve only their own members and care little for the fate of farmers outside of their own membership. Most small sugar cane farmers have no access to the market. The industry is characterized by complex and opaque market structures, unfair subsidies and price adjustment mechanisms (that even agro-economists struggle to understand) and a labyrinth of import and export rules and quota systems. It's all designed to serve and protect the market of Northern sugar beet farmers (20 percent of the world's sugar comes from beet sugar), large plantations and the privileges of food and energy multinational corporations (and sometimes co-operatives) that require cheap sugar to make everything sweet: cookies, chocolate, candy, sodas, animal feed and, more recently, biofuels. Outside of a few exceptions, such as in Cuba in the 1950s or Peru with President Juan Francisco Velasco Alvarado's land and agricultural reform in the 1970s, rare are the moments where sugar cane farmers were at the centre of any positive reforms that benefited them and alleviated this condition.

The acceleration of the organic and fair trade movements in the early 2000s brought Manduvira a flow of activists and consumer-citizens eager to work with them, with the ambition of transforming the food system and international trade. This allowed farmers in Paraguay, Belize, Costa Rica, Mauritius, Malawi and elsewhere to travel and participate in market fairs and seminars, to learn and gradually better understand the colonial and political dynamics that shaped their past and the possibilities that could transform their future. Having relationships that went beyond purely merchant preoccupations and extended into the social, environmental, political and spiritual sphere allowed them to develop their autonomy and their own strategies to access high-value niches, while eliminating, as much as possible, intermediate market structures.

Circumventing these intermediaries can be quite complicated, especially in the chocolate and sugar industries, where the financial and technical barriers to processing and marketing are important and out of reach for small, marginalized farmers. More often than not this is simply impossible because of national public policies designed to protect inherited colonial privileges and keep sugar cane the "poverty crop," the cheap input to make sugar — one of the ten most traded commodities on the planet, with coffee, gold and corn — a very lucrative trade that, like cocoa and coffee, leaves a trail of economic exclusion.

The idea of processing its own sugar and eventually diversifying into other industrial activities became Manduvira's obsession. Its members were ridiculed in their own country and called dreamers, but in silence they continued advancing, keeping their eye on their objective. In 2003, the co-operative's only option was to sell its sugar to a major regional mill. This family operation was paying very little money to the farmers and was constantly trying to break their solidarity and disrupt any form of organization. While a fair trade organization would pay the premium directly to the co-op on the cane they supplied, the sugar had to be bought from the mill, which would systematically pressure the producers into selling at the lowest possible price. This contradiction is possible because, with the exception of the Small Producers Symbol (SPP), which has a minimum floor price of $850 per metric ton, there is no minimum Fairtrade-certified price for sugar. The fair trade premium of $60 per metric ton of sugar ($80 per metric ton for certified organic sugar) is the main economic metric that matters for certification, in addition to the negotiated price. This means that some multinationals can easily make back whatever premium they paid by simply lowering the price on their remaining purchases. (This is also a practice commonly seen in cocoa and coffee, although there is a minimum for those commodities). But having access to international buyers and consumers meant Manduvira had a better understanding of the market trends and dynamics. The co-operative realized that its product was unique and more importantly that its work as responsible caretakers of their its corner of the earth was valued by the citizen-consumers. The co-operative decided to organize and demand higher prices. It asked Andrès Gonzales to lead a sugar strike and become its general manager. Andrés agreed under the condition that the protests be carefully planned out and, more importantly, that they remained peaceful and non-violent. He knew too well the sugar oligarch would use any form of violence to repress the community. One hundred families volunteered in the name of the community to conduct a non-violent strike. Despite the peaceful nature of their protest, they suffered death threats and other forms of intimidation and humiliation. But they were able to maintain the solidarity, and after three weeks of the "sweet revolution," as they call it, the mill owner conceded on price. This was one of the first examples of a peaceful negotiation and settlement between organized famers and the Paraguayan agro-industrial complex, and this empowered the members. They continued their march toward the dream of owning their mill, and in 2005 they rented a 100-year-old sugar mill.

This allowed them to gain independence from the local mill owner but also to prove to themselves and the world that they were able to operate and market their own finished goods.

In 2008, while they continued working in the rented facility, they set out to build their own state-of-the art mill, which generates its own electricity. They designed it on a circular production model, ensuring to upscale all the refuse from the mill into fertilizer. It was inaugurated in 2014 and is still today the most modern and ecological industrial operation in the country's sugar industry. On that inauguration day, the dreamers were proud. The Paraguayan sugar industry was no longer controlled by only six families but by more than one thousand, and that number is still growing today as the co-operative has extended its reach to other farmers and is collaborating with neighbouring organized farmers in the region.

This is a story that the La Siembra and Equal Exchange worker-owners know well, as the destinies of our three co-operatives were closely tied to the Fairtrade organic hot chocolates that La Siembra had introduced into the market shortly after launching in 1999. In 2002, at the Expo East Natural Products show held in Washington DC, Kevin Thomson, one of La Siembra's early worker-owners and co-executive directors received in the co-op's name the prestigious socially responsible business award. This highly acclaimed recognition gave our little co-op, still an unprofitable start-up at the time, tremendous international visibility, which sparked substantial international demand for our unique organic fair trade hot chocolate.

Requests were pouring in from the United States, New Zealand, Japan and Australia, most of them coming from fair trade organizations and co-operatives, like us, 100 percent committed to fair trade. Besides access to working capital, which our co-op obtained from solidarity investors Desjardins Credit Union and Shared Interest, our main barrier to materializing these partnerships was finding enough organic and fair trade sugar, a rare commodity in what was just a budding organic market. Manduvira became our supplier, and this has tied us together to this day. During the following two decades, our hot chocolate exports would grow to more than $2.5 million annually, fueling a huge demand for Manduvira's golden light sugar.

Processing cane sugar can be done at different scales and can come in different shapes and sizes. These choices are often linked to geography. In northern Peru, in the high mountains of the Piura region, Norandino, a second-level co-op, unites over 90 base groups and over 4,000 farmers. In Piura, sugar cane was originally grown as a subsistence crop or a source of alcohol. It is now grown as an alternative crop to coffee or cocoa and transformed into the specialty sugar muscovado, or panela, as they call it in South America.

In the case of Norandino, the high mountains led it to design a different model than that of the low plains of the Paraguayan Paraná. Instead of a large mill at the centre of the agricultural zone, the Peruvian farmers built more than thirty small *modulos*, small production units technically similar to the Canadian sugar shack. Each community has its own processing facility, and, in Piura, the co-op has a sifting and packaging plant that ensures quality control and manages the export process. Producers are paid not for their cane but for the actual sugar, and they need to participate in the processing. While this development model is relatively recent in Peru's history, it is spreading. It was first and foremost possible because of an agricultural and land reform led in the 1970s by the Velasco government, which broke the sugar oligopoly, making sugar the "primera industría sin patron" (first industry without a boss), an important symbol for the Peruvian small farmer that is still referenced today.

In this highly successful model, the advantage to the farmer is not only diversifying income, but also spreading out the work, as the harvest seasons are different from coffee, which helps to mitigate climate uncertainty. Norandino's panela has become a popular ingredient in the European slow food movement, a gourmet delicacy regarded like a fine wine or craft cheese.

While Manduvira's and Norandino's successes are unequivocal, sadly they are rare accomplishments in the world of fair trade sugar. Much remains to be done for the small sugar cane farmers of the world. In most cases, climate change and industry consolidation are making things much worst. Despite the apparently impressive numbers in Fairtrade sales,[2] the proportion of Fairtrade sugar sold around the world is less than 1 percent of the overall volume consumed worldwide.[3] The majority of the sugar we consume is invisible. It is in our foods, beverages, alcohol, animal feed and the biofuels in our gasoline. Even within fair trade networks, I would estimate, based on years of experience and the most recent data from Fairtrade International, that many co-operatives sell less than 10 percent on Fairtrade terms. Conventional sugar is also hard to sell on fair trade terms, especially outside of the United Kingdom — the only large

Table 12.1: Fair Trade Facts

FLO Standards	SPP Global Standards
Minimum price: none	Minimum sustainable price: 850 US$/MT
Fairtrade premium: 60 US$/MT	SPP Incentive (premium): 80 US$/MT
Organic premium: 20 US$/MT	Organic premium: 210 US$/MT
Quality premium: to be determined	Quality premium: to be determined
Number of producer groups: 101	Number of producer groups: 10
Premiums paid in 2018: over US$ 10 million	N/A

Sources: Fairtrade International <https://www.fairtrade.net/> and International Organization for Standardization <https://www.iso.org/home.html>.

market where, unlike Canada, Germany, Italy and France, the fair trade movement is uncoupled from organic networks.

Being able to sell 100 percent of production of sugar under fair trade terms (SPP or FLO) is limited to a select few who generally share these two common characteristics: (1) they handle processing on their own and can control their market and sell finished goods directly; and (2) they are certified organic or biodynamic — markets that most often demand fair trade as an obvious complement and offers an additional premium.

While all these producer accomplishments are rooted in tremendous solidarity from Northern worker and citizen-consumer based organizations, it is important to know that it is not at all one-sided. In 2013, after a few bad years in the market and some badly timed decisions, our co-op, La Siembra, faced possible demutualization and bankruptcy. This was highly publicized after La Siembra tried to leverage financing by participating in the popular television show *The Big Decision*. During the period leading to that crisis, Manduvira and other producer groups like Norandino continued to supply us and directly financed us through supplier credit. While trying to cope with these financial hardships, La Siembra was in no position to honour timely payments, let alone pre-harvest financing, one of the most important fair trade principles. In the end the broadcast gave us a lot of media attention and mobilized our members, but no real applicable solution emerged out of that experience. Years later, in a great gesture of solidarity, an investment in money and human capacity from our friends at Equal Exchange allowed us to steer back to profitability and regain our true identity.

In the wake of this crisis, at a Paraguayan truck stop where we went to drink a soda and eat a slice of pizza, Pablo Cachenot, the Manduvira export manager who we have worked closely with since the very first days, told Josiane and I that despite their concerns, they had never considered stopping supplying us. He reminded us that in 2006, Just Us! and La Siembra co-operatives had been the only partners to "blindly" purchase the first containers Manduvira produced themselves. "You took a big risk by prepaying those containers" he said, laughing. "The same way you believed in us, we believed in you — there is no way we would have let you down."

To this day, telling this story still brings back strong emotions. In moments of doubt, if nothing can lift me up, I think of the *manduvira* tree and the sparkle in our friends' eyes when they were showing us their new mill for the first time.

Notes
1. *Geoffroea spinosa* Jacq. / Manduvirá
2. 170 million tonnes in 2018 <https://info.fairtrade.net/product/sugar>.
3. 172.441 million tonnes in 2018 <https://www.isosugar.org/sugarsector/sugar>.

Recommended Resources
Camino, La Siembra Cooperative, https://camino.ca/
Coscione, Marco. 2014. *In Defense of Small Producers: The Story of* CLAC. Blackpoint, NS: Fernwood Publishing.
Van der Hoff Boersma, Francisco. 2014. *Manifesto of the Poor: Solutions Come from Below*. London, UK: Permanent Publications.

13

"Wear It!"

Moving the Fashion Industry Forward

Erin Bird

This chapter discusses how the fashion industry can move toward more ethical and sustainable choices, including an explanation of how the circular economy can be applied to fashion, using cradle-to-cradle design and current growing trends around reusing, reducing, thrifting, alterations and mending. This chapter also looks at how society can make a stronger connection to producers along the fashion supply chain.

> "Fast Fashion isn't free. Someone, somewhere is paying the price." — Lucy Siegel, journalist for the *Guardian*, in the movie *The True Cost*

As I was starting out on my fair trade journey and becoming aware of why fair trade was important, I remember taking a trip to the mall. I was looking to purchase new dress shirts for my husband and decided to check out the places where I would normally shop. The Bay was a store I frequented, as I felt proud that the store had Canadian roots, and I felt certain that I would be able to find what I needed. In rummaging through the racks, looking at styles, colours and sizes, I started paying attention to the labels and where the shirts were made. Now that I was part of a fair trade community, I wanted to be more aware of where my clothes were made. Made in Cambodia, made in Bangladesh and made in Vietnam are what I found.

With the Rana Plaza factory collapse in Bangladesh fresh in my mind, I knew that I could not buy any of these items. I looked at brands from Canada and the United States, but every shirt I looked at in the store had been made in a country in Asia. I knew that there were problems with labour standards in many of the countries in the Global South, and though some of the styles were what I wanted, I just could not bring myself to buy them because I didn't know if I would be supporting exploitive working conditions.

I reluctantly started to walk through the store and noticed the Olympic mittens and scarves on display, marking the upcoming winter Olympic games. Surely at least these items, celebrating Canadian athletes, would be manufactured in Canada? It was disappointing to see the "Made in China" tag on every single Olympic item. I left the store that day without having bought a single thing. I felt sad, angry and a bit overwhelmed. But amid this hopelessness was a burning feeling that there was a need to bring awareness to this reality and to what actions could be taken.

A COMPLEX SUPPLY CHAIN

When we buy a shirt off the rack at a local store, we may not realize the journey that the garment has taken in order to reach us. It's easy to get caught up in the excitement of the colour, style, latest fashion trends and the feel of a new piece of clothing, without looking at the label or thinking about how it was made. A garment would probably collect many more Air Miles than most people do in a year or two. Due to the number of steps involved in the process of making a garment, and the many hands that touch it, it might seem too hard to trace its journey. But that is exactly what we will try to do here. The steps to create a garment are as follows:

1. Growth of raw material crops
2. Raw material collection (in this case, let us use cotton, which is picked by hand)
3. Material cleaning (cotton ginning and cleaning)
4. Spinning
5. Weaving or knitting
6. Dyeing
7. Cutting
8. Sewing
9. Artwork, embellishments
10. Finished product

The raw material collection and ginning into yarns may be done in a different location than the spinning, weaving or knitting. For cotton, 6.42 million metric tons are grown in India, with China a close second, at 5.93 million metric tons.[1] Cutting, sewing and dyeing tend to be done in factories, usually in Bangladesh, Vietnam or China.[2] Depending on the

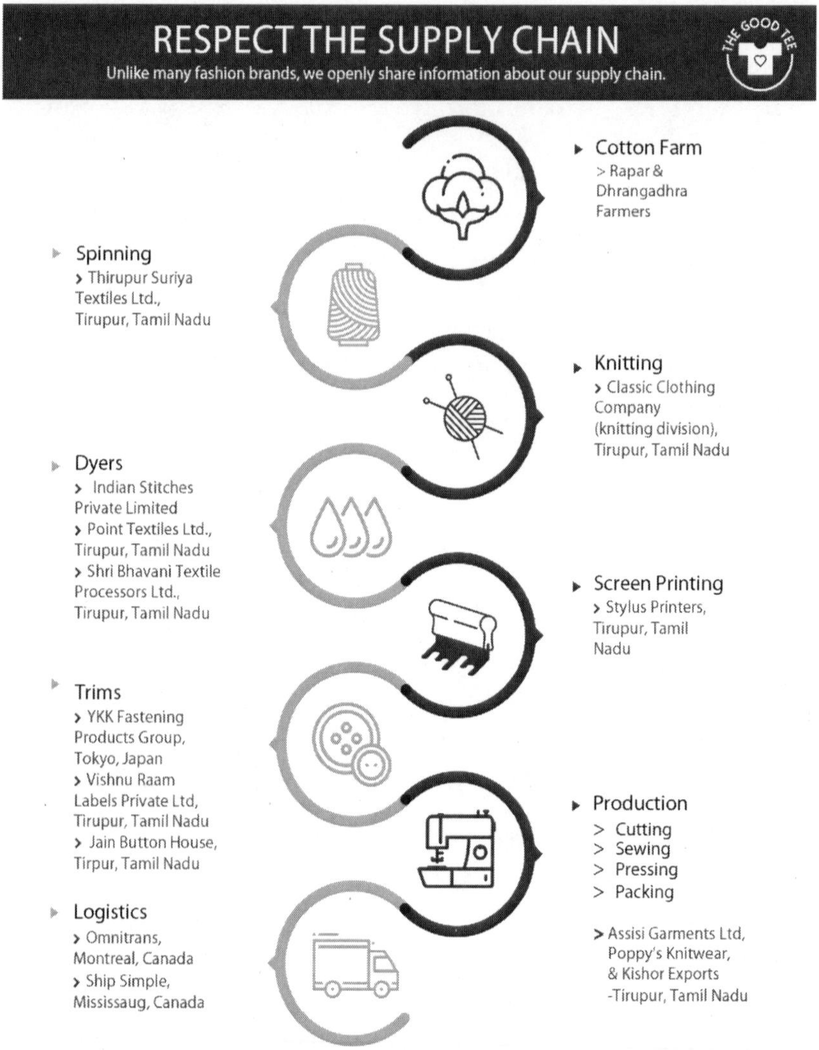

RESPECT THE SUPPLY CHAIN
Unlike many fashion brands, we openly share information about our supply chain.

▸ Cotton Farm
> Rapar &
Dhrangadhra
Farmers

▸ Spinning
> Thirupur Suriya
Textiles Ltd.,
Tirupur, Tamil Nadu

▸ Knitting
> Classic Clothing
Company
(knitting division),
Tirupur, Tamil Nadu

▸ Dyers
> Indian Stitches
Private Limited
> Point Textiles Ltd.,
Tirupur, Tamil Nadu
> Shri Bhavani Textile
Processors Ltd.,
Tirupur, Tamil Nadu

▸ Screen Printing
> Stylus Printers,
Tirupur, Tamil
Nadu

▸ Trims
> YKK Fastening
Products Group,
Tokyo, Japan
> Vishnu Raam
Labels Private Ltd,
Tirupur, Tamil Nadu
> Jain Button House,
Tirpur, Tamil Nadu

▸ Production
> Cutting
> Sewing
> Pressing
> Packing

> Assisi Garments Ltd,
Poppy's Knitwear,
& Kishor Exports
-Tirupur, Tamil Nadu

▸ Logistics
> Omnitrans,
Montreal, Canada
> Ship Simple,
Mississaug, Canada

Figure 13.1: Transparency and the Fashion Supply Chain—The Good Tee. Source: Adila Cokar, The Good Tee, https://www.thegoodtee.com/pages/fashion-supply-chain

type of clothing, additional artwork and embellishments may be added either at the factory, or locally, before being sold.

With internationally certified products, Fairtrade International requires that all Fairtrade products be 100 percent audited at every step of the supply chain. Certification takes a hard stance on this requirement, which makes it very robust. However, it also makes it hard to achieve. With so many steps in the supply chain, traceability and transparency must be present at every step. Currently, only cotton is certified as Fairtrade.

There are other designations that will certify single steps in the supply chain of a garment. Fair Trade USA uses labels such as "Fair Trade Factory" and "Fair Trade Cotton" to identify the steps they have certified as meeting their requirements, but there are concerns with the standards against which the Fair Trade USA certifications are applied. Fairtrade International has rolled out a single ingredient label within a composite product; however, this designation does not yet apply to clothing. Fairtrade International launched its Fairtrade Textile Standard in 2016, but the standard is limited to cotton and has not yet been adopted in many of the countries where change needs to happen. Complexities around instilling a living wage and possibly pushing companies that want to support the standard into being non-competitive is a challenge; systems change is needed but may be gradual to happen.[3]

ARTIFICIAL VERSUS NATURAL

The fabrics that make our clothing can be either human-made (artificial) or natural materials. When talking about natural materials, those most commonly used in clothing are cotton, silk, wool and leather. More sustainable natural fibres are gaining popularity, such as bamboo, Tencel (made from ethically sourced wood fibres or cellulose), hemp and jute (vegetable fibre used to make burlap). New and innovative natural materials include those made from plant and food waste, creating materials such as pineapple and peel leathers.

An advantage of using natural materials for clothing is that they can decompose over time. Artificial materials, such as polyester, spandex, acrylic and nylon, on the other hand, are polymer-based, which come from petroleum products. The advantages of using artificial materials centre on the stretchiness of fabrics, as they can more easily be made waterproof and smooth. On the negative side, artificial materials never decompose. Blended materials that use both natural and artificial materials (i.e., polycotton) provide a more flexible fit initially, though they lose their shape after multiple wash-dry cycles. Polycotton garments are made faster and cheaper, but the end product is harder to recycle.

Fairtrade certification can be applied only to clothing made entirely of cotton material, including thread and all components. Perhaps in the future, other natural materials could be certified, but so far, that is not available.

GMO COTTON SEED

Internationally certified Fairtrade products cannot use genetically modified organisms (GMOs). It may seem like this requirement is purely environmental, but the rationale also includes the social well-being of farmers in the cotton industry. A serious concern in the agriculture industry is around the potential monopoly created by using GMO seed and the ways in which small-scale farmers lose access to open varieties of seed for their crops. According to the Berlin-based non-profit organization RESET, "the ten largest seed corporations dominate three quarters of the commercial seed market. The top three of these, Monsanto, DuPont and Syngenta, represent more than half (53 percent) of the market."[4] The seed control issue is no less prevalent in the cotton industry. The allure of GMO seed is in providing a faster growing cotton crop that is more pest-resistant, but the resulting effects on both people and the environment are a tragic trade-off.

By monopolizing access to seed, landowners and giant corporations, such as Monsanto, control the sales of crops and pesticides required to yield maximum harvests. The plants are engineered to not reseed, so seeds need to be bought again every year, which is an unsustainable process and a constant expense to farmers. GMO plants have been modified to withstand heavy use of pesticides. Roundup is a popular brand of pesticide used on cotton crops, conveniently developed by Monsanto. Several lawsuits have been filed against Monsanto from cancer patients who were exposed to RoundUp while the company had claimed it was safe for human contact.[5] Conventional cotton remains one of the most pesticide-heavy crops in the world, yet the promises of GMO cotton seed limiting chemical application does not equate to reality. Many pests have become tolerant to the pesticides, and secondary pests have been introduced into ecosystems.

Cotton is one of the oldest and most popular materials for clothing. It may be seen as one of the most "dependable" materials around the world for making strong, comfortable and durable clothing. However, over time, this natural crop has been greatly altered from what it was in the days of the Industrial Revolution. Advances in technology have not always come with benefits. Farmers who must buy new GMO seed and pesticides each year may rely on loan sharks in order to afford the purchase. Farmers are often paid less than a living wage in cotton sales, and go further into debt each year, conditions that are exacerbated with variable weather conditions and volatility in the cotton market. Cotton farmer suicides are especially prevalent in India, as farmers spiral into debt and lose hope. The 2011 documentary *Bitter Seeds* depicts the bleak situation for cotton farmers in India.

Fairtrade International has been vocal in its opposition to GMO seeds for all agricultural crops: "Fairtrade believes that the dependence of producers on GMO seeds and the companies that market them is against their long-term interests and outweighs any short-term benefits the crops may bring" (Gelkha Buitrago, head of standards at Fairtrade International).[6]

FROM LINEAR ECONOMY TO CIRCULAR

A linear economy supports a culture that produces and consumes without conscience. A linear economy is the process of how we use our products, from raw materials being taken for production to create usable things to then discarding them when we feel their useful life is over. We buy new, we use, and we dispose. In a linear consumer culture, there is no real thought to how a product is made, the length of useful life and how that product is disposed of after we are done with it. It is a culture of convenience and of entitlement, rooted in colonialism and a colonial view, where people in power exploit others to get what they want cheaply and without accountability. The serious toll the linear economy is taking on our world, both socially and environmentally, is becoming more and more evident.

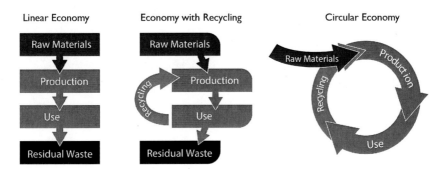

Figure 13.2: From a Linear to a Circular Economy. Source: Government of Netherlands, https://www.government.nl/topics/circular-economy/from-a-linear-to-a-circular-economy.

For fashion, the extensive use of artificial materials, which never decompose in landfills, is creating a serious waste problem. Most clothing is also made of blended materials, making recycling a complex process that is cost-prohibitive and rarely available for consideration. In addition, the concept of "fast fashion," where brands often release 52 fashion seasons a year, encouraging consumers to treat clothing as a disposable short-term commodity, exacerbates the social and environmental strain immensely. The culture of fast fashion has increasingly put stress on raw material producers and factory workers to work quickly and cheaply. The trend over the past 30 years has been for more and more countries in the Global North to outsource clothing manufacturing to countries in the Global South that have lower minimum wages and less oversight on labour and environmental standards. Global Labor Justice carried out two studies in 2018 detailing how exploitation and mistreatment — including physical abuse, sexual harassment, poor work conditions and forced overtime — of Asian female garment workers in two major North American supplier factories created a climate of fear.

Moving from a linear economy to a circular economy means that thought must be given at the start of design and production to how the end product and its composite materials may need to be disassembled, repaired or reinvented into new products and uses at the end of each useful life. The concept of circular economy removes the word *waste* from our vocabulary and rather looks at how materials can be used and reused perpetually for different purposes. Every step of the design, use and reuse process can be continuously optimized, including the cycles of byproducts and the uses of energy, economy and human effort.

The Circular Economy Leadership Coalition is a Canadian organization whose aim is to accelerate sustainable, profitable and zero-waste solutions. The Government of Canada will be co-hosting the World Circular Economy Forum with the Finnish innovation fund Sitra in 2021 (delayed from October 2020 due to COVID-19), the first time the forum will be hosted in North America. The Circular Economy Club is another non-profit organization that advocates for circular economy practices. There are grassroot city chapters in various parts of the world, including seven chapters in Canada: Vancouver, Calgary, London, Toronto, Ottawa, Montreal and Quebec.

Fashion Takes Action is a Canadian non-profit organization that was founded in 2007 by Kelly Drennan to advance sustainability in the fashion industry through education, research and collaboration. The organization hosts the World Ethical Apparel Roundtable (WEAR) in Toronto each year. WEAR has delved into environmental and social issues related to fashion and has invited representatives from Fairtrade Canada to present at its conference. The event is currently being offered as a monthly webinar series and has a strong focus on how fashion should be transitioning from a linear to a circular economy. Fashion Takes Action's website has many resources, including information on the 7Rs of fashion: recycle, rent, reduce, repurpose, repair, reuse, resale.

FASHION REVOLUTION AND #WHOMADEMYCLOTHES

You can't talk about fast fashion without remembering the Rana Plaza factory collapse in Bangladesh on April 24, 2013. Over 1,000 workers were killed and 2,500 injured. As the fourth largest industrial disaster in history, news of this event went viral, casting a light on the unsafe, unethical working conditions of garment workers and calling out popular brands that were involved.

Fashion Revolution was founded in response to the Rana Plaza collapse by Carry Somers and Orsola de Castro, who both have extensive fashion backgrounds and were advocates for transparency in the industry. The main message of Fashion Revolution is to focus on #WhoMadeMyClothes and to demand transparency across garment supply chains. As a fair trader, there are many aspects that should be looked at with respect to Fashion Revolution. In addition to bringing awareness to the conditions in factories and sweatshops and the exploitation of textile workers, fair traders also strive to address the conditions of workers who harvest raw materials. Child labour in the fashion industry is another big problem. Often children are desired for embroidery work as their fingers are small and they can perform intricate stitching. When families feel they have no other option than to send their children to work and help out with family finances, it creates a vicious cycle, as children who must work rather than learn tend to perpetuate multi-generational poverty. Toxic dyes for textiles are also a problem. Few workers are offered protective coverings, yet exposure to dyes can lead to serious health issues. Used dyes are often dumped in waterways that may also be providing the only source of drinking water for thousands of people. *The True Cost* and *River Blue* are two powerful documentaries that highlight the social and environmental issues in the fashion and textile industries.

THE MAKER MOVEMENT

With growing awareness around the serious issues in the fashion industry, more consumers are reassessing their values and shopping habits. Awareness of problems in the fashion industry has enticed more local makers to enter the arena. The mindset is that if we can't trust the big brands to provide transparency, let's do it ourselves locally where we have more control.

Many makers and consumers are embracing the romance of handmade items with a sense of local pride and ownership. The maker movement has definitely increased the appreciation for the time and effort it takes to design and sew an article of clothing. However, the origin and nature of the raw materials isn't always considered; there still seems to be a disconnect between the raw fibres and how they become a piece of clothing. And a fine balance still remains between the desire to support local makers and the culture of convenience.

The time and effort required to create a locally sewn customized piece of clothing is not always something an impatient consumer is willing to wait or pay for. Pressure within the maker community to mirror the fast-fashion expectations of conventional clothing brands and their respective customers can result in shortcuts. There is a wide spectrum of local makers who may claim to be sustainable and ethical but are only able to be transparent within one step of the supply chain. Fair trade consumers who support local makers need to be aware of greenwashing and be willing to challenge the product if transparency is not evident. While the image of sweatshops often evokes factory workers in countries in the Global South, the disappointing reality is that sweatshops happen universally, including in North America and other countries in the Global North. Migrant workers are sometimes taken advantage of — working in confined, unsanitary conditions for negligible salaries — to the extent that the work may be indentured servitude.[7]

The Made in Canada label itself can be misleading, as it is not required to acknowledge where the raw material for the fabric comes from, only the country of final assembly. Even if the majority of a piece of clothing was outsourced for cutting and sewing in a country in the Global South at a fraction of the cost, but the design and final embellishment was done by a Canadian designer, you will still see the Made in Canada label. Goods with the Made in Canada label have had the last transformation of the garment done in Canada and 51 percent of the direct cost incurred in

Canada.[8] With the low cost of materials and labour in countries in the Global South, it isn't very hard to achieve Made in Canada status, despite the fact that a large percentage of effort was done in another country.

When supporting a local maker, fair traders should ask about the products' source materials. Where was the raw material harvested (if natural) and how were the workers treated? What other standards does the material meet (i.e., Global Organic Textile Standard)? How much of the final product was made locally versus internationally? Developing personal relationships with producers is at the core of the fair trade movement, and pushing designers and makers to disclose the quality of the relationships they have with suppliers, sewers, factories and growers should be a responsibility that we advocate within the maker movement.

CELEBRATING A CULTURE SHIFT TOWARD FAIR TRADE FASHION

Before the Industrial Revolution, clothing was hand-sewn by individual makers for their own families and community. Indigenous cultural handicraft such as weaving, beading, embroidery, felting, tanning, distressing and knitting are traditions that have been passed down from generation to generation. Countries and unique communities are often identified by these traditional forms of craft. With the advent of more mechanized and automated clothing manufacturing, traditional handicraft has been limited to small, isolated segments of the population, or in some cases lost altogether. Cultural designs are taken, replicated by industrial machinery and passed off in other cultures as novelty.

However, new trends aligning with fair trade principles, such as support for the Sustainable Development Goals, Fashion Revolution, the maker movement, the buy local movement, the climate movement, minimalist movements and the revitalization of sewing and quilting circles are all working to help reset expectations around what is acceptable for the fashion and textile industries. As well, pleasure in the art of renewing a lost cultural craft or reinventing it for current society is exciting and hopefully a path for the future. Fair trade member organizations such as the Fair Trade Federation and the World Fair Trade Organization have helped promote robust standards for fair trade clothing and handicraft that align to the principles of fair trade.

Fair trade advocates must draw the parallels between other socially and environmentally conscious messages, movements and trends to leverage change. Through education, advocacy and sincere appreciation; listening to the stories that Indigenous makers share about their handicraft; appreciating the time, effort and love it takes to sew an article of clothing; creating a deeper appreciation for each and every piece of clothing we own; insisting that each piece be well made; and respecting the people and environment clothing comes from, we can and will create a fair trade fashion future.

Notes

1. "Side-by-side top 4 Asian countries for manufacturing garments," Manufacturing and QC Blog <https://www.intouch-quality.com/blog/side-by-side-top-4-asian-countries-for-manufacturing-garments>, Oliver Knack, 2017-08-15.
2. Leading cotton producing countries worldwide in 2019/2020, from "Global cotton production 2019/2020, by country" <https://www.statista.com/statistics/263055/cotton-production-worldwide-by-top-countries/>, M.Shahbandeh, 2020-10-06.
3. "Fairtrade's New Textile Standard: A New Option for Consumers," *Fair Trade Magazine*, Erik Johnson, Summer/Fall 2016.
4. "The Privatization of Seeds." RESET. <https://en.reset.org/knowledge/privatisation-seeds>.
5. Katy Moncivais, "Roundup Lawsuit," *Consumer Safety* <https://www.consumersafety.org/product-lawsuits/roundup/>.
6. "Understanding the continued opposition to GMOs," Linda Cornish, *Devex*, 22 January 2018. <https://www.devex.com/news/understanding-the-continued-opposition-to-gmos-91888>.
7. See Clean Clothes Campaign, *Exploitation of Migrants* <https://cleanclothes.org/fashions-problems/exploitation-of-migrants> and Kristi Ellis and Khanh Tran, 2016, "Sweatshops Persist in US Garment Industry," *WWD News* <https://wwd.com/business-news/government-trade/sweatshops-persist-in-u-s-garment-industry-10716742/>.
8. Made-in-Canada Guidelines <https://en.wikipedia.org/wiki/Made_in_Canada>.

Recommended Resources

Circular Economy Club <www.circulareconomyclub.com>.
Circular Economy Leaders <www.circulareconomyleaders.ca>.
Fashion Revolution Canada <https://www.fashionrevolution.org/north-america/canada/>.
Fashion Takes Action <https://fashiontakesaction.com/>.
Source My Garment by Adila Cockar <https://www.thegoodtee.com/products/how-to-manufacture-clothing>.

14

Fair Trade, Firsthand

Connecting Northern Consumers with Southern Producers

Jennifer Williams

Fair trade impacts the lives of millions of farmers and their families in deeply complex and profound ways. To understand these impacts, we need to hear stories about change and transformation — firsthand, from producers. These stories connect our morning coffee with the people who grow the beans, and this connection is nearly impossible to make through articles, blog posts and, especially, marketing material.

In 2016 the Manitoba Council for International Cooperation piloted the first fair trade origin trip from Canada, taking Canadians to visit farmers, workers and co-ops in Peru. The goal was to provide an indepth experience about global commodity production and fair trade and also create a connection between producers and consumers.

Participants included business owners who source fair trade products, staff of the Canadian Museum for Human Rights, procurement specialists with the provincial government and daily consumers of coffee, chocolate and other commodities. We visited northern Peru to spend a week with cocoa, coffee, sugar, mango and banana farmers and hear firsthand the stories of transformation and change that have come through fair trade trading relationships.

Our 2016 trip to Peru set in motion a series of annual origin trips led by the Canadian Fair Trade Network (CFTN). Over a four-year period, I joined four different groups of consumers, buyers, students and advocates. We visited northern Peru twice, Ecuador and Costa Rica. We explored fair trade products such as coffee, cocoa, panela (sugar), flowers, mangos and bananas. The majority of the producers we met can be described as small-scale producers, owning under five hectares of land. Most are organized into producer associations or co-operatives. The one exception occurred in Ecuador, where we met workers at family-owned, cut-flower companies that were committed to applying fair trade standards to working conditions.

The trips often started with a visit to the central offices of an organization to meet with staff and get an understanding of its history, how it operates and the opportunities and challenges it faces. Next, we would typically tour processing facilities to gain insights into the transformation of agricultural products. From there we would visit the farms and communities of producers to gain an understanding of their realities and chat with them about their farms, fair trade, the associations they belong to and the challenges they face.

While fair trade may have emerged from a development mentality, one of providing assistance to those in need, criticized for the colonial legacy that remains at times, these origin trips have consistently demonstrated that fair trade has become a truly international system with active involvement and leadership from Southern partners. The fair trade system provides much-needed checks and balances in the trade of commodities that protects the livelihoods of small-scale farmers and provides environmental safeguards that mitigate against climate change. Without this system in place, the drive for profit at all costs by corporations would leave behind many in the Global South.

FROM MOUNTAINSIDE TO CAFE: EXPERIENCING THE COMPLEX CHAIN OF FAIR TRADE

Fair trade, and all that it touches, is incredibly complex. Millions of farmers and workers around the world are organized into co-operatives or associations that allow them to export their products and attain fair trade certification. These organizations are member driven. This means that each farmer has a role to play in the governance of their organization. They have the right to vote in elections, they have the right to be a representative of the organization, and they have a say in how the organization uses its profits and its fair trade premiums.

Some of these organizations are quite small. For example, 130 farmers comprise the El Guabo Banana Co-operative in Ecuador. Each member of El Guabo cultivates, on average, six hectares of land, and the co-op directly exports fair trade organic bananas to international markets, including Canada, Switzerland, the United States and the United Kingdom. Other organizations, however, can be quite large and complex. Take Norandino

Folks on an origin trip from four universities, one fair trade town, one fair trade business and Fairtrade Canada sit down for a group dinner in Piura, Northern Peru. Source: Sean McHugh

for example, in northern Peru. Norandino is a second-tier co-operative (a co-op of co-ops) made up of more than 6,000 farmers. These farmers produce coffee, sugar cane and cocoa in regionally organized associations, and Norandino provides the processing and value-add production and exports the products. You can find Norandino's products in cafes worldwide, and it frequently wins international competitions for quality.

While the members of these co-ops or associations are farmers, hired staff run the business of the co-op. The employees often come from the region and have an education background in business, agronomy or engineering. In the international market, the staff drive the business on behalf of members, attending trade shows and conferences. To sell as a Fairtrade-certified organization, farmer-led co-ops need to be certified by FLOCERT to Fairtrade International standards. There are strict standards to adhere to, as well as minimum pricing and premium structures based on regional and commodity specific realities.

For anyone interested in understanding fair trade and cutting through its complexities, an origin trip can help put the pieces of this giant puzzle together. Visiting producers and their communities makes it easier to relate to a farmer growing coffee on the side of a mountain in Peru. A trip to an origin allows you to experience the chain of custody — the systems, people, transportation and processing — between the farm and your cup of coffee. On our origin trips, we experienced the roads the

Making Complexity Tangible: A Concrete Example

On one of our origin trips, upon arriving at a fair trade co-operative known for its leadership and commitment to fair trade, we were told that the co-op had just received notice that its Fairtrade certification had been suspended and then revoked due to non-compliance.

This occurs from time to time, as it can be difficult to keep up with the various processes and procedures related to running a business, growing and exporting products, and ensuring good and transparent governance, all things mandated under Fairtrade standards. We learned that the co-op had sold product outside of proper protocol and current contracts, as a higher price was offered by an outside buyer. We also heard rumblings that the person completing the audit, the same person who made the decision to decertify the co-op, may have had a personal issue with the co-op's general manager, hence the somewhat drastic measure to jump straight to decertification by FLOCERT.

The consequences of being decertified were steep. The co-op's fair trade buyers were no longer able to buy from them if they wanted to continue selling this product as Fairtrade-certified. This was of course difficult for the co-op, as they lost customers, and also challenging for the buyers, who have to choose between buying from a co-op they know, and finding an alternative source. This experience opened our eyes to the complexities of fair trade: the day-to-day realities of price, contracts, production and export; the inherent contradictions that often exist; and even how personal interactions play a role.

This experience was also one of our deepest, as we got to see firsthand how these systems work. We spent time with the co-op members, who were happy that we stuck with our plan and carried through with our visit. We even went out for lunch together in a large group that included the general manager of a different co-op. He was planning to outstretch his hand — with not only cash, but technical support and staffing time — to support the co-op's efforts to resolve its issues and get back on its feet. This visit brought fair trade, from what can sometimes be seen as systems, standards and procedures, back to the ground, and back to the people behind it all.

products travel on, visited the processing centres where products are readied for export and, most importantly, met the growers. These trips wove together the human experience of fair trade to make the complex system tangible and accessible.

THE DEPTH OF IMPACT OF FAIR TRADE

Most people who buy a fair trade cup of coffee think they have made a difference because they paid slightly more. This is only the tip of the fair trade iceberg. The increased price paid for that coffee is only a very small part of the impact fair trade has on the lives of farmers and their communities. Origin trips allow participants the opportunity to dive below the surface and see what lies beneath the story of price. On the surface, the impacts of fair trade can be difficult to understand. Through origin trips, we can experience the transformational change that accompanies fair trade and gain an indepth understanding of how key themes work together. We select the groups we visit, the products we observe and the topics we raise, and then we allow the producers and the associations to share their experiences. Here are some of the insights over the years that show the depth of impact of fair trade as experienced on the origin trips.

Yield and Quality Are Key to Increasing a Farmer's Income

Most marketing material about fair trade talks about the price paid to the farmer for their commodity and how that enables them a better quality of life. This is true; there is a minimum price in fair trade and there is a social premium, which is paid as part of every fair trade product, which goes back to the co-op or association to be used as they see fit; this money often gets invested in health, education, infrastructure and/or training for their members. These additional funds are important elements of the fair trade system and should not be overlooked.

However, at the grower, co-op or association level, one of the greatest successes of fair trade has been the ability for growers to invest in their production quality and yield. For a small-scale farmer with, on average, one to five hectares of land, there are limited ways to increase income. Over time the most successful fair trade organizations have demonstrated that by continuously investing in several areas they have been able to greatly increase member income through yield and quality.

Staff lead the group through coffee cupping at Norandino Coop's main facility in Piura, Peru. Everyone got a chance to try their hand at the infamous slurp used by Q graders. Source: Sean McHugh

Investment in the Plants Themselves

Farmers are constantly dealing with changing realities, such as plagues, disease, drought, flooding and climate change, all of which have a great impact on a farmer's ability to produce any product. Farmer organizations are regularly investing in research and testing of different plant varieties that will withstand these changes and offer better yields and improved quality. Much of the success behind fair trade comes in the form of tree nurseries, where members can access seedlings to revitalize their land.

Training and Support

To improve plants' productivity, a farmer needs access to training and support to know what methods work. Most fair trade organizations invest in training and support, which in turn enables farmers to increase the quality of their product and the quantity produced.

On origin trips, we hear from producers who have been able to transition to organic and fair trade because they are now able to get a better price for their crops. This increased price comes not only from the fair trade price but also for the higher quality products farmers are offering the market. In addition, proper upkeep and fertilization of the land has allowed farmers the ability to increase their production of their crops, so much so that this has a significant impact on their incomes.

Quality Enhancements: Processing

Most producer groups have invested in processing of their raw products to improve the consistency and quality of their products. The processing of coffee cherries, from the tree to the green bean that is exported in the international market, requires many steps to ensure a high-quality product. When farmers worked on their own, not in fair trade, they did not have access to the knowledge, equipment or processing facilities to properly undertake the processing of their products to ensure a high-quality product for export. As such their product would receive lower prices in the market. With the investment in these enhancements, farmers are able to get a better price for what they produce and bring in a greater income for their household.

Government Services

The basic services provided by governments in the Global North are often not provided regularly by governments in the Global South. This includes services and infrastructure for water, sewage, electricity, roads, health care, schools, and so on. Many NGOs on the ground are working to provide these services, and over the years, producers and their communities have used fair trade premium money to invest in many of these basic services.

Fair trade has played an important role in providing these services. In the early years of an association, fair trade premiums are often used for communications facilities, health care and schools, dental clinics and centralized water distribution. Then, as a fair trade organization becomes an important exporter in the national economy and a key source of foreign currency and jobs, local and national governments take notice and start investing in much needed infrastructure in the region where the organization is based.

During fair trade origin trips, we often saw electrical poles being installed or roads being repaired, and heard stories of how the roads and bridges have changed dramatically in recent years. We visited communities that used to be cut off from the rest of the region when the rains would come as there were no bridges to enable transport over the water. Yet with the year-round need to transport sugar cane for export, these communities now have better roads and bridges that not only facilitate export but also make it easier for people to acquire goods and services. Fair trade has put these rural communities on the map in their own countries and has forced their governments to pay attention to them and provide much needed basic services and infrastructure.

Political Shift

Through participation in their local fair trade organizations, fair trade producers have the opportunity to become active politically. For these producers, serving on a co-op's board or representing an organization internationally are the first steps to standing for election in the local region. In addition, as large contributors to their country's GDP and export revenue, small-scale farmers and rural communities now wield political power they did not have before. Politicians are more apt to listen and, as a result, rural communities involved in fair trade are more likely to have their needs met than ever before.

Training, Development and Self-Worth

Consistently on these trips we hear stories from farmers who speak of the pride of being part of a global fair trade community, of the pride of knowing that their coffee, cane, cocoa, etc. are in demand in foreign markets. We hear stories of gratitude for being part of an organization that is doing something meaningful for its community.

Producers have opportunities to learn, grow and develop that would not have been available for most rural farmers without the existence of the fair trade system, which requires participation and governance. Fair trade offers personal and professional development that would otherwise be lacking for a rural farmer; this in turn supports emotional well-being and has transformed the lives of thousands.

Solidarity

These trips, and fair trade as a whole, enable conversations, relationships and friendship. They work to break down barriers between the North and South by finding commonalities and mutual interest. Rural farmers feel a sense of pride when outsiders express interest and are willing to collaborate to make something work. This goes for farmers all over the world, and people in general all over the world. When we get past our differences, and the many challenges that each of us faces, we realize we're more similar than we are different, and we have the same goals of living a meaningful life of dignity, eating good food, having a roof over our head and having access to health care and education and the ability to take care of our family, friends and community. Fair trade helps break down barriers and allows for solidarity and respect.

The Spin-Off Benefits

The international fair trade system creates a benchmark in regions where there are fair trade organizations, such that fair trade pricing becomes a standard in the region and provides protection for other farmers to receive fairer prices for their commodities, even if they are not part of a fair trade co-op. In Costa Rica, the Indigenous Cocoa Association has set a pricing standard in the region, so other cocoa farmers, even if they are not involved in fair trade, use the price being paid by APPTA (Asociación de Pequeños Productores de Talamanca – Small Producers Association of Talamanca) as a tool to negotiate prices with buyers who would otherwise pay significantly less. Fair trade pricing and associations set a standard on how to treat farmers — this has the benefit of spinning off to all farmers in regions where fair trade producers are based.

We Are All Connected

One of the most common challenges farmers discussed with us in recent years was climate change. Farmers everywhere in the world are grappling with the changes in weather patterns right now. We met coffee farmers who have had to plant and harvest much higher up the mountains than in years prior, to simply maintain their crops. We met cocoa farmers who are looking to diversify their crops and cocoa associations that have had to buy driers for their cocoa beans because the weather has become too unpredictable and wet. In hearing these struggles, we know that we also face these challenges, though differently.

CONCLUSION

At its very core, fair trade is about honouring each individual on this planet as worthy and equal, and in doing so, ensuring they receive a fair wage for the work they do — so we can enjoy our morning coffee or afternoon bite of chocolate. Fundamentally, origin trips take us to that humanity, to that moment of knowing that the farmers who grow the products we enjoy in Canada deserve to be treated with fairness, equity and respect. By hearing a farmer tell their story of how fair trade has impacted their life, from their own mouth, in real life, we can understand how our actions matter and how we will never see a cup of coffee the same ever again.

Recommended Resources

Bowes, John, ed. 2011. *The Fair Trade Revolution*. London: Pluto Press.
Canadian Fair Trade Network. Trips to Origin. https://cftn.ca/trips-origin/.
Cooperativa Agraria Norandino. https://coopnorandino.com.pe/.
Meet the People Tours. https://www.meetthepeopletours.co.uk/.

Part Three

Pursuing Global Justice

Brazil, with its vast warehouses receiving 3.5 million metric tons of green beans in 2020, is by far the most important coffee producing country, providing about one-third of the coffee consumed around the world. Dirley, a warehouse worker, in the state of Minas Gerais, Brazil. Source: Éric St-Pierre

15

The Sustainable Development Goals as a Global Framework

Where Fair Trade Fits

Sean McHugh and Nell Jedrzejczyk

THE NEED FOR GLOBAL REORIENTATION

There are 7.8 billion people on planet Earth, a number that is expected to rise to 9.7 billion by 2030. We share the same basic needs and wants, yet many people around the world lack access to clean water, healthy food, quality education, adequate shelter, security and basic health care. Additionally, a fair portion of the world's citizens are denied basic rights and freedoms, such as freedom of association, the right to peacefully assemble, the right to vote and the right to travel. Hundreds of millions of people struggle from day to day on little to no income. Farmers and workers toil on farms and in factories, often while living in poverty.

Meanwhile, resources are concentrated in only a few hands: the wealthiest individuals hold far more wealth than that of the rest of the world's population combined. With this concentration of capital comes power and control, resulting in an ability to create circumstances that benefit individual interests. This injustice has created a tangled mess for marginalized populations, trapping many vulnerable communities into vicious cycles of worker exploitation, ongoing environmental degradation and unhealthy living and working conditions.

If we seek to ensure dignity and prosperity for all, societal objectives and practices must shift away from individual capital accumulation. After decades of unfettered capitalism, it is clear that the notion of trickle-down economics has not worked. The global system, as we know it, has led us to a tremendously unequal place. If we hope to address the world's problems, we will need to reorient everything we do and set new, broader and community-based goals. We will need individuals, public institutions, businesses and governments to prioritize and embed sustainability into everything.

The road that brought us here is complex. It will not be easy to change course and leave behind the systems that created our present circumstances. How do we empower people to stand on their own feet? How do we put the right protections in place to ensure a soft landing in times of uncertainty? How do we redistribute wealth so that everyone has enough? How do we build a global community where global health and happiness are at the forefront of our efforts? What if there was a plan that could ensure every person had their needs met, and could live in an equitable society?

FOCUSING ON THE SUSTAINABLE DEVELOPMENT GOALS

It might be hard to imagine, but the United Nations 2030 Agenda for Sustainable Development is that plan. The agenda, adopted by world leaders on September 25, 2015, outlines 17 major Sustainable Development Goals (SDGs) that address specific targets. The SDGs address a range of issues from poverty and community development to environmental protection and beyond. The UN calls the SDGs a "blueprint for peace and prosperity for people and the planet, now and into the future" (United Nations n.d.). These goals are steps toward establishing prosperity, dignity

Source: United Nations Sustainable Development Goals <https://www.un.org/sustainabledevelopment/>. The content of this chapter has not been approved by the United Nations and does not reflect the views of the United Nations or its officials or member states.

and a healthy planet for all. With its significant scope, the 2030 Agenda implies that nobody should be left behind; it also implies that nobody can stay on the sidelines. To succeed, we must be more than bystanders.

It is important to note that the agenda outlines goals rather than clear-cut instructions for the most efficient way of reaching global sustainability. Of course, total clarity on society's most complex issues is hardly possible — do a little thinking about the issue of poverty, for example, and you will also need to consider education systems, inclusive employment, racism and other root causes. To amplify these complexities, the relationships between issues vary to unique degrees between geographical locations and scales. As such, the SDGs outline targets and goals that are formatted to allow for broad interpretation through whatever system is most appropriate per region. Therefore, because of the interconnected complexities of world problems, a central component to the agenda is the connectivity between the SDGs. Without multidisciplinary thinking and support from a broad set of actors targeting many goals, the agenda will not see much success.

While leaving the SDGs open to interpretation allows flexibility, this openness also creates a lack of emphasis on the significance of creating interlinked implementation strategies that prioritize systemic advancement over the cherry-picking of goals. It will not work if actors are allocated certain responsibilities and work independently on different targets. Rather, the SDGs require "attention on interlinkages in three areas: across *sectors* (e.g., finance, agriculture, energy and transport), across societal *actors* (local authorities, government agencies, private sector and civil society), and between and among low, medium and high-income *countries*" (Stafford-Smith et al. 2017). If we hope to be successful, we must first realize that the efforts of individuals, organizations, sectors and governments on their own will not be enough. This must be a multilateral, all-hands-on-deck effort that relies on holistic, systems-thinking approaches engaging with broader, interrelated contexts.

HOW FAIR TRADE ALIGNS WITH THE SDGS ON A GLOBAL LEVEL

When the idea of fair trade first came around, its supporters saw it as an alternative to the inequalities of mainstream trading systems and worked to create changes to how businesses sourced goods. The movement largely focused on growing consumer awareness of production and supply chains exploiting impoverished communities, of businesses that sourced differently and of third-party certification systems that ensured product authenticity. Fair trade not only focused on empowering farmers and workers, it also revealed purchasing power to buyers in the Global North and created support for better trade policies and legislation. As the years progressed, a proliferation of various fair trade labels explained to buyers that these fair trade products were indeed different. Predictably, as consumer awareness grew, fair trade sales increased, better policies were adopted at municipal and institutional levels, and the number of companies supporting fair trade expanded.

With the growing impact of fair trade, there emerged a need to adopt a wider approach for empowerment of producers in the Global South. While ensuring farmers and workers receive better pay does directly combat poverty, historically exploited communities face a slew of other challenges; to name a few: environmental degradation, gender inequity and lack of access to education. It became clear that fair trade initiatives needed to adopt increasingly holistic, systems-thinking approaches that target the diversity of interrelated challenges (Fairtrade Foundation 2015). Thus, fair trade certification systems began embedding sustainability initiatives into their practices.

For example, Fairtrade International's mission is to attain a happy, healthy life for producers in the Global South through "a model of trade that ensures better prices, decent working conditions, no child labour, sound environmental practices and strong business relationships" (Fairtrade Canada 2021). While Fairtrade's mission is to reduce poverty through methods of better trade, there is an explicit awareness that it cannot succeed without targeting an array of issues. This integrated approach to interconnected problems overlaps heavily with the perspective in the UN's Agenda for Sustainable Development. When we look at the Fairtrade International certification system, we can see how it specifically targets multiple SDGs.

Goal 1: No Poverty

The best way out of poverty is to pay farmers a decent income and make sure workers get a fair wage. The Fairtrade minimum price acts as a safety net for when prices crash, helping producers make ends meet. In addition, every Fairtrade-certified product comes with a Fairtrade premium, which is money that goes directly back to the co-op or association (as discussed in other chapters). Currently, the premium for coffee is $0.20 per pound and $1.00 per box of bananas, for example. With sugar, these premiums are even higher under the Small Producer Symbol (SPP) standards (see Chapter 12).

Communities decide for themselves how they invest that money and often use it to meet needs in their communities. While the premium addresses poverty, it goes further by reinforcing community agency.

Goal 2: Zero Hunger

Farmers help to feed the world, but only if they get a decent income to invest in their farms and their futures. For example, the agricultural sector is the largest source of livelihoods in India, with the country being a major global producer of milk, cattle, rice, wheat, sugar cane, cotton, groundnuts, fruits and vegetables (Food and Agriculture Organization of the United Nations n.d.). Despite their major role in providing food for millions of people, there is a remarkably high rate of poverty and suicide among Indian farmers (Kennedy and King 2014). Building exasperation among Indian farmers has led to mass rallies against controversial agricultural legislation that further threatens farmers lives. Unfortunately, this pattern of financially insecure, overworked and unsupported farmers can be observed globally. This has resulted in the average age of farmers increasing as fewer younger people are willingly take over family farming businesses; instead they opt for more secure lines of work. Without producers, the global population will not be fed. Fairtrade supports farmers and workers to make sure they do not have to give up their farms or relocate from their communities in search of better paying work.

Goal 5: Gender Equality

Fairtrade standards prohibit discrimination, sexual harassment and sexual violence. Fairtrade also funds and supports projects such as gender leadership schools, where women are empowered to become entrepreneurs and managers. Opportunities for education and pre-financing offered by these programs helps women to buy their own land and become confident leaders in their communities. While in some countries it is still not acceptable for women to own land or handle money, these kinds of programs change the norm. The importance of gender equity has been a growing concern for Fairtrade, which still has a way to go to promote women's participation (see Chapter 4).

Goal 8: Decent Work and Economic Growth

Even today, millions of farmers and labourers work long hours in hazardous conditions. Things like child labour and forced labour are unfortunately common and can be challenging to recognize. For example, consider the blurry line between child labour and common family farming operations: A child working alongside their parent to learn the tools of the trade to eventually take over the family business may or may not be acceptable depending on circumstances. Fairtrade standards prohibit abuses in order to promote health, safety and worker's rights, while also increasing training for auditors to better identify cases of abuse.

Goal 12: Responsible Consumption and Production

Fairtrade producers, distributors and businesses all comply with tough social, economic and environmental standards throughout the supply chain. On a macro level, Fairtrade focuses on first ensuring that farmers and workers have sustainable modes of production and then on promoting sustainable consumption through education and engagement of individual consumers, businesses and institutions.

Goal 13: Climate Action

Fairtrade standards include requirements for environmentally sound agricultural practices. The focus areas are minimized and safe use of agrochemicals, proper and safe management of waste, maintenance of soil fertility and water resources, and no use of genetically modified organisms. Fairtrade also helps increase resilience to diseases, extreme weather and other climate-driven impacts by working with producer communities to encourage tree planting, improvements to irrigation and waste management, diversification of crops and the pursuit of varied sources of income.

Goal 16: Peace, Justice and Strong Institutions

"Members of the international Fairtrade system meet once a year at the General Assembly. This assembly combines 50 percent producer representation with 50 percent national Fairtrade organization representation, and decides on membership issues, approves the annual accounts, and ratifies new Board members. There are also annual assemblies for each national Fairtrade organization and the producer networks. The Board of the international Fairtrade system is elected by the General Assembly and includes: four board members nominated by the three producer networks, four board members nominated by the national Fairtrade organizations, and three independent board members" (Fairtrade International 2021). While the 50/50 split does not eliminate uneven power relations between representatives of the South and North, it does represent a unique model, compared to others, and is a huge step forward.

Goal 17: Partnerships for the Goals

Fairtrade brings together farmers, workers, consumers, trade unions, businesses, governments and campaigners to deliver real impact and sustainable economic growth through a variety of methods. By looking at the relationship between fair trade and the SDGs, we can see the interconnections between strategies: Each goal benefits another through association. Even at this scope, it is necessary to incorporate a systems-thinking approach for success. Thus, achieving the Sustainable Developments Goals on a larger front will require integrated implementation strategies that work together across sectors, cultures and borders. It will require all tools in the toolbox.

While we have a long way to go, there are signs that the world is starting to realize that staying the current course is not going to cut it. Below are four examples of broad, systemic change occurring recently in relation to fair trade that show change is possible when we work in partnership:

Modern slavery acts

Several countries, including the United Kingdom, Australia and Finland have put in place modern slavery acts, legislation that focuses on human rights due diligence. This legislation mandates companies to understand their supply chains and address issues as they arise. While this type of legislation is in its early days and has been adopted by only a handful of countries, it lays a strong foundation for future policies to build from.

Value-add at origin

A few of the leading fair trade companies have begun shifting production or the finishing of products, often where much of the value lies, from the Global North to South, at long last moving beyond the colonial structures of raw commodity export. For example, the Norandino Cooperative in Peru now exports packaged sugar and processes its own cocoa. Manduvira in Paraguay set up its own mill, and now processes its own sugar. These are encouraging developments; they contribute to multiple SDGs and empower people for the long term.

National leadership

Over 70 percent of the world's cocoa comes from Ghana and Côte d'Ivoire. After decades of low prices and exploited farmers, in July 2019 Côte d'Ivoire's Coffee and Cocoa Board and the Ghana Cocoa Board successfully imposed a pricing mechanism to help producers earn a living wage. This is another example of essential, collaborative groundwork conducive to setting similar policies in motion across different sectors and levels of governments.

Using trade as a tool for change
Shortly after the signing of the Paris Climate Agreement, the European Union made the decision to make trade with the bloc contingent upon ratification of the agreement, putting significant pressure on those wanting to trade with the European Union. Countries are steadily reorienting toward the SDGs, making national, international, economic and business decisions based on them.

FROM GRASSROOTS MOVEMENTS TO SOCIETAL ADOPTION:

Systemic changes such as the aforementioned examples rely on public support, often originating from and gaining momentum from grassroots movements. Using collective action from the local level to effect change at the local, regional, national or international level, grassroots movements are associated with bottom-up — rather than top-down — decision making and are sometimes considered more natural or spontaneous than more mainstream power structures. The Canadian Fair Trade Network (CFTN) encourages community members to use self-organization to contribute to the fair trade movement by taking responsibility and action for their community through designation programs. In their cumulation, these programs and grassroots activism for fair trade have supported large-scale change across Canada.

The Growth of National Fair Trade Designation Programs

In 2011, the CFTN was founded to strengthen grassroots movements in support of fair trade by tying together individual actions and enabling community members to speak with a louder, more coordinated voice. At the time, Canada had only one national fair trade designation program, the Fair Trade Town program, with fifteen designations. Originally started in the United Kingdom in 2001, the program was brought to Canada in 2006 to recognize efforts made by municipalities and advocates for their support for fair trade and was the catalyst for national expansion of new fair trade designation programs.

Building off the steady growth and success of Fair Trade Town, the Fair Trade Campus program launched in 2011, Fair Trade School in 2014, and Fair Trade Event, Workplace and Faith Group after that. All six national programs recognize efforts made in the name of fair trade.

To earn designation, groups need to meet several requirements: the establishment of fair trade steering committees, consistent sourcing of fair trade products and sharing educational materials on fair trade. There have been over 360 designations since 2011, and the number is growing as students, businesses and communities identify the significance of their support of fair trade.

This bottom-up approach has been critical for the success of the CFTN, which now encompasses individuals, volunteers, advocates, businesses and institutional and government leaders, as well as non-profit partners and academics. By convening various sector actors through the designation programs, the CFTN is an example of a successful, cross-sectional approach needed to achieve the SDGs. While much has been achieved through local initiatives in terms of garnering demonstrated support for the movement, there is much to do.

The CFTN seeks to continue establishing better support for fair trade through influencing community policy and purchasing, driving education, promotion and group sustainability and working to increase the number of designations. Beyond designations, the grassroots movement must seize tangible opportunities to advance fair trade across a larger scale by increasing pressure on the private sector and nudging governments forward on a range of sustainable legislative goals. While fair trade offers a vehicle for promoting discussion and awareness around global issues and rethinking our production and consumption systems, the related support from Canadian grassroots activists occupying various niches is vital to creating a fair and sustainable world. This is said not to impose total responsibility on the individual: It is a reflection of the steady progression of societal adoption needed to help create a robust platform for global reorientation of fundamental values.

With its long history among niche markets, fair trade is relatively new for mainstream consumers. Fair trade is still evolving, and the fair trade of today will not be the fair trade of tomorrow. However, by engaging with the movement in the various roles we hold — whether it be as consumers, businesses, institutions or certifiers — we can ensure that notions of fair trade continually meet the challenges of global development. By supporting the awareness and availability of fair trade products and facilitating an adoption of greater accountability and transparency measures, we encourage a more responsible vision for the future while contributing directly to the 2030 Agenda.

Simon Fraser University — Leading the Way

Universities play a significant role within society. As institutional spaces, universities are tasked with preparing young generations with the diverse skill sets and values needed to tackle rising social, economic and environmental tensions. At their core, these institutions have an obligation to foster innovative ways of thinking about sustainability within enrolled students and the surrounding community.

Simon Fraser University (SFU), located in Burnaby, BC, has an extensive history of political activism and contributions to the natural and social sciences Currently, SFU proclaims a diverse array of sustainability commitments, policies, pedagogies and projects that inform and inspire the campus community, including the 20-Year Sustainability Vision, the Zero Waste Initiative and the ongoing development of Living Labs, just to name a few. A strong example of SFU's work toward the SDGs is its role as one of Canada's leading Fair Trade designated campuses, the country's only campus to have achieved Gold status (as of April 2021).

SFU has championed fair trade for a decade, after students pushed SFU authorities to engage with the fair trade movement in 2011. SFU efforts have resulted in a major corporation such as Starbucks offering Fairtrade-certified espresso at campuses across Canada. These initiatives host a ubiquitous availability of fair trade products on campus, a steering committee to improve fair trade product procurement and community knowledgeability and a passionate student group that advocates for the movement through community outreach projects. So, why is fair trade that is so important to SFU?

When SFU supports fair trade, the university is doing more than just helping someone get fairer pay. The campus community is actively fighting hunger, encouraging responsible, just and healthy development for communities across the globe and teaching climate resilience practices — all through a framework that relies on transparent, multi-stakeholder engagements. This is only one method of advancing the SDGs, but these kinds of big-picture movements are exactly what institutions should expand support for. By further bolstering holistic values within university frameworks, institutions can continue adding to the growing international momentum seeking to create a sustainable global community.

SFU is one university within a growing community of Canadian campuses driving real change. As of April 2021, there are 41 Fair Trade designated campuses in Canada.

CONCLUSION

With increasing risk of environmental and social catastrophe associated with the climate crisis, widening wealth gaps between the richest and poorest, and the persistent battle millions fight to meet their basic needs, there is an urgent necessity for societal goals to be redefined. While the SDGs are lofty, ambitious goals, they create a comprehensive guide that encourages alignment across sectors, actors and countries. This alignment is necessary to tackle the globe's wicked problems. In targeting numerous SDGs, fair trade is an excellent model of this holistic, systems-thinking approach while laying groundwork for future cross-sector partnerships vital to SDG advancement. While governments, elected officials, trade agreements, businesses and large scale institutions are key to us achieving our goals, grassroots movements and non-profit organizations are crucial to the adoption of these kinds of societal changes. With these comprehensive and collaborative efforts building, our trajectory is set in motion as we navigate toward a more just, sustainable tomorrow.

Recommended Resources

Fairtrade Foundation. 2015. *Delivering the Sustainable Development Goals Through Trade – A Five-Point Agenda for Policy Coherence.* London: Fairtrade Foundation. <https://www.fairtrade.org.uk/wp-content/uploads/2020/07/Delivering-the-SDGs-through-Trade_Five-Point-Agenda_FINAL.pdf>.

Government of Canada, Employment and Social Development. 2021. *Taking Action on the 2030 Agenda for Sustainable Development.* <https://www.canada.ca/en/employment-social-development/programs/agenda-2030.html>.

Stafford-Smith, M., Griggs, D., Gaffney, O. et al. 2017. "Integration: The Key to Implementing the Sustainable Development Goals." *Sustain Sci* 12. <https://doi.org/10.1007/s11625-016-0383-3>.

UN Department of Economic and Social Affairs. *Transforming Our World: The 2030 Agenda for Sustainable Development.* <https://sdgs.un.org/publications/transforming-our-world-2030-agenda-sustainable-development-17981>.

United Nations. N.d. *The 17 Goals.* <https://sdgs.un.org/goals>.

16

The Case for Shaping the Business and Human Rights Agenda

Elena Lunder and Sergi Corbalán

Fair Trade is a trading partnership, based on dialogue, transparency and respect, that seeks greater equity in international trade. It contributes to sustainable development by offering better trading conditions to, and securing the rights of, marginalized producers and workers — especially in the South. Fair Trade Organizations, backed by consumers, are engaged actively in supporting producers, awareness raising and in campaigning for changes in the rules and practice of conventional international trade. (Definition of fair trade agreed upon by international fair trade networks in 2001, taken up by the International Fair Trade Charter 2018)

Fair trade is often perceived as a market-based movement to "level the playing field" by empowering disadvantaged producers, such as small farmers, artisans and workers, to fully enjoy the benefits of international trade. We find this too reductionist. Most worrying to us is the possible interpretation that simply producing and selling more fair trade products may suffice to achieve the fair trade movement's vision of a world in which justice, equity and sustainable development are at the heart of trade structures and practices.

One third of the world's 7.6 billion people are smallholder farmers and their families. There are 1.4 billion poor people living on less than US$1.25 a day. One billion of them live in rural areas where agriculture is their main source of livelihood. If the women and men that grow nearly 70 percent of all food consumed worldwide can't maintain a decent and dignified livelihood through their work, the problem is not merely about specific disadvantages that some of them face — we have a serious structural problem.

In manufacturing, women in the Global South make up 60 to 80 percent of export workers and three-quarters of the 60 to 75 million workers in textile, clothing and footwear supply chains, where human rights violations and poverty wages are widespread, not to mention the fact that women continue to earn on average only 60 to 75 percent of what men earn, according to CARE International (2017). In parallel, the ongoing climate crisis is not impacting the world in an even way. Small producers in the Global South are among the hardest hit. For example, as much as 50 percent of the global surface area currently used for coffee farming may no longer be suitable, due to the changing climate (Climate Institute 2016). When it comes to emissions, the Global North is disproportionately causing climate change compared to nations in the Global South. For instance, 21 people from Côte d'Ivoire have the same carbon footprint as one person in the United Kingdom, according to the Fairtrade Foundation.[1]

To make things worse, the world's ten richest men have seen their combined wealth increase by half a trillion dollars since the COVID-19 pandemic began; the 1,000 richest people on the planet recouped their COVID-19 pandemic losses within just nine months. It could take more than a decade for the world's poorest to recover from the economic impacts of the pandemic, according to a 2021 report by Oxfam International.

It has been a recurring pattern that companies placing their products on the market in the Global North have decided to offshore their production to the Global South. Examples include Bangladesh for textiles (Clean Clothes Campaign 2020), the Philippines for electronics (Björnsson 2020) or Malaysia for gloves (Vanpeperstraete 2021; BHRRC 2020), where cheaper production is rooted in lower human rights and environmental standards or weaker enforcement of rights that exist on paper (De Schutter 2020). In addition to looser regulatory frameworks, suppliers and producers are further pushed to produce as cheaply as possible to avoid losing powerful buyers. A survey conducted by the International Labour Organization (ILO) found that more than a third of producers accepted orders worth less than the cost of production, which translated into negative impacts on worker's labour rights and remuneration (Vaughan-Whitehead and Pinedo Caro 2017; Ethical Trading Initiative 2017). Factory owners and producers operate on thin margins and sometimes with extremely limited resources, making it more difficult for them to comply with international labour standards and provide sustainable protection or remediation to affected workers (Anner 2019). The impact of the stark power asymmetry is especially evident during the COVID-19 crisis, where many global brands and retailers simply cancelled orders of goods that were already produced (Anner 2020).

Against this appalling background, the magnitude of the change that is needed and the vested interest by those that benefit from the status quo, we believe it would be naive to think that incremental market-based solutions on their own will be sufficient to achieve the fair trade movement's broader vision.

As a matter of fact, trade and market rules are rigged against the fair trade movement's values. By promoting competition on the basis of low prices, market rules create a race to the bottom, where the most competitive businesses are those that maximize short-term profits for the sake of shareholders. By being blind to the negative "externality" costs of unsustainable consumption patterns on human rights and the environment, governments are indirectly subsidizing companies that put profit before people and planet, rather than mission-driven companies, such as fair trade enterprises.

BUT NOT ALL IS DOOM AND GLOOM!

Over the last three decades, the impact of business on human rights and the environment has become more and more visible. Governments and regional and international organizations, like the United Nations (UN), have taken steps to address, albeit partially, some of these issues. One the most relevant international policy frameworks is the Business and Human Rights Agenda. In addition, there is also an uptake of public attention to the irresponsible business conduct in global value chains. Different stakeholder groups are calling for binding regulation (Smit et al. 2020; Investor Alliance for Human Rights 2020; BHRRC 2019), and the international trend of lawsuits has developed (Taylor 2020). One such example is the case *Nestle USA, Inc. and Cargill v. Doe,* which was originally filed in 2005 and made its way to the Supreme Court of the United States in 2020. The question before the court is whether the defending companies can be held responsible for the violation of the human rights of the claimants, six "John Does," who, as children were abducted and forced to work on cocoa farms in Côte d'Ivoire. The defendants argue that they cannot be held liable for what happened to these children as the law (Alien Tort Statute) should only apply to individuals and not corporations, in addition to the fact that United States courts might not have any jurisdiction over a violation which happened abroad and not by a US national. It remains to be seen what the Supreme Court will decide, while keeping in mind that Stephens (2014: 1518f) demonstrates that as of 2012, sixty cases alleging violations of international law were filed under the Alien Tort Statute, and only twenty made it to extended litigation.

In an amicus brief, filed by those with strong interest in a case but not party to the action, in *Doe v. Nestle*,[2] eighteen small- and medium-sized (SME) companies demonstrate that they are producing cocoa without the use of child labour. As an important difference to the production process of the defending companies, the SMEs pointed out that their suppliers do not use child labour in part because they pay a premium price for the cocoa, enabling small farmers to earn a living wage. They additionally point out due diligence as a useful tool to detect the risk of forced and child labour and do their best to prevent it.

WHAT'S HUMAN RIGHTS GOT TO DO WITH FAIR TRADE?

The aim of the fair trade movement, to contribute "to sustainable development by offering better trading conditions to, and securing the rights of, marginalized producers and workers — especially in the South" (International Fair Trade Charter 2018: 11) is inextricably connected to the aim of advancing human rights. Considering the immense negative human rights impact of the unequal power relations in global value chains, it is clear that respect and promotion of human rights is an inherent part of the movement.

For example, the focus of the Fairtrade system on advancing a price that covers the average costs of production and the provision of a Fairtrade premium enabling the communities to invest in what they see is needed in their environment has the potential to lead to economic empowerment and in turn the fulfilment of human rights, such as the right to adequate remuneration, adequate housing and numerous other economic and social rights.[3]

Although the impact of fair trade supply chains and fair trade enterprises on the fulfilment of human rights needs to be assessed on a case-by-case basis, taking into account the specific context and target group, in general, the movement has a lot to offer to the business and human rights discourse. There is a need for a paradigm shift leading to companies being more mindful of their impacts on people and the planet instead of solely focusing on the risks to companies themselves, and for that, we need regulatory change. Even within a movement with a purpose to empower all actors in global supply chains, there is a need for constant vigilance to assess the adverse impacts on human rights and the environment. The focus on cheap production processes is so deeply engrained in the international trade systems that a thorough and coherent redefinition of the relationship of companies towards their value chains is needed.

UN BUSINESS AND HUMAN RIGHTS AGENDA

The UN Guiding Principles on Business and Human Rights (UNGP 2011)[4] have crystallized the global consensus that companies have a responsibility to respect human rights. The UNGP adapt an otherwise corporate concept of due diligence to human rights due diligence (HRDD), which refers to a continuous process aimed at identifying, mitigating, remedying and reporting actual or potential adverse impacts in their own operations, business relationships and value chains.[5]

Since 2011, several countries have adopted national action plans (NAPs) (Office of the United Nations High Commissioner for Human Rights n.d.), and a few countries have gone a step further and adopted some form of national legislation. The United Kingdom and Australia have each passed modern slavery acts, which is a reporting regulation obliging companies of a certain size to report on their due diligence to address modern slavery in their supply chains.[6] In France a duty of vigilance law covers all large companies who have to conduct HRDD and can be held liable for both inadequate HRDD process and egregious violations happening despite the process (Macchi and Bright 2019). The European Union (EU) is drafting a future sustainable corporate governance law, which will include human rights due diligence for all companies operating in the European Union market. At international levels, following an initiative by the government of Ecuador in September 2013, in 2014 the UN Human Rights Council adopted Resolution 26/9, which established the new Intergovernmental Working Group (IGWG) to develop an international legally binding instrument to regulate transnational corporations (TNCs) and other companies with respect to human rights (Friends of the Earth International n.d.).

These developments have the potential to be a huge milestone in reaching greater equity in global value chains. A mandatory HRDD framework, including a strong liability regime and effective access to remedy, would make a big difference for many victims of corporate violations in seeking justice (Cranston et al. 2020). The legislation would force companies to face the impacts of their supply chains and lead to more transparency, while the possibility of litigation could lead to better compliance with the framework.

However, when talking about voluntary or mandatory HRDD, we should strive for more than just legal compliance. The fair trade movement knows that respect for human rights cannot be achieved by a checklist approach, passing all responsibility (and costs) for compliance on to the weakest parts of the value chain. Human rights due diligence frameworks should be carefully designed and implemented to avoid unintended consequences and ensure that they have a positive impact on the most vulnerable parts of the chain. Research has shown that companies tend to focus on those human rights risks that are easiest for them to address and not on those that are the most salient for their stakeholders. Often, the existing voluntary HRDD schemes have ended up as a tick-box exercise, focused on reporting, and companies fail to take genuine action that would have an impact on the ground. Another risk is that companies may cut and run from suppliers and shift their sourcing to less-risky countries or to larger suppliers, rather than working with vulnerable suppliers to address human rights risks together. Finally, companies tend to impose human rights and environmental requirements onto their suppliers without accounting for the costs of compliance in the price they pay (Nelson, Martin-Ortega and Flint 2020).

The suppliers are put under pressure to ensure better production standards in their own facilities, monitor their own suppliers and maintain the same low prices, speed and reactivity of the production process (Smit et al. 2020: 83–86). Unfair purchasing practices, while not absolving supply chain actors from their own responsibility to respect human rights and the environment, lead to human rights violations as they burden and weaken suppliers, factories and small farmers, who cannot earn a living income, pay their workers and employees a living wage or ensure worker safety and environmental protection. In some cases, there is even a correlation between low prices and an increased risks of modern slavery (Cockayne 2021: 21). To enable actual change on the ground, there is a need for a more integrated approach with attention given to companies' own purchasing practices, including price, and not only imposition of codes of conducts to their suppliers (Smit et al. 2020: 83–86).

ENSURING THAT HUMAN RIGHTS DUE DILIGENCE RULES UPTAKE FAIR TRADE VALUES

To ensure that HRDD frameworks, internationally or nationally, lead to actual change on the ground, they need to adopt the following proposals:

- HRDD must cover at least all internationally recognized human rights, with clear guidance on how to assess the severity of risks, including root causes, such as a lack of living wages and living income, either as rights themselves or as preconditions for fulfilment of other human rights (Nelson, Martin-Ortega and Flint 2020: 30).
- Rightsholders, including workers, artisans and small farmers, need to be engaged at every level of the process so that the mitigation, remediation and future prevention actually address their most pressing concerns.
- The framework should explicitly cover purchasing practices, including, but not limited to, pricing as a key factor affecting human rights risks and recognizing that poor practices will often lead to human rights abuses.
- HRDD frameworks need to recognize that voluntary certification and accreditations schemes have a role to play to accompany companies to prevent and address human rights violations, yet rules must clarify that companies placing products on the market are the main responsible organization and cannot discharge their liability to such voluntary schemes.
- The price companies pay to their suppliers, and ultimately to the producers, needs to enable them to produce with respect for human rights and the environment, pay living wages to workers and, for small farmers, to earn a living income. It needs to encourage development of long-term sourcing relationships with suppliers, to enable actual investment in a sustainable production process.
- Simultaneously, it needs to be recognized that human rights violations are often linked to structural economic, social and cultural contexts and require companies to support their suppliers in respecting human rights, rather than abandoning or avoiding high-risk sourcing areas.
- Finally, a regulatory framework as well as the HRDD process itself

must include and empower those who fight against human rights violations, such as trade unions, civil society, farmer groups and human rights organizations.

CONCLUSION

Well-intended, classical human rights and "corporate accountability" advocates are right to speak out for binding HRDD frameworks. However, for these frameworks to be effective and lead to a change in status quo, the advocates need also to frame their demands through a trade justice lens, recognizing the endemic power dynamics leaving groups like small farmers in a drastically more vulnerable position. For example, we need to assure that at, in the implementation of such HRDD rules, small producers are not pushed to comply with even more bureaucratic paperwork, while still being paid dirt-low prices for their produce. Prices that cover at least the costs of production, living incomes and living wages are essential to enable all actors in global value chains to comply with human rights and environmental protections.

We need to make sure that respect for human rights is a shared responsibility in the value chain. It is thus key that the fair trade movement takes an active role, together with allies, such as NGOs, trade unions and farmer groups, in support of business and human rights regulatory frameworks that are not blind to the root causes of human rights violations. In doing so, it is essential that, as a global movement, we raise awareness among policymakers, business leaders and civil society about the perspective of small farmers, artisans and workers in value chains and support having their voices heard in important policymaking debates. The fair trade movement must therefore not only embrace the UN Business and Human Rights Agenda, it is essential that the fair trade values shape the rolling out of future binding rules for companies to ensure this agenda delivers positive impacts for small farmers, artisans and workers in supply chains.

Notes

1. Our World In Data. 2019. *Where in the world do people emit the most CO2?* <https://ourworldindata.org/per-capita-co2>, as cited in Fairtrade Foundation. 2020. *A Climate Of Crisis* <https://www.fairtrade.org.uk/wp-content/uploads/2021/02/A-Climate-Of-Crisis_Fairtrade-Foundation_Feb-2020_HR.pdf>.
2. Brief of small and mid-size cocoa and chocolate companies as *amici curiae* in support of respondents, Nestle USA, INC. v. John Doe I et al., and Cargill, INC., v John Doe I et al, NOS. 19-416 & 19-453 (21 October 2020).

3. UN General Assembly, *International Covenant on Economic, Social and Cultural Rights,* 16 December 1966, United Nations, Treaty Series, vol. 993.

4. Human Rights Council, *Guiding Principles on Business and Human Rights: Implementing the United Nations 'Protect, Respect and Remedy' Framework: Report of the Special Representative of the Secretary-General on the Issue of Human Rights and Transnational Corporations and other Business Enterprises* (21 March 2011) UN Doc A/HRC/17/31.

5. Since the publication of the principles, a more or less global consensus has been reached that HRDD also includes environmental aspects.

6. UK Modern Slavery Act 2015 (UK MSA); Modern Slavery Act 2018 (No. 153, 2018).

Recommended Resources

De Schutter, Oliver. 2020. *Towards mandatory due diligence in global supply chains.* Prepared by Prof. Olivier De Schutter at the request of the International Trade Union Confederation. <https://www.ituc-csi.org/IMG/pdf/de_schutte_mandatory_due_diligence.pdf>.

Nelson, Valerie, Olga Martin-Ortega and Michael Flint. 2020. *Making Human Rights Due Diligence Frameworks Work for Small Farmers and Workers.* University of Greenwich Report Commissioned by the Fair Trade Advocacy Office and Brot für die Welt. Chatham: UK.

Vaughan-Whitehead, Daniel, and Luis Pinedo Caro. 2017. *Purchasing Practices and Working Conditions in Global Supply Chains: Global Survey Results.* International Labour Organisation INWORK Policy Brief No. 10.

17

Uneven Outcomes

The Tensions, Contradictions and Challenges in the Search for Fair Trade

Mara Fridell, Ian Hudson, Mark Hudson

Fair trade has not set a goal that, once achieved, would allow everyone to dust off their hands and declare mission accomplished. Rather, Fairtrade as a labelling project and fair trade as a social movement contain many objectives, from the easily achievable to the decidedly daunting. In this chapter, we list and evaluate some of the more important goals that have been identified by Fairtrade International and its affiliated organizations and producer networks. We then evaluate the contradictions that exist for Fairtrade, as well as its potential to realize its objectives.

FAIRTRADE'S GOALS

An obvious goal of Fairtrade is increasing sales. On this front, it has been remarkably successful. From its extremely humble beginnings characterized by informal trading out of car trunks, churches and charity shops, Fairtrade saw global retail sales of its products grow to around US$11 billion (€9.8 billion) in 2018 (Fairtrade International 2019: 2). The variety of commodities bearing the Fairtrade label and the number of organizations in each sector being licensed as Fairtrade producers have grown rapidly over the past two or three decades. Today, Fairtrade consumers connect economically with 1.66 million farmers and workers in over 1,500 Fairtrade producer organizations across 73 countries. The total number of Fairtrade-certified producer organizations increased 32 percent in the five-year period between 2013 and 2017 (1,210 to 1,599). Global sales of Fairtrade coffee, one of the longest-standing Fairtrade products, increased from 20,000 metric tonnes in 2003 to 214,000 in 2017 (see Figure 17.1). This is even more impressive considering that the 2003 number included sales in the United States, but the 2017 numbers

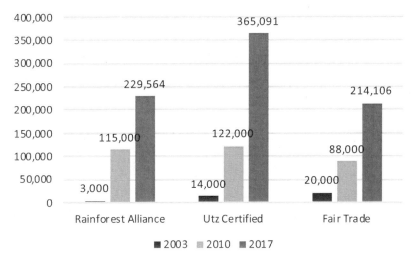

Figure 17.1 Global Sales of Certified Coffee in Metric Tonnes
Note: Rainforest Alliance and UTZ Certified merged in 2018

do not, after Fair Trade USA split from the international Fairtrade organizations in 2012.

Increasing sales is instrumental in achieving Fairtrade's most visible goal: increasing the incomes of workers and farmers in the South. Yet research on the impact of Fairtrade suggests that while more and more farmers and workers are producing under Fairtrade certification, their earnings have only modestly improved, and many of them remain in poverty, at least in terms of cash income.

Fairtrade also quietly contains a number of other non-income, socioeconomic goals that are embedded in its production criteria. For example, Fairtrade includes a price premium that must be spent according to the results of a democratic process — through co-operatives in the case of small-scale producers and voting by workers in the case of hired labour — which suggests that Fairtrade also values increasing economic democracy. Most studies do show some degree of success in achieving these non-income goals. Fairtrade enhances security of land ownership or access, improves access to credit and stabilizes price fluctuations. In some instances, though unevenly across workplaces and co-ops, it provides social and political benefits such as improved organizational capacity for co-operatives, improved gender equality and a sense of democratic control of both the premium and a broader sense of political agency (Hudson et al. 2013; Fairtrade International 2019). In addition, some economic benefits, including Fairtrade-funded infrastructure improvements like schools and roads do spill over from Fairtrade co-ops.

However, if the goal of Fairtrade is to improve the condition of workers and farmers in the South generally, rather than the more modest goal of improving the condition of Fairtrade-certified producers, it has considerable work to do. Most of the income benefits go only to the very small portion of producers who sell their products under the Fairtrade label. Despite its impressive growth, Fairtrade coffee, for example, amounted to a little over 2 percent of total global coffee sales in 2017. Other Fairtrade products constitute an even smaller portion of the market. And, of course, there are many products in which Fairtrade does not operate. Fairtrade has so far concentrated mostly, and understandably, on products with relatively simple supply chains. Although it is not completely impossible (the Fairphone does exist <https://www.fairphone.com/en/>), establishing the criteria for products, such as a car, with many stages in the production process, with countless different raw materials, production methods and labour relationships, is inherently more difficult than for a product like coffee. As a result, the Fairtrade model has not been able to reach workers and producers in many major global industries.

To expand Fairtrade in the products in which it exists, and to more products, an additional goal must be to educate consumers about the problems created by production and exchange in the conventional market. Indeed, the overarching goal of early fair traders was to overturn the injustice of the world trading system and the power of multinationals. A clever example of this type of education campaign was Fairtrade Canada's "banana stamps," which activists placed on conventional bananas in supermarkets with messages such as: "Most banana workers don't earn a living wage" and "Women have no protection from harassment on banana plantations."

Ambitiously, Fairtrade attempts to get consumers to understand that consumption has political, economic and social consequences that people need to recognize, care about and act on. This is no small task. It amounts to nothing less than a transformation of how people consume, setting them the difficult task of moving from individually based, fairly straightforward decisions about how the products they buy benefit them, to complex, solidaristic decisions based on the normally invisible processes of production that lie hidden behind each commodity. Indeed, Fairtrade really asks people to abide by the credo of John Ruskin, who, writing in the late 1800s, claimed: "In all buying, consider first, what condition of existence you cause in the production of what you buy" (J. Ruskin and C. Wilmer 1986 [1860]). Fairtrade competes in the market, but it also critiques the market — at least as it exists in many products. As the percent of the total market still dominated by conventional production suggests, mainstreaming this criticism has been an uphill struggle. However, describing Fairtrade as a failure for not realizing such an ambitious goal would be churlish in the extreme. In fact, Fairtrade should be commended for even placing such a transformative goal on its agenda, no matter how incompletely it has been realized.

Many apparently ethical labels are just another form of marketing, with no substantive improvement in the process of production from the conventional market. However, Fairtrade was started by activists driven by a social justice mission, not by an industry group or a corporation trying to cash in on a niche market. It stressed partnership and cooperation across the North-South, consumer–producer divide from the outset, including (though not perfectly) in its organizational structure. It relies on rigorous third-party certification and the development of standards across a broad cross-section of issues (organizational requirements, labour standards, minimum prices, duration of contracts, environmental standards, gender equity, etc.). So, Fairtrade is ethical labelling's best-case scenario. However, attempting to deliver benefits to producers by both simultaneously criticizing and participating in the market creates some important contradictions in Fairtrade that make it difficult to both scale up to a larger share of the market and continue to stand apart as a genuine alternative to conventional production.

SCALING UP, WATERING DOWN?

One possible source of downward pressure on the underlying ethical substance behind labels is the desire or perceived need to engage with big market actors. One way of reaching more consumers, and thus supporting more farmers, is through the large corporations that have access to supermarket shelves or other retail spaces, as well as large current market shares. In the United States, where this has been most aggressively pursued, growth in Fair Trade USA coffee sales is largely attributable to its availability at big corporate retailers like McDonalds, Walmart, Starbucks

Timmy's Holds Out Against Fairtrade

As Fairtrade mandates minimum purchasing prices, it inevitably raises the cost of coffee. As a result, coffee sellers have implemented their own cheaper, watered-down certification alternatives that still give them the ability to brand themselves as ethically responsible corporations. The Canadian icon Tim Hortons is one such corporation. In 2005, Tim Hortons created the Tim Hortons Coffee Partnership, which involves teaching farmers in South America to sustainably improve the quality and quantity of their coffee yields. The partnership uses a market-based pricing approach, as they baselessly argue that with minimum prices farmers have "little incentive to improve the quality of their coffee." Tims' partnership approach focuses on business training for coffee farmers, and its environmental actions are limited to regulating how much pesticide its farmers are using, making it less rigorous than other certifications that have a focus on minimum prices, democratic control of the production process and protection of natural habitats. From 2005–2013, Tims invested a mere $7 million in the partnership. To put the numbers in perspective, Tim Hortons' revenue in 2017 alone was an estimated $3 billion. Despite this small impact, Tims rolled out an extensive marketing campaign highlighting the partnership, which included Partnership Blend bags of coffee sold at their locations. Since 2015 it has become even more difficult for Tim Hortons to improve the sustainability of its coffee and lives of its coffee farmers, as it is now owned and controlled by the massive Brazilian-American investment fund, 3G Capital, notorious for its mean and lean budgeting process.

Note: Research by Rylan Ramnarace

and Costco. Fairtrade Canada singles out Costco as a major driver of increased sales. While the major coffee roasting companies initially tried to ignore and then discredit Fairtrade as a means of alleviating poverty (and some still do, see above Box), specialty markets, including certified coffees, have been a major growth sector. As a result, some of the big players were forced to engage with Fairtrade, buying at the same price, and from some of the same co-ops as other Fairtrade companies. However, while they want to have control over a secure supply, and they would like a share of the specialty markets, major corporations don't really want to bind themselves to costly and strict rules about how the coffee or cocoa they buy gets produced, by whom and at what price they must buy it — all aspects of Fairtrade standards.

The way forward has tended to be through negotiation. Throughout these negotiations, companies have criticized the inflexibility and complexity of Fairtrade's standards and enforcement processes. Fairtrade International has been at pains to accommodate these concerns, as emphasized by its then-CEO Dario Soto Abril, who said, "We're making a big effort to listen to companies and adapt and innovate within our model" (Ionova 2017).

This process of mainstreaming Fairtrade has raised concerns that the standards and terms that consumers associate with the label have been or will be watered down. Seen relative to the radical goals and objectives of early Fairtrade supporters, it is clear that much of its radical content fell by the wayside. In 2011, as the tensions within the Fairtrade movement over mainstreaming were coming to a boil, the Dutch Fairtrade pioneer and Max Havelaar co-founder Frans Van der Hoff predicted that mainstreaming would "just end in fair-washing and smokescreens" (Clark and Walsh 2011). Jeroen Douglas, the executive director of the NGO Solidaridad (a key player in the establishment of Max Havelaar and FLO), has recently claimed that certification is "not at all delivering on significant, let alone systemic, change any more. They are really there to message a feel-good factor that's not at all connected to reality" (Nieburg 2019).

Fairtrade certainly made a big effort to listen to Starbucks, which offered a huge opportunity to scale up Fairtrade. In 2000, the company made a limited commitment to purchasing Fairtrade, which — even though it was only a very small portion of their purchasing — significantly upped the volume of Fairtrade sales. In getting Starbucks to agree to do so (which it did albeit under pressure of a threatened global boycott), Fairtrade allowed Starbucks to sidestep a rule proposed by Equal Exchange that only companies making a minimum 5 percent commitment to Fairtrade as a portion of their total purchasing could carry the label. This was greeted with considerable hostility and skepticism from smaller companies that were 100 percent Fairtrade (Jaffee 2010). While Starbucks' purchase of Fairtrade did create the desired scaling up, its commitment to ethical sourcing deliberately sought to limit its relationship with Fairtrade. Starbucks eventually developed its own set of standards (called "C.A.F.E. standards") allowing it to claim that 99 percent of its coffee is "ethically sourced." However, the C.A.F.E. standards are set up to encourage "continuous improvement" rather than create set of standards by which its suppliers must abide. The "Zero Tolerance" criteria for suppliers, which must be corrected if they are not met, are mostly violations of the law, like paying a "nationally or regionally established minimum wage" or prohibiting "the use of forced, bonded, indentured, convict or trafficked labor"[1] (Starbucks 2016). Practices that improve on already existing minimum legal requirements, such as "workers are not required to pay a recruitment fee as a condition for employment" are part of a large social and environmental checklist that do not have to be met. If suppliers score more than 80 percent on this checklist they get a "strategic" classification. If they score less, they are classified as "verified" and encouraged to improve (Starbucks 2020). A critic might argue that C.A.F.E standards are designed with considerable "wiggle room" for compliance.

A SHIFTING TENSION: MARKET ENGAGEMENT + ACTIVISM

Fairtrade fosters consumers' knowledge about the problems of conventional production and encourages them to collect enough information to enable them to voluntarily choose products that are more sustainable for both producers' livelihoods and the environment. Relying on voluntary consumption decisions to improve environmental and social production processes raises two key questions: Who can or will participate in this remedy? What is the precise nature of the remedy?

Turning first to who will participate, Fairtrade creates a "free rider" problem. Generally, the free rider problem occurs when someone enjoys the benefits of something that they have not contributed to or paid for. An obvious example of this happens when companies free ride on the time and effort of the fair trade movement's successful efforts to develop a conscientious consumer market by selling "ethical" products at premium prices. A less obvious issue revolves around the fact that those who buy Fairtrade pay for benefits on which others inevitably free ride. The conscientious and caring who buy Fairtrade pay for benefits of reduced poverty and a better environment (such as Southern social, economic and environmental stabilization and the reduction of migrant and immigration crises) from which non-Fairtrade purchasing free riders benefit. Should the caring and compassionate subsidize the ignorant and uncaring? Free riding is the main reason that many collectively enjoyed goods are moved out of the realm of the market and into the realm of the state.

As for the nature of the remedy, consider an alternative, *global* solution to international inequality, a solution that relieves consumers of the exclusive responsibility for addressing poverty, prevents free riding and increases the incomes of producers and workers in the South: state-based regulations. Interstate organizations and international agreements like the International Coffee Organization and International Coffee Agreement once maintained a minimum international coffee price that helped prop up producer incomes. This producer support eliminates free riding. But global price solutions to producer poverty can be insensitive to *consumer* poverty, with bad political consequences. Where higher prices exclude poor consumers from any form of the product, the regressive distributional consequences of minimum prices are often used as an argument against regulation, portraying Walmart-style supplier squeezing as championing the interests of low-income consumers.

Fairtrade has also been accused of being a venue in which only more affluent consumers can engage. Compared to the conventional market, Fairtrade encourages consumers to determine how they may shift their resources to solidarity and environmental protection. Some find they cannot choose to do so because of economic maldistribution. Fairtrade is limited by market income inequality (as would a state-based solution that increases the price of a product) because that inequality minimizes the increasingly consumer-based freedoms of the poor, including poor consumers in the North. Poor consumers, unable to afford the Fairtrade markup, are left only with the option of supporting corporations' predatory conventional production processes, which heavily exploit labour and the environment. On the other hand, compared to a regulated price minimum, Fairtrade nicely accords with the ability-to-pay principle in which those with higher incomes pay more for socially beneficial goods and services. The crux here is whether the political and economic implications of market inequality can be clarified by Fairtrade organizers, or whether it is obscured by corporate marketers reducing Fairtrade to a status symbol, a fall guy for poor people's market exclusion

Also at stake is whether people know what kinds of conditions are fostered through their consumption. When labelling and certification were pursued by Fairtrade organizations as guarantees for a wider consuming public, their success was partially checked by rival ethical-consumption labels (in coffee, Rainforest Alliance and utz grew more rapidly than Fairtrade — see Figure 17-1) with different production criteria and by conventional businesses' marketing departments. Rival fairwashing labels flooded the consumer market to disrupt the ethical signal and beckon consumers back to conventional commodities painted with words of virtue, such as "corporate social responsibility."

By the second decade of the twenty-first century, there were 113 ecolabels in Canada. New efforts were mobilized to disentangle the signal jam. Ecolabel Index, an online inventory of ethical labelling schemes, allows consumers to purchase the capacity to compare the contents of 457 labels and certifications across 199 countries and 25 industries. Other efforts to separate the social responsibility label and ecolabel wheat from the chaff have identified hundreds more, from independent third-party certifications like Fairtrade, to government-regulated labelling schemes like organic, to business "first party" brand labels and labels manufactured by businesses' subsidiary fairwash organizations.

This proliferation has been thrown into the spotlight recently by chocolate companies shifting into developing their own sustainability and labelling schemes. Particularly high-profile was the removal of the Fairtrade label from Cadbury's chocolate bars and its replacement with the firm's own Cocoa Life seal. The UK Fairtrade Foundation and Fairtrade International cheered the private label for involving more farmers, and agreed to act as an auditor, consultant and partner for Cocoa Life, even briefly agreeing to put a "Partnering with Fairtrade Foundation" label on the backs of packages before activists raised a ruckus about it. Cadbury (owned by Mondelez International, owned by Kraft Heinz) was following along with Mars and cocoa processing giant Barry Callebaut. Some have suggested that private labelling takes the Fairtrade transformation into the corporate heart of the tea, cocoa and coffee sectors.

In boxing out Fairtrade's intermediation and replacing the independent activist aspect of fair trade, however, these corporate ethical labels amass for corporations the capacity to gut Fairtrade organizations. The shift to private labels raises serious concerns about who controls goals and information. Will producers have a voice in establishing the terms of "sustainable" or "ethical" trade relations with these multinationals, as they have laboured to win within Fairtrade International's governance structure? Will the "transparency" promised by these in-house schemes translate into consumers really understanding where their coffee, tea and cocoa come from, and under what terms?

It is as yet tough to say what the impacts of private labelling schemes are. Cocoa Life involves a $400 million "commitment" over ten years to improve the sustainability of cocoa farming. There is no price guarantee to compare to Fairtrade's minimum $US2400/metric tonne. There are "loyalty payments" (reported as $US80 per tonne, compared to the Fairtrade premium of $US240 per tonne) paid on top of the market price. Increased volume of cocoa transacted under Cocoa Life's terms are supposed to ensure that the "value per farmer" of the program is at least equivalent to what it was under Fairtrade (Fairtrade Foundation and Mondelez International 2018: 3). There is funding for training in farming, financial literacy and business management for farmers' organizations; there is funding for "community action plans" for community infrastructure, such as schools and clinics. Some of the funding for this is from Cadbury; some is from organizations such as CARE International, World Vision, Save the Children International and Cargill. They produce impact reports that feature a variety of metrics, but the reports produced by their verifiers, Ipsos and FLOCERT, are not public. The real concern is that everyone in agribusiness will follow the model, excluding Fairtrade and its rigorous standards, and sticking their own label on the product. It is not auspicious that Kraft Heinz's biggest shareholders are Berkshire Hathaway and 3G Capital, some of the most ruthless financial capitalists striding the globe.

Observers of the move to corporate in-house certification in chocolate expressed concern that this might lead to a confusing proliferation of brand-specific ethical labelling. Ethical labels operate within a competitive market environment, and, given that shoppers have a hard time telling labels apart on the basis of their underlying "ethical content" (the substance and strictness of their standards, or their means of verification), this leads to a troubling dynamic. Products made through well-compensated, independent, democratically organized and environmentally friendly forms of labour tend to be higher cost. That is to say, all things being equal, labels, such as Fairtrade, with higher labour and environmental standards are going to be stuck to more expensive versions of what otherwise appear to be the same things. When states neglect their consumer-protection role, leaving consumers to the mercy of thronging labels in the supermarket aisles), consumers will tend to buy the cheaper item, and, over time, the market will select for the cheapest product whose label looks "ethical" but which has the least substance behind it.

The critical attention paid to this and to other sketchy dealings (like partnering with Nestlé, once voted the world's least responsible company) suggests that at least some Fairtrade consumers are vigilant about the political content of the label. This supports other evidence that highly engaged consumers work, with some degree of success, to differentiate between labels on the basis of what lies behind them and to resist being bamboozled by fairwashing (Lekakis 2012). Activism returns as the crux of Fairtrade's viability, expanding the limit of people's engagement in the work required to peer behind the plethora of labels on the shelves and to evaluate and treat these labels as substantively different (which they are) rather than as small variations on a shared commitment to "care." Some of these changing relationships between Fairtrade and large corporations have led some NGO partners of Fairtrade, like Solidaridad, to suggest that certifiers turn toward becoming watchdogs for state regulatory schemes — including state-based regulation of labour and environmental conditions (Roozen 2017).

CONCLUSION: STRATEGIC DEVELOPMENT

The current corporate global food system creates largely hidden but nonetheless brutal effects on producers, the environment and consumers. Fairtrade still has an important role to play in creating producer–consumer connections and limiting capitalist excesses, and it will always require agile strategy and activism.

The proliferation of labelling schemes is the result of organized Fairtrade incursion on commodity markets, pushing capitalist corporations to defensively protect their supply chains and markets by engaging, aping and subverting ethical signalling. The strategy of proliferating labels allows corporations to jimmy and jam production-information signalling, to reclaim some of their lost control. Next steps for Fairtrade may include continuing to use the trust it has earned to assist consumers with conceptual transformation toward activism aimed at re-tasking states with setting boundaries on capital; watchdogging state regulation; and internationalist social movement mobilization to institute an intergovernmental organization supporting sustainable food production policy supports across states. Scaling up should be geared toward moving fair trade principles, values and standards into treaty and law, rather than focusing overly on gaining specific market advantage to certain players. Fairtrade's focus on ensuring sustainable producer livelihoods must be a floor, not an aspirational ceiling for processors, traders and retailers.

Note

1. It has been reported that the Brazilian government found at least two Starbucks-certified plantations to be employing slave labour (Camargos 2019).

Recommended Resources

Ecolabel Index. <http://www.ecolabelindex.com/>.

International Guide to Fairtrade Labels. <https://fairworldproject.org/wp-content/uploads/2019/12/international-Guide-to-Fair-Trade-Labels-2020-Edition.pdf>.

Law and Political Economy blog. <https://lpeblog.org/>.

Reference Guide to Fairtrade and Worker Justice Certifications. <https://fairworldproject.org/choose-fair/certifier-analysis/reference-guide-to-fair-trade-and-worker-welfare-programs-2/>

18

COVID-19, Trade and Corporate Power

Sujata Dey

M any have remarked how COVID-19 spotlighted various weaknesses: in health care systems, old age homes, food and water systems and social safety nets. Wrecking economies and livelihoods, the crisis ground travel almost to a halt and put a large dent in international trade, so much so that the World Trade Organization estimated that trade declined in 2020 by 13 to 32 percent (Alberti 2020). As the crisis temporarily unravelled international supply chains and as countries competed to procure protective equipment, ventilators and vaccines, COVID-19 shed light on another global failure: the powerlessness of global trading rules to encourage international cooperation to prevent and combat the virus.

It shouldn't be like this. As travel and trade increase in normal times, so does our exposure to pandemics. Business travel, international trade and tourism accelerate the propagation of viruses. Like many previous pandemics, the spread of COVID-19 can be linked to international trade. As Andrew Nikiforuk (2020) has written, global trade has always played a role in pandemics, such as the plague and the Spanish flu:

> The Silk Road brought rats and fleas to 13th-century Europe, resulting in a demographic collapse in which one in four people died. The slave trade bombarded two continents with epidemics. Waves of cholera epidemics followed European trade routes from the Ganges Delta to the slums of major cities. Global steamship traffic dutifully carried influenza around the world and played a key role in spreading the deadly Spanish flu pandemic.

And yet, while international trade and travel increase the risk of global pandemics, international trade agreements do not provide frameworks to prevent or cope with them. Focusing on rules to facilitate, streamline and standardize trade, such agreements offer little to deal with the social or environmental fallout of international trade.

Projection on the Supreme Court of Canada protesting corporate trade deals.
Source: Council of Canadians

Our global trading system, embodied in so-called free trade agreements, multiple arrangements under the WTO and numerous investment agreements, is supposed to form the rulebook for international trade, at times protecting us from unilateral and unfair trading decisions. These rules are supposed to be neutral, creating one trading system for all. But instead, they straightjacket national states, preventing them from implementing the very policies that could protect them from a pandemic. International trade agreements were never equipped to deal with the negative externalities of enhanced international trade, whether climate change, increased global inequality, tax evasion, corporations evading environmental and social legislation or, in this case, a global pandemic. Designed to liberalize and deregulate, these agreements empower corporations to evade and challenge government regulations. As I demonstrate, the international trade framework systematically reduces national sovereignty and democracy, disempowers governments that seek to enact policies to protect people and the planet and encourages governments to flatten public safety and environment rules, not improve them.

So, what does an international trade agreement contain? While governments promote trade agreements as a key to economic prosperity, they are guided less by economic analysis than by international trade laws and rules and political considerations (Sinclair and Trew 2019; Barlow and Dey 2015). Usually, a trade agreement has a chapter that proposes changes to duties and quotas for various products in agriculture and other sectors (Spinney 2020). Wildlife trade was a factor in the COVID-19 outbreak. Trade in agricultural products is a major vector of disease propagation. Agreements often reduce significant tariffs on agricultural goods, thereby ramping up international agricultural trade and encouraging monolithic agribusiness rather than local food systems (Dey 2019). But this is just a small part of a free trade agreement. For example, in the so-called Comprehensive and Progressive Agreement for a Trans-Pacific Partnership (TPP11), signed in 2018 between eleven partners, including Canada, only one of the thirty chapters deals explicitly with tariff elimination. Typically, free trade agreements prescribe rules — neoliberal rules — well beyond tariffs. Following are some examples.

PROTECTING MONOPOLY RIGHTS FOR MULTINATIONAL CORPORATIONS

Many agreements extend or criminalize breaches of patent and copyright legislation. While free trade is theoretically designed to promote fair international competition, patent rights grant monopoly rights to patent holders, prohibiting competition in certain products. For example, this protects large multinational entertainment and pharmaceutical companies from competition, resulting in higher prices and fatter profit margins. In the health care field, this makes life-saving treatments increasingly expensive. The recently enacted Canada-European Union Comprehensive Economic and Trade Agreement (CETA) increased the length of patent protection by two years, delaying the development of cheaper generic drugs. Canada's independent parliamentary budget officer predicted that the federal government would pay $270 million more per year in drug costs because of CETA (Duggan 2018). Promoted by American drug companies, the partially ratified TPP11 would add patent-like protection on biologic drugs. Biologics are medications or treatments made from human or animal tissue. They can treat conditions like arthritis or ulcerative colitis, but prices are exploding. Biologic treatments can cost upwards of $20,000 to $30,000 a year. In some cases, the cost can go as high as $100,000 *(Husser 2018)*. And guess what? Vaccines are biologics covered by patents that are heavily protected in trade agreements. While some countries have pooled funds to develop a free COVID-19 vaccine, corporations that create vaccines are under no obligation to offer them at affordable prices. Giant pharmaceutical companies, for their part, make enormous profits from this system. By one estimate, "between 2000 and 2018, thirty-five big drug companies received a combined revenue of $11.5 trillion, with a gross profit of $8.6 trillion" (Lynch 2020).

While the COVID-19 crisis shows that everyone, whether slum dwellers in Mumbai or the president of Brazil, needs to be protected by empowered public health systems to beat the virus, trade rules lead in the opposite direction. In October 2020, India and South Africa proposed to the World Trade Organization to suspend some of the intellectual property rules in order to make some of the vaccine and treatments affordable and available to all, a proposal defeated by Canada and other developed countries. To defeat COVID-19, we have to do something that we have needed to do for a long time: protect the international commons. We need to play a new survival game: a game of international cooperation, sharing scientific knowledge and equipment, and bolstering public health systems.

CORPORATIONS HAVE A VIP SYSTEM
TO CHALLENGE GOVERNMENT RULES

When the new Canada-United States-Mexico (CUSMA) agreement came into effect in 2020, Canada achieved a milestone: the removal of the Investor State Dispute Settlement Provisions (ISDS), the infamous Chapter 11 in the old NAFTA. The epitome of corporate power, Chapter 11 provisions have allowed multinational corporations to sue governments over changes in policies or regulations that affect their profits. This was a historic win. For decades, the Council of Canadians and its former honorary chairperson, Maude Barlow, campaigned to remove this chapter. Ironically, while Canada and our former Trade Minister Chrystia Freeland championed this agreement, it was removed at the request of United States President Trump's White House. As a result of Chapter 11, Canada was the most sued country in the developed world, with over $300 million in settlements and $2.6 billion in challenges (McCall 2020). While the United States never lost a case, Canada bore the brunt of the NAFTA challenges (Sinclair 2018).

According to the Canadian Centre for Policy Alternatives, two-thirds of the challenges against Canada concerned environmental regulations and resource management, such as Québec's moratorium on fracking and

The NAFTA Civil Society Summit, September 2017. Sujata Dey, second from the left. Source: Council of Canadians

oil exploration around the St. Lawrence River, and Nova Scotia's refusal to issue a quarry permit to a project that would compromise the Bay of Fundy ecosystem (Sinclair 2018). Chapter 11 provisions were used mostly by large companies, and many have documented how it has been used to threaten states into compliance even without an actual claim, through the "chill effect" on policy makers (Van Harten 2016). Unfortunately, the death of Chapter 11 is not the end of the ISDS. For one thing, it will be around until 2023 as it winds down. Second, it still applies to Mexico in the CUSMA. And more importantly, it is still alive in over 3,200 agreements worldwide (Barlow 2015). In fact, the same year that the CUSMA went into effect, the world reached a dubious milestone: the one thousandth ISDS case was filed (UNCTAD 2020).

And while things may be bad in Canada, in the Global South, matters can be even worse. According to the Transnational Institute, there are over 300 ISDS claims currently pending in the world, the majority brought against Latin American, Asian and African countries. Most cases that have been completed have been settled in favour of investors, with significant financial consequences. The completed cases in Latin America, for instance, have resulted in states being ordered to pay a total of US$31 billion to private investors (Olivet and Müller 2020). ISDS was created to discipline developing countries and to deter them from putting restrictions on international investment. The first agreement, between Germany and Pakistan in 1959, was intended to promote investment in poorer countries. However, there is no evidence that this actually helped (Berger 2015).

AS COVID-19 KICKS IN, CORPORATIONS CASH IN

At the time of writing, almost two million people had died of COVID-19 worldwide, and there was no telling what the final death toll would be. Around the world, people have made sacrifices to protect one another in an inspiring display of solidarity. In March 2020, as people were staying home and limiting their social contact, and as Italian authorities rationed respirators, making heartbreaking and crucial decisions as to who would live and who would die, corporations put forward more selfish concerns around how life-saving government actions could be subject to ISDS suits.

In the *Global Arbitration Review*, lawyers discussed how Italy's emergency measures could face corporate challenges under ISDS. Corporations are exploring ways to sue governments for taking action to protect people:

> Both sets of emergency measures are likely to affect investments made in Italy by foreign investors. Indeed, they may result in harsh limitations on investors' property rights; fundamental and unpredictable changes to the "normative environment" of the investment; potential discriminations between domestic and foreign companies; and, possibly, failures to provide investors and their managers or employees with the safeguards they need to carry out their activities…More generally, they may lead to a suspension of basic entrepreneurial freedoms and to distortion of competition. (Benedetteli 2020)

These comments show the perversity of the ISDS system, which rewards corporate bad behaviour and penalizes necessary government actions. That is why over 630 organizations all over the world are joining forces to ask for a moratorium on ISDS during the COVID-19 crisis. This was headed for debate in the British Parliament (see Open letter to governments on ISDS and COVID-19). But it may be too late. Peru participated in a robust lockdown, and already, international law firms have been challenging the necessity of its actions. In particular several road toll concession holders threatened to initiate ISDS proceedings because Peru suspended toll collection in the wake of the crisis. In order to avoid an ISDS case, Peru reversed this policy. ISDS arbitrators have refused to suspend expensive legal cases for poorer countries in the midst of the COVID-19 crisis (Olivet and Müller 2020).

GETTING RID OF THOSE PESKY CHEMICAL AND SAFETY RULES

Trade agreements devote a lot of attention to government regulations, seeing them as barriers to trade or red tape that blocks companies from seamlessly moving from one market to another without worrying about adjusting to new standards or rules. In many agreements, this is contained in chapters on sanitary and phytosanitary provisions, technical barriers to trade or increasingly, including in the new CUSMA, on regulatory and good regulatory practices. Governments pitch this as voluntary conversations between regulators to discuss rules when they affect trade. What harm could friendly conversation between regulators cause? Unfortunately, what they are discussing are our chemical, environmental, food safety and other regulations. They are doing so without parliamentary oversight and often with corporate lobbyists around the table. Rules on food inspection or food protection or on safe treatments or agricultural practices could be important in combatting pandemics. However, there is strong evidence to suggest that these regulatory cooperation committees are less a matter of raising national standards to protect the public than of lowering standards to benefit corporations. In a 2020 report, the Council of Canadians and Foodwatch Netherlands revealed how one CETA regulatory cooperation committee was being used to undermine European Union food safety regulations on pesticides and herbicides. Canadian regulators were using the committee to challenge regulations and get assurances from the European Union that, eventually, it would abandon the "precautionary principle," the notion that, when there is unknown risk, regulators should err on the side of caution (Council of Canadians and foodwatch 2020).

Under the CUSMA, regulatory cooperation is no longer voluntary. It is has become a permanent, binding process that all three countries must follow. Unelected "stakeholders" now have a back room in which to shape regulations, with no public participation or oversight. In regulatory cooperation, corporations are given advance notice of new regulations. So-called interested persons are notified ahead of time about planned government regulations and are allowed a consultation process before any regulation goes through a legislative process.

The chapter requires that regulations be "science-based." In other words, regulations cannot be prescribed for ethical or social reasons. The emphasis is on the regulator to prove that a regulation is backed by "science" and not on the corporation to prove that their product does no harm. The precautionary principle is precluded by this approach. Regulators must defend proposed regulations vigorously and are even required to suggest alternatives that do not involve regulating. They have to provide extensive analysis, including cost-benefits to industry. Regulatory cooperation is also subject to dispute resolution, meaning corporations can directly challenge government actions. As corporations push for genetically modified organisms and glyphosate, and against health labelling, cigarette labelling, food inspection rules and many public safety rules, they have forums not only to be heard but also to contest regulations behind closed doors.

DISMANTLING THE STATE

While COVID-19 has shown us the importance of public health systems, government intervention, income supports and a social safety net, trade agreements prescribe the opposite. To a trade agreement, these public sectors need to be liberalized. Government monopolies, whether in health care or state-owned enterprises, go against the idea of liberalized trade, where companies can make a profit anywhere. However, governments — at their best — have important considerations besides profit: protecting the commons, ensuring wealth distribution and equal opportunity, ending discrimination and trying to protect and look after the public. In trade agreements, chapters on trade in services often invoke "standstill" or "ratchet" clauses. These clauses prevent services, once they have been privatized, from being put back in national or municipal ownership. While states can privatize more, they cannot undo privatization.

Since the 1980s, many governments have privatized state corporations, government services and parapublic bodies. For example, in Canada, nursing assistance, old age homes and hospital laundry and catering services have been shifting towards private ownership. And yet many of these private old age homes and private nursing services have been among the weaknesses in Canada's COVID-19 response. Any attempt to bring them under public control could be challenged, depending on the agreement. Trade agreements also go after public contracts by preventing government entities from buying local or keeping contracts in the local economy. They do not allow governments to distinguish between national companies and international companies, thereby favouring large foreign multinationals. As well, the agreements go after state-owned enterprises such as electrical utilities, Canada Post and others, by forcing them to behave like market entities.

COVID-19 AND THE CRISIS OF THE UNMANAGED COMMONS

COVID-19 is a perfect example of what happens when cooperation and sharing are subverted by an international economic system aimed at individual or national self-interest. At the very basic level, everyone must cooperate in maintaining social distancing levels and not pursue their individual selfish interests, to grow their economy by ignoring them, or the virus spreads. As well, with finite protection equipment and finite scientific expertise, we all have a global common interest in ensuring that the prices of this equipment and resources remain affordable. We also have a global interest in having health and sanitation protections to prevent further outbreaks. Since every individual member of the globe is a potential carrier and spreader of the disease, we do not eliminate COVID-19 unless the Earth's nearly 8 billion people have immunity. To provide billions of vaccines, we need a common non-profit, international response. If we allow private pharmaceutical and high-tech industries to sell us back cures developed in public labs, we cannot survive as a planet.

In a 2020 *Foreign Affairs* article, Thomas Bollyky and Chad Brown write about "The Tragedy of Vaccine Nationalism" and the need for an international treaty to provide a common, accessible vaccine. They argue that it is in every nation's self-interest that an effective and low-cost vaccine be found and distributed globally. And that it requires a global trade treaty to ensure cooperation and not competition:

> That sort of "vaccine nationalism," or a "my country first" approach to allocation, will have profound and far-reaching consequences. Without global coordination, countries may bid against one another, driving up the price of vaccines and related materials. Supplies of proven vaccines will be limited initially even in some rich countries, but the greatest suffering will be in low- and middle-income countries. Such places will be forced to

watch as their wealthier counterparts deplete supplies and will have to wait months (or longer) for their replenishment.... In their quest to obtain vaccines, countries without access to the initial stock will search for any form of leverage they can find, including blocking exports of critical vaccine components, which will lead to the breakdown of supply chains for raw ingredients, syringes, and vials.... The result will be not only needless economic and humanitarian hardship but also intense resentment against vaccine-hoarding countries, which will imperil the kind of international cooperation that will be necessary to tackle future outbreaks — not to mention other pressing challenges, such as climate change and nuclear proliferation.

While some countries have pooled their resources in mechanisms such as GAVI and argue for a vaccine as a global, public good, in practice, most richer countries, in the European Union, as well as the United States and Canada, have gone on their own making exclusive deals with pharmaceutical companies to procure vaccines for their own residents. Bollyky and Bown propose a trade agreement that would ensure that every country works together in a global pool. Participation in such a trade agreement would be ensured by the fact that most countries are interdependent and rely on multiple supply chains to produce vaccines. Every country would also have a self-interest because there is no guarantee that their national champion would succeed, so by pooling resources, they would be guaranteed a successful vaccine. The trade agreement could sanction non-cooperating countries with retaliatory tariffs (Nadeau 2020).

Such a vision, however, is far off from the present trade rules, which elevate the power of corporations and discourage states from acting at all, much less cooperating with other states to do so. In essence, even if states were to agree to such a system, corporations could argue that this is paramount to expropriating their profits under the protections of trade agreements. With the rest of the trade apparatus intact, it would have to have carve-outs to supersede all other trade agreements (Van Harten 2015).

AND ENVIRONMENT AND LABOUR WITH THAT?

Nowadays, trade agreements have many chapters that did not exist previously — sustainable development or environment chapters, labour chapters, gender chapters. In the CUSMA negotiations, the Canadian government unsuccessfully floated the idea of an Indigenous rights chapter. In the CETA agreement, a separate non-binding interpretative agreement outlined principles the signatories hoped the agreement would follow without writing them into the text. These chapters exist primarily to curb public opposition to trade agreements. But with the exception of the labour chapter and, to some extent, the environment chapter in the CUSMA, these the chapters are not binding, are aspirational in character and do not set any standards that need to be upheld. They are merely window dressing in a corporate-first agreement.

THE RESULT: PLUTOCRACY

In the end, trade agreements cement neoliberal rules onto sovereign democratic states and push for less government and more multinational space. They attack democratic rules implemented by states in order to maximize corporate power. As Maude Barlow (2019) has written:

> Modern free trade agreements, along with deregulation, privatization and the slashing of governments' ability to act as an antidote to a corporate free for all, have led to the greatest wealth disparity since the robber barons at the turn of the twentieth century. Of the world's top economies, thirty-one are countries and sixty-nine are corporations. Apple's revenues exceed the GDP of two-thirds of the world's countries. Walmart's annual revenues exceed the GDP of 157 countries. BP is bigger than Russia. Exxon is bigger than India.

Not everyone is suffering during this pandemic. A 2020 report from the Institute for Policy Studies showed that, while unemployment skyrocketed, the wealth of billionaires in the United States grew by $580 billion during the first months of the crisis, an increase of 20 percent. In Canada, the top five billionaires saw their wealth grow 9 percent, while offering around 0.09 percent of their income to charity (TaxCoop 2020).

Even without trade agreements, corporations have enormous power to shield themselves from nation-state regulations and policies by shopping for jurisdictions with looser regulations, lower corporate taxes or juicy fiscal incentives. And no international legal framework can stop them or stop states from competing downwards. Corporations have the financial power to lobby and to push their agendas with friendly lawmakers and manipulable governments. With the possibility of using mechanisms in trade agreements, they have an extra card in their hand in lobbying governments in countries where they do set up shop.

We must have a balanced trading system to combat this unprecedented global concentration of power. After all, it could lead to human annihilation. Governments must act nationally. But we also need an international overhaul of our trade agreements and constraints on corporate power. One way to proceed would be to eliminate all trade agreements and instead establish a charter to end corporate impunity, as proposed at the United Nations (Wetzels 2019). Another, more reformist in tone, is to remove corporate rights systematically from trade agreements and add binding commitments with sanctions to penalize corporations that do not meet social or environmental standards in existing agreements. Now more than ever, we need international solidarity and international cooperation, not corporate solidarity. We must defend the commons — our air, our water, our health —internationally from corporate greed. New rules and a new international order need to be developed quickly: not just to address COVID-19 but to provide food, water, education and health care to a growing world population. And to prevent human extinction.

Recommended Resources

Barlow, Maude. 2019. *What Trade Would Look Like with a Different Set of Values*. Council of Canadians. <canadians.org/analysis/what-would-trade-look-different-set-values>.

Sinclair, Scott. 2018. *Canada's Track Record Under NAFTA's Chapter 11*. Canadian Centre for Policy Alternatives. Ottawa, January. <policyalternatives.ca/sites/default/files/uploads/publications/National%20Office/2018/01/NAFTA%20Dispute%20Table%20Report%202018.pdf>.

Vaillaincourt, Claude. 2019. *Le libre-échange aujourd'hui : Bilan des accords de libre-échange soutenus par le Canada*. Pointe Calumet: M Éditeur.

19

Demanding Justice

Can Trade Policy Be Fair?

Gavin Fridell and Kate Ervine

The Fair Trade movement won't be able to realise its vision only through a market-based approach. Shaping the rules of the game … and tackling imbalances of power in supply chains is essential to realise our movement's vision, where justice and sustainable development are at the heart of trade structures and practices.
— Sergi Corbalán

Over the past few decades free trade agreements have spread rapidly across the globe, entrenching the conditions under which goods, services and investments can flow with minimal friction and maximum profitability. While unprecedented wealth has been generated, its extreme concentration has led organizations like Oxfam, and even the International Monetary Fund (IMF), to identify the growing gap between the rich and poor as a major threat to global stability and prosperity. Free trade agreements have overwhelmingly favoured investor rights, with labour, human, gender, racial and environmental rights sidelined, ignored and trampled.

The rise of fair trade has been a response to these injustices. But, as Sergi Corbalán, executive director of the Fair Trade Advocacy Office (FTAO) in Brussels acknowledges above, the reach and impact of fair trade as a consumer-based movement remains limited. A challenge for fair traders is to create a vision for how the principles of fair trade — democracy, justice, dignity, human rights, a living income and environmental stewardship — can be used to inspire a new generation of trade agreements where human and planetary well-being are prioritized in the spirit of solidarity.

United Nations Office at Geneva, just down the road from the World Trade Organization. Source: Gavin Fridell

A MULTILATERAL WORLD ORDER?

A starting point for building a fair trade agreement could be to look at existing multilateral institutions that deal with everything from trade and investment rules to issues of global poverty, sustainability, public health, human rights and climate change. These institutions have vastly different degrees of influence and effectiveness, often depending on the extent to which their goals align with those of powerful countries and corporations. As a result, issues of social and ecological justice are rarely prioritized or enforced.

The 2015 Paris Climate Agreement illustrates this point. Climate breakdown represents one of the gravest threats to humanity, and it demands bold and decisive action. Ratified by 189 countries, the Paris Agreement emerged from years of difficult negotiations led by the United Nations Framework Convention on Climate Change. The agreement represents the main multilateral framework for globally organizing state action on climate breakdown, and yet, it does not have the status of an official treaty and lacks any legally binding emission reduction or financial commitments. The *voluntary* commitments made through the agreement, moreover, have been widely assessed as inadequate to avoid catastrophic climate change. The Climate Action Tracker projects possible warming of over 3°C under current commitments, significantly higher than the agreement's target to limit warming above pre-industrial levels to well below 2°C.

In contrast, the World Trade Organization (WTO), the world's top intergovernmental trade body, has enforceable trade liberalization rules with legally binding commitments, a Dispute Settlement Body to handle violations and a range of penalties carrying political and economic weight. Certainly, the threat posed by climate breakdown warrants a multilateral agreement that is vested with these sorts of powers, or those held by global financial institutions like the IMF and World Bank, which regularly make decisions impacting the global economy and the livelihoods of millions. In practice, no such agreement exists for the environment.

Certain examples do demonstrate that multilateral action among states can be harnessed to support fairer outcomes. In the post–World War II era, a range of projects emerged that supported fairer prices and incomes for small farmers and rural workers. This included the International Coffee Agreement, lasting from the 1960s to the 1980s. Through a quota system that regulated higher and more stable coffee prices, from 1976 to 1989, millions of farmers worldwide received prices that would today be considered equivalent to the minimum price guaranteed by Fairtrade standards.

In another case, beginning in 2004 a group of ten Latin American and Caribbean countries formed the Bolivarian Alliance for the Peoples of Our America (ALBA) as an alternative to free trade agreements, emphasizing collaboration, cooperation and recognition of the asymmetries of size and power between different partners. This initiative has trained doctors, engaged in health-care internationalism, provided extensive literacy programs, subsidized petroleum for lower income members and provided low-cost financing to partners in need.

In one case, the Caribbean nation of St. Vincent and the Grenadines, one of the smallest nations in the world, was able to construct a vital international airport during a time of economic downturn, with support from ALBA partners Cuba and Venezuela. This included low-interest loans and millions of dollars of unique, in-kind assistance, including free engineering services, construction equipment, wind stations and an on-site laboratory — equivalent to nearly 40 percent of the airport cost. Completed in 2017, the airport is a critical source of global connectivity for this small island state. At the same time, ALBA has had its challenges, including an over-reliance on oil exports to fund its projects. This has

Exporting Health and Well-Being

You may be surprised to learn that Cuba's most valuable export is people. Built over many decades, Cuba's program of medical internationalism combines solidarity, diplomacy and economic interest, sending health professionals to the poorest countries at no cost and charging those able to pay on a sliding scale. In 2018 Cuba earned over $8.6 billion through medical internationalism, with 28,000 of its highly trained doctors, nurses and other health professionals working in close to 60 countries before the COVID-19 pandemic began. By the end of May 2020, continuing a long tradition of aiding countries facing health crises and natural disasters, Cuba had already sent 2,000 health professionals to 23 countries to support their fight against COVID-19. By trading in services the world needs and providing them free to the most vulnerable, Cuba's medical internationalism provides an example of how trade can be reimagined to serve human need and well-being, prioritizing solidarity over profit (Augustin 2020).

resulted in a decline in initiatives during the economic downturn, when the price for oil and other commodities has dropped significantly.

While positive examples of multilateral cooperation exist, the norm in global politics is to show little interest in social and ecological justice. Some international law experts argue that multilateral negotiations offer an opportunity for smaller or more marginalized nations to bind together and make collective demands on more powerful ones. The work of the Alliance of Small Island States in securing broad diplomatic support to include an aspirational limit of 1.5°C of warming above pre-industrial levels in the Paris Agreement is a case in point. However, when measured against the actual emission reduction commitments made by governments, and the lack of legal force around them, these successes appear mostly symbolic. All too often, multilateral forums are perceived as places where progressive agendas go to die, hindered by opposition or disinterest from powerful states who prioritize their perceived national interests over those of the common good.

GOING IT ALONE: THE UNILATERAL OPTION

Frustrated with the pace of things at the multilateral level, unions, social justice organizations and human rights groups have often lobbied for unilateral action from their own national governments. Generalized systems of preferences (GSPs) are one example. Used in particular by the United States and the European Union (EU), GSPs allow developing and least developed countries to gain preferential access to Northern markets in return for fulfilling obligations with respect to labour rights, human rights and sustainable development. While some gains have been documented, GSPs are often criticized as unilateral, paternalistic impositions on Southern nations, in a manner that can hamper their economic competitiveness without providing genuine partnership, mutual dialogue or shared responsibility for the costs associated with improved standards (higher wages, technical training, expanded labour inspections).

To avoid some of these concerns, social justice groups have placed increased efforts on pushing their own governments to adopt policies that demand accountability from their domestic-based transnational companies for the negative impacts along their global supply chains. Modern slavery legislation has been particularly notable in and widely adopted by countries such as the United Kingdom, France, the Netherlands, Norway and Australia. In Canada, a coalition of groups led by World Vision, Fairtrade Canada, UNICEF Canada and Save the Children successfully lobbied the government to table legislation for a modern slavery act in 2020.

According to the ILO, in 2016, modern slavery affected 40 million people, unable to refuse work due to threats, violence, coercion, deception or abuse of power. Modern slavery legislation requires large corporations to report steps they have taken to ensure there is no forced labour in their supply chains. While this legislation has been a welcome victory for human rights advocates, a great deal remains to be done. In the United Kingdom, corporations must report the steps they have taken, yet the legislation has not required much more than this; it even allows corporations to simply state that "no such steps" have been taken. The legislation in Canada, if it receives final approval, as well as new legislation in the works globally, could go beyond this by directly prohibiting the importation of goods produced by forced or child labour.

RIDING ON FREE TRADE AGREEMENTS:
FROM SIDELINES TO MAIN GAME?

Efforts to include social rights chapters in trade agreements have been among the most prominent options over the past few years. These agreements have long contained extensive regulations on everything from investment rights, intellectual property rights and rules of origin to public procurement and state enterprises. As passionate free trade proponent economist Jagdish Bhagwati argues in *Termites in the Trading System*, under the cover of being "trade-related," these agreements have expanded vastly to include a wide range of rules that have "nothing to do with the freeing of trade." Not only do these agreements extend beyond freeing trade, but they are also heavily slanted in favour of corporate interests. Investment rights chapters, for instance, have clear and binding rules, penalties for violations and dispute panels that can be launched unilaterally by transnational corporations. As a result, they have been used extensively. According to a 2017 United Nations Conference on Trade and Development (UNCTAD) analysis, *Investor-State Dispute Settlement*, from 1987 to 2017, a total of 855 investor disputes were launched against states, awarding billions of dollars to corporations, with the average award amounting to $125 million.

Labour chapters, in contrast, when they exist at all, contain general language and significant barriers to enforcement. As a result, only one major labour case has ever been brought before a trade tribunal, through the Dominican Republic-Central America Free Trade Agreement (CAFTA-DR) with the United States. In this case, the tribunal infamously determined in 2017 that the Guatemalan government had violated labour laws at eight separate workplaces, but that the actions did not "affect trade," so the case was dismissed.

Can this bias in trade agreements be shifted? A range of groups, in particular unions, as well as policymakers, academics and some governments have offered proposals with this in mind, advocating for new trade chapters, as opposed to the side agreements that have been the norm historically, on labour, gender equality, the environment, Indigenous rights and human rights. While many of the best ideas remain on paper, some important gains have emerged in trade negotiations at the bilateral and plurilateral levels. Perhaps most important has been an expansion of trade agreements with labour chapters that might have enforceable mechanisms. This includes the renegotiated NAFTA, which, in 2020, became the new

Canada-United States-Mexico Agreement (CUSMA), with a labour rights chapter that goes beyond previous models, including stronger labour standards, a more direct path to dispute panels and a new "rapid-response" enforcement mechanism with the power to investigate labour violations and impose penalties. The inclusion of this chapter builds upon years of tri-national union lobbying, which, according to Angelo Di Caro, national representative of Unifor, Canada's largest private sector union, aimed at "a very ambitious approach to reforming how labour standards are addressed in free trade agreements." In a recent interview, Di Caro said, "I think what they have proposed in NAFTA really does break the mould in terms of what we've seen in other free trade accords."

Other new social rights chapters, while offering some promise, appear to lack genuine enforceability and could end up like the empty chapters of the past. The CUSMA's environment chapter, Chapter 24, while technically enforceable, fails to directly mention climate change and contains key loopholes that suggest it is unlikely to be rigorously enforced. For instance, while any group can raise a complaint if they think a country has failed to follow its own environmental laws, the complaint "may" be considered by an environmental commission if it meets various criteria, including that it "appears to be aimed at promoting enforcement rather than at harassing industry."

In other agreements, the government of Canada under Prime Minister Justin Trudeau has been keen to promote new gender chapters as part of its "progressive" trade agenda. This has led to new gender additions to the pre-existing Canada-Chile Free Trade Agreement (CCFTA) in 2017 and the Canada-Israel Free Trade Agreement (CIFTA) in 2018. Only the Canada-Israel chapter is, in theory, subject to enforcement and dispute resolution. In both cases, however, the language is vague, offering general commitments to promote gender-responsive policies and foster financial inclusion, leadership, entrepreneurship and capacity building for women. It is difficult to imagine how these commitments could be meaningfully enforced or transcend the general pledges typically made by governments. They also run the risk of perpetuating and promoting free trade agreements without regard for their negative impacts that disproportionately affect women, such as cuts to public spending, increasing costs for medicine and the feminization of low-paid precarious work (Bissio 2017).

A FAIR TRADE VISION FOR BILATERAL AGREEMENTS?

One of the more interesting models to emerge in recent years is that of voluntary partnership agreements (VPAs), which advance a vision for bilateral agreements that are not about free trade, per se, but rather about achieving specific social and ecological goals among trading partners. According to Sergi Corbalán, of the FTAO, VPAs offer an opportunity to imagine what fair trade agreements could look like. To this end, the FTAO has worked in partnership with sustainable forestry groups to advocate for VPAs modelled off those that exist between the EU and timber-exporting countries. Under the terms of the EU's Forest Law Enforcement, Governance and Trade (FLEGT) Action Plan, initiated in 2003, a series of VPAs have been adopted between the EU and its timber suppliers where the latter gain easier access to the EU market in exchange for demonstrating that the timber has been legally and more sustainably produced. As the VPA is a "partnership," the EU has stepped up to provide capacity-building to assist timber exporters in setting up licensing schemes and improving enforcement.

Despite slow progress at the start, as of 2019, the EU had VPAs with nine countries and several more in the works. Duncan Brack, in his report *Towards Sustainable Cocoa Supply Chains: Regulatory Options for the EU*, concludes that the VPAs have "in some cases significantly improved governance and law enforcement, making the forest sector more transparent and accountable, and reducing illegal logging." At the same time, FLEGT has been criticized for its role in criminalizing and negatively impacting small timber suppliers that lack secure land tenure (Rutta, Myers, Ramcilovic-Suominen and McDermott 2018).

The FTAO and its partners believe the concept of a VPA could be applied to other products, like cocoa, which is a major driver of deforestation in West Africa, while its shortcomings could be addressed through a wider mandate aimed at the needs of smallholders and workers through fair trade standards. This could be combined with other existing and proposed EU policies, such as sustainable procurement, supply chain legislation and corporate due diligence laws, for maximum impact.

Moving the discussion away from the EU, Canada could explore similar models, with fair trade and ecological justice as the key objectives. One of the benefits of the VPA vision is that it shifts away from unilateral imposition toward partnership, shared responsibility and mutual benefits, with both countries negotiating an agreement designed to meet their needs. It also lifts things out of the sometimes-amorphous world of global agreements, where grand statements and general commitments are often made without clear, direct objectives and a precise way to measure real impacts.

Imagine, for instance, a VPA for coffee between Canada and its major coffee-exporting partners. While coffee is a globalized industry, Canada imports nearly 68 percent of its unprocessed coffee beans from just Brazil, Colombia and Guatemala. Starting with Guatemala, the most economically vulnerable of the three, Canada could negotiate a coffee VPA aimed at assisting coffee farmers in addressing the impact of climate change, which threatens the entire region due to unpredictable weather patterns, warmer climate and increased vulnerability to coffee disease and pests, while also achieving fair trade standards for farmers and workers. The initial VPA could be reproduced to include other coffee exporters and provide a clear mechanism for multi-stakeholder engagement between governments, farmer representatives, unions, nongovernmental organizations and industry. Fair trade could be scaled up to the level of intergovernmental relations through a model aimed at avoiding the paternalist impositions of the past.

STEPPING UP FAIR TRADE

The COVID-19 pandemic shines a light on the profound dangers of an international economic system whose rules are designed to safeguard investor and business profitability and, in doing so, diminish the capacity of far too many, including the world's most vulnerable, to withstand the crisis. While fair trade advocates have highlighted this fact for decades, grinding poverty remains a daily reality for an unacceptably high number of the world's small producers. A major challenge, both politically and economically, is to imagine how fair trade principles might serve as a starting point to reimagine trade as a tool for achieving human and planetary well-being.

While this chapter's overview of specific examples showcases their promises and limitations, it also shows that there is no silver bullet for making trade truly fair. As activists, practitioners, scholars, consumers and policymakers, the task ahead demands of us an honest naming of the injustices that mark the contemporary free trade regime, an openness to learn the lessons from existing initiatives and a willingness to refuse business-as-usual.

Recommended Resources

Bissio, Roberto. 2017. "Is 'Gender' a Trojan Horse to Introduce New Issues at WTO?" *Third World Network*. <dawnnet.org/2017/12/is-gender-a-trojan-horse-to-introduce-new-issues-at-wto/>.

Brack, Duncan 2019. *Towards Sustainable Cocoa Supply Chains: Regulatory Options for the EU*. Fern, Tropenbos International, Fair Trade Advocacy Offices. <fern.org/news-resources/towards-sustainable-cocoa-supply-chains-regulatory-options-for-the-eu-1978/>.

Canadian Foreign Policy Institute. <foreignpolicy.ca/>.

Sinclair, Scott, Manuel Pérez-Rocha and Ethan Earle (eds.). 2019. *Beyond NAFTA 2.0: A Trade Agenda for People and Planet*. Canadian Centre for Policy Alternatives, Institute for Policy Studies, the Rosa Luxemburg Foundation. <policyalternatives.ca/publications/reports/beyond-nafta-20>.

Zini, Sylvain, Éric Boulanger and Michèle Rioux (eds.). 2021. *Vers une politique commerciale socialement responsable dans un context de tensions commerciales/Towards a socially responsible trade policy in the context of commercial tensions*. Québec: Presse de l'Université du Québec.

20

Taking Fair Trade to the People

Education and Advocacy for Social Change

Zack Gross

It was a long time ago, 50 years to be exact, and I was just beginning a career that would span my lifetime. I had always been interested in global issues. In elementary school, I participated in Model United Nations assemblies that our Grade 6 teacher organized. In high school, I led our Current Affairs Club and benefited from the support and mentoring of a particularly progressive principal. And then, at 20 years of age, I was in university studying politics and history and encountering — given that it was the 1960s and '70s — a deluge of radical ideas, such as that there should be no war and no gap between rich and poor. That led me one fall evening in 1969 to be part of a "delegation" of young people that headed to the Winnipeg International Airport to greet (he might have thought confront) External Affairs Minister Mitchell Sharp, part of the Pierre Trudeau–led Liberal cabinet. We wanted to ask why Canada had not yet lived up to its pledge, based on a United Nations resolution, to provide 0.7 percent of our gross domestic product (GDP) to Official Development Assistance (ODA). We handed Mr. Sharp a petition or letter, I don't remember which, and felt that it was bound to make a difference.

Half a century later Canada's commitment to ODA, at this writing, is 0.27 percent of GDP, just one-third of what was hoped for way back then. In recent years only a very few Western European countries have attained 0.7 percent or a bit higher. This haunts me still. How can we educate and advocate on global issues, such as fair trade, in ways that actually bring about positive, concrete action and change? How can we not just be busy, not just try, but actually accomplish our goal of fundamental change?

I know that I am not alone in this, that activists from across our country and around the world are doing effective work to bring about change in how humanity develops economically, socially, culturally and environmentally. We seek justice, equality, transparency, fairness, participation and more. The great challenge for those of us working at the education and advocacy level is to choose our message and take it effectively — along with the messages of our partners in the Global South — to target sectors of our society.

While fair trade is important to pursue in itself as a set of principles and actions, it is also a vehicle or tool in what we call international development, which for many of us has been anti-colonial work and the creation of opportunities for marginalized peoples to improve their economic and social positions. Aside from the macro side of fair trade — to change global economic systems — there is a more individual side: to support lifestyle change in the consuming North.

Maintaining our current lifestyle will certainly destroy our planet. Old style development thinking says that a better world will be created when changes are made in the Global South. Colonial development thinking says that we should exploit the resources and labour available in the Global South. Today's United Nations Sustainable Development Goals argue that the changes that need to take place in our world need to happen in rich countries as well as poor. The North's consumption of resources, our policing of the world to make sure it operates to our economic and political advantage, our abuse of the natural environment that sustains us all, our belief in our own ascendancy and our practice of cultural domination are profoundly self-defeating in our age of pandemic, climate change and nuclear weaponry.

One of the challenges in writing this chapter is that a variety of fair trade groups are working on education and advocacy at different levels. Some specialize in school programs; others focus on business. Some operate at the local level, others at the national. Some have adequate resources; others operate with little financial support. Action on fair trade is uneven across the country, with much being accomplished in some jurisdictions and less in others. A book, not just a chapter, could be dedicated to this work. Thus, here are snapshots of what can/could/ought to be done.

FOR IMMEDIATE RESULTS, WORK WITH GOVERNMENTS

There is much to be accomplished by ramping up our communication with elected officials from all levels of government — national, provincial, municipal and school board. At least once per year, a meaningful exchange should take place between fair traders and elected governing members in every possible jurisdiction, with a set of reasonable asks, such as specific policy changes or program creation, as the framework for that discussion. In Manitoba, where I am from, we were able to do this in past years, in part, because our Fair Trade Manitoba program was part of the educational side of the Manitoba Council for International Cooperation's public engagement effort. Our requests included funding for our educational programs, making our legislative building a Fair Trade Workplace, inviting elected officials to join trips to producing countries and supporting the serving and sale of Fairtrade products in government-run establishments, such as legislators' offices, liquor marts and casinos.

As we had the human resource capability to work with cities and towns, schools and campuses, workplaces and faith communities, we were also able to connect with some members of Parliament and the Legislative Assembly, mayors and their councils, school board trustees, and the professional civil service for all of these political institutions with some success, and the inevitable frustrations as well. There is much to learn from jurisdictions such as Scotland and Wales, each a designated Fair Trade Nation, including how they have made fair trade a part of their governments' regular policy discussions and agenda. Unfinished business includes our own attempt to move toward becoming a Fair Trade Province. Just the exercise of defining what that would mean is well worth the effort.

Direct asks of the provincial government, such as for Manitoba Liquor & Lotteries to showcase and sell Fairtrade-certified wines, beer and spirits, were met with immediate positive action by a New Democratic Party (NDP) government and then with continued support from a Progressive Conservative (PC) government when power changed hands. Some members of the legislature from all parties participated in carrying Fairtrade-certified coffee in their offices and the Manitoba Legislative Building cafeteria itself served a number of fair trade products.

The provincial government offered a small grant to support Winnipeg's hosting the National Fair Trade Conference in 2016, and underwrote through Statistics Manitoba our being able to poll Manitobans on fair trade through a provincial survey conducted by a professional research company on several occasions. (Having these kinds of official statistics greatly enhanced our credibility in the eyes of government and business.) Our premier, cabinet ministers and legislative members attended and spoke at a number of our fair trade or related events.

FAIR TRADE TOWN COMMITTEES
CAN ACT AS LOCAL CONSCIENCE

Across Canada, not just in my own home province, Fair Trade Town committees have led successful designation campaigns in close to 30 towns and cities, and my experience has been that there is strong support from elected officials and the bureaucracy. A coordinated effort between local and national fair trade organizations would make an impression on members of Parliament. Meanwhile, school boards, which often aim to build youth citizenship, sustainability and inclusion in their districts, would seem ready to hear from the fair trade movement, especially via their own passionate students. The message from advocates is twofold: Be more mindful of the harm done by conventional consumerism and be aware of the alternatives available through more ethical and green choices.

Moving fair trade to the front burner is a challenge for educators and advocates. When I visited Duane Nicol, chief administrative officer for the City of Selkirk, Manitoba, now a Fair Trade Town, he showed me the pile of files on his desk that cried out for his scrutiny. They covered issues and initiatives such as infrastructure repair, social housing, mosquito abatement and more. The challenge is that if fair trade is perceived as an optional activity after the "compulsory" work is done, many just won't get to it. In a joint presentation that Duane and I made at a school assembly to local students and officials, he told them that a municipal office is there to take care of the basic needs of its citizens. If the Earth is our home, just as Selkirk is, then a municipality also has some responsibility to support citizens around the world through initiatives such as fair trade.

In a local paper, the media will celebrate a fair trade project but at the national or international level, as even they would admit, there is coverage only if something seemingly negative can be exposed. As with politicians and government, we need to create the occasions and stories, develop relationships with journalists and build strategies that create awareness and action. How do we get a greater percentage of the public, business people, decision makers and other groups to look for the latest stories about ethical production and consumption?

Even with the successes that have been met in some jurisdictions, what we haven't had to my knowledge is notable progress toward a deeper discussion of how to change trade policies. How can we persuade provincial and federal governments to take a critical look at their trade relationships with other nations? Some more unfinished business includes researching, reporting and acting on how fair our trade is with poorer countries and what we can do, as a country, to better support those who grow our coffee, cocoa, cotton and bananas and sew much of our clothing?

For more than a half century, the international development community has delivered countless presentations in classrooms, community halls and places of worship. Having an entertaining and interactive presentation is a must. A dry lecture might be filled with information, but those wandering minds might not pick up much of it! Simulation exercises, videos, guest speakers with on-the-ground experience and stories, and samples (especially chocolate!) are the ticket. I was once struck by a PowerPoint that illustrated how the people who produce so many of our most cherished products live at the bottom of the United Nations Human Development Index. The question of "Why?" should motivate students to focus their lives on social betterment. Significantly, that was the message that hooked me as a student a long time ago, and, sadly, it is still relevant today.

ENLISTING THE PASSION OF YOUTH

In my experience in taking world poverty to the school system, there are certain issues that catch the attention and passionate support of students, and one of them is fair trade. This is also true at the postsecondary level. But, a fair trade speaker could be in two classrooms per day — or maybe more — every school day of the year, and then do it all over again the next year with a new batch of young people, and still possibly fair trade would not be much further ahead without policy and practical action. So, given the relatively meagre resources of the fair trade community and the vast number of students, we must find strategies that maximize our impact.

An alternative is to no longer deliver fair trade presentations without including a strong ask, that a class or school commit to something concrete. This might be to hold a "Fair Trade Grad," or become a Fair Trade School, or sell fair trade products in their business class or school store, or write letters or start an online petition to push a government or business to adopt fair trade. Persistently but politely follow up to see what happens and make every effort to help them achieve that benchmark. Some very exciting outcomes have been documented in schools across Canada, and it's exciting to see that a discussion of fair trade and action in support of it have sometimes become the starting points for broader and deeper involvement in social change in some communities.

Integrating Active Citizenship into Community Life

Rob Jantz, who teaches in the Evergreen School Division in the Interlake Region of Manitoba, demonstrates how fair trade can be part of an overall effort by and for youth to confront social issues and strengthen their role in social decision making. Alongside school personnel and community members, Rob helped launch the Youth Community Partnership, an initiative that enhances leadership opportunities for local youth. The partnership has created greater awareness for a number of issues, and its efforts have led to improvements to the Lake Winnipeg ecosystem; support for LGBTQ students in the face of bullying; the designation of Gimli, Manitoba, as a Fair Trade Town; and the addition of a youth representative on the local municipal council. There were, for a number of years, fair trade coffee houses with music by students and teachers; regional school conferences on fair trade and other social issues; visioning sessions on the future of our local area; report-back sessions for students, parents and community leaders; and the twinning of Gimli, which is mixed fishing, farming and tourism, with projects in East Africa. Additionally, the partnership created a video on LGBTQ issues. Thus, fair trade can become part of the daily fabric of a community and one of the issues that elected leaders and the public address as they improve the lives of citizens at home and abroad.

One of the great challenges as we do our work is turnover of the personnel involved, and with that change, which is a constant in our society, not all of these exciting programs will continue. In our own local area, with the election of new mayors and councillors, with the retirement or moving on of some teachers, administrators and board officials, and with the graduation and exit of activist students, the level of social action has diminished. But the history and the option are still there. This can happen again, where it did and somewhere else.

In any movement, there are champions — people who take on responsibility, people you can count on to make things happen. So it is with fair trade, and through designations — Fair Trade Town, School, Campus, Faith Group and Workplace. Whether it is in Victoria, Vancouver, Calgary, Olds, Edmonton, Regina, Winnipeg, Brandon, Toronto, Ottawa, Montreal, Hudson or Halifax, there might be one or a very small number who play this role. Identifying those champions and supporting them is an important job for leaders at the national level (who are also dotted across the country). The CFTN has effectively taken on the role of a national convenor of local leaders.

GETTING OUT OF OUR COMFORT ZONE

Call me naive. People who work for social justice often see the business community as opposition. Yet there are many who work for companies or own businesses who are — or are open to — carrying, selling or serving ethical and fair trade products. Some of them truly care about sustainability, equity and human rights. These include what we call 100 percenters, who only trade in fair products, and many whose corporate roles include sustainability management. In recent years, many companies have created these positions, while university and college commerce and MBA programs have added sustainability and ethics courses to their syllabuses.

Zack Gross promoting fair trade in the "infamous" banana suit.
Source: Canadian Fair Trade Network

Other businesses see fair trade products as a niche market. They know they can make some money if they carry Fairtrade-certified (or fairly traded) goods. We can't shy away from engaging with the business community, whether it is the local branch of a large company or a one-off small business. We can't only, as the old saying goes, preach to the choir — let's expand our reach! A number of years ago, fair trade staff and volunteers in Winnipeg blitzed downtown cafes, dropping off sample products and introducing fair trade. In a reverse initiative, busloads of students, teachers and civic officials in Selkirk and Brandon, with media in tow, toured local supermarkets, cafes and health food stores to document and promote the fair trade products they sold.

Larger enterprises support sustainability for that combination of altruism and self-interest noted above. Whether it is Costco, Federated Co-op, IKEA, Loblaws or others, building relationships at the local level and supporting national and global connections is important. Large venues such as convention centres, sports arenas, casinos and more also need to hear from us. Two of us with the Fair Trade Winnipeg committee met with the catering manager of the RBC Convention Centre, the city's largest, to promote the idea of their carrying fair trade products for the many conferences, weddings and graduations they host. We even dressed up! Before we could warm up to our spiel, the executive we met with said, "You don't need to convince me. You need to help me do it." Over the next several months, we connected her with product suppliers, helped in their development of a menu and promoted their initiative, whereby people using the Centre could choose Fairtrade-certified products off their menu, such as wine, coffee and flowers.

The increasingly mainstream position of fair trade means larger enterprises purchase from the Fairtrade system and carry these products, sometimes to the detriment of producers and of smaller shops. Ultimately, selling more fair trade product is in the best interests of our producing partners but this is an issue to monitor to make sure we are bringing about real and lasting change.

WHY DOESN'T EVERYBODY JUST "GET IT"?

It made a lasting impression on me years ago when I heard a speaker talking about why our message as NGOs doesn't galvanize people to action in support of our causes. We know that we have "right" on our side, so what's the problem? How can we talk to people in ways that engage and recruit them, rather than putting them off or scaring them off? Start with where your audience is coming from, not from where you are. For me, it is about creating a relationship with the person in question, who might be a school principal, a media reporter, a business owner or a civil service manager, so that they trust you and adopt your cause in part because they have adopted you. It can be slow work but it is fundamental to real change. And, of course, it doesn't always work.

For many people who hear the fair trade message, there are reasons why they won't be signing on. The usual reasons are that our products are too expensive, or not available where they shop, or not available in sufficient quantity if they are thinking larger scale. It might also be that they don't understand or identify with the ongoing neo-colonialism that affects primary producers in the Global South. It might be that they don't see what's in it for them. Or they just have their own smaller world they are focusing on. No social movement captures 100 percent of support.

As I said earlier, there is much more to be discussed and written about how to most effectively educate and advocate on behalf of fair trade. This chapter is part of an ongoing discourse, and I welcome people's stories, comments and suggestions. How can we take fair trade to the public, to youth and to our leaders in business and government? It is a similar dilemma to how to best bring about awareness and action on climate change or human rights. They are all connected and they are all urgent.

Recommended Resources

D'Alisa, Giacomo, Federico Demaria and Giorgios Kallis. 2015. *Degrowth: A Vocabulary for a New Era*. New York: Routledge.

Green, Duncan. 2016. *How Change Happens*. Oxford University Press.

Raworth, Kate. 2017. *Doughnut Economics: Seven Ways to Think Like a 21ˢᵗ Century Economist*. Vermont: Chelsea Green Publishing.

Rosling, Hans. 2018. *Factfulness: Ten Reasons We're Wrong About the World – And Why Things Are Better Than You Think*. New York: Flatiron Press.

21

Fair Trade 2030

Gavin Fridell, Zack Gross and Sean McHugh

The consumer walks into the grocery store and heads for the coffee section. It's just after opening time at the store, and they just realized, after waking up, that there was no coffee in the house. Now the headache that comes from delayed caffeine intake is starting to percolate. Down the coffee aisle, there are so many, too many, choices but they search out the fair trade options, pleased that the options with the most rigorous certification process are prominently and clearly displayed. The consumer pays a bit more but is glad that the producers use ecologically sustainable methods and get paid a living wage.

Unlocking the door at opening time, the cafe owner eyes the lineup outside. Another busy day is in the works. Some customers just want to kill time over a cappuccino, others settle in to write term papers or do office work, while others prepare to meet with clients or colleagues. The owner knows that the customers buy this coffee because it's fair trade and prepared the right way. It satisfies their social conscience and their taste buds. And the owner feels that they are doing well financially while doing good globally.

The supply chain manager is looking to sign a long-term contract for large amounts of coffee. As a post-graduate student before taking this job, they learned that the coffee we drink not only offers an energy boost to employees but impacts global poverty levels, climate change, health and human rights. The bottom line is not only about profit but also covers the state of our society and our environment. They will choose fair trade and pay the best possible price, keeping in mind that there is an acceptable cost to growing, trading, processing and consuming our coffee the right way.

The coffee co-op manager in a Global Southern country is pleased that their crop is not only selling well this year but that generous contracts have been agreed upon into the future. They know that a quality product that meets the highest standards of economic, social, cultural and environmental sustainability is now what the market is looking for.

Growing recognition of the colonial crimes of the past have led to a new sense of common purpose as the world tackles both longstanding and new challenges. For the co-op, they see that coffee and its producers are no longer ignored; their knowledge and hard work are recognized. Each cup people sell or drink no longer repeats the cycle of global injustice but brings us one step forward to something better on the horizon.

Maybe it was the COVID pandemic back in the early 2020s that got people more engaged in dealing with these big issues around health, environment, fair wages and worker safety. Somehow, we didn't entirely go back to our self-centred ways but — whether driven by fear or by a new spirit of cooperation — decided as governments, businesses, institutions and families to create true global partnerships and make the changes that would keep us alive and allow more people to thrive. But even in 2030, there is still much to be done and we see that a fair trade mindset can help to lead the way forward.

Or, maybe it was the tireless effort of active citizens, socially conscious business people, critical-thinking academics and many others — including those in the fair trade movement — who generated a global discussion of how to create a better world for all that led to where we could be in 2030. It seems that often, when it comes to the best of ideas, no one can remember who thought of it first!

In that spirit, we hope *The Fair Trade Handbook* can help drive us toward the future we urgently need. We offer here six overarching lessons from the book and its contributors that we think are essential to get fair trade, and hopefully other movements and groups as well, on the road to this future.

1. DECOLONIZATION AND SOLIDARITY

Decolonizing trade, and fair trade, remains one of the greatest challenges that lies ahead. In economic terms, fair trade has been a leading movement demanding change to the unequal terms of trade between rich Northern nations and poorer Southern ones, and between powerful transnational corporations and small farmers and workers within these nations. As Haroon Akram-Lodhi has so well documented (in Chapter 3), colonialism was "little more than a global confidence game" leaving behind a global trading order rooted in monopoly privileges for capital, racialized discrimination, extreme social hierarchies and uneven trade and investment flows, all of which become locked-in under the premise of "free trade." These inequalities continue unabated; Zak Cope (2019) has estimated that $1.2 to $2.8 trillion of value was transferred in 2012 alone from the Global South to the Global North as a result of unequal exchange.

Fair traders have sought to challenge these injustices by directing more wealth and income into the hands of the farmers and workers who make the products in the first place. Their direct impact has been limited thus far. As Mara Fridell, Ian Hudson and Mark Hudson observe in Chapter 17, fair trade has had a modest impact on income and working conditions globally, although it continues to play an important role as a movement raising awareness and limiting capitalist excess. Fair trade is about more than just the economics, of course. It is also about global solidarity, local democracy and social justice. Here, too, more remains to be done to decolonize fair trade, abandoning the paternalistic approach of the past in favour of a new vision that places producer agency front and central to fair trade's vision and goals.

As Nelson Melo Maya and Joey Pittoello (Chapter 7) and Jerónimo Pruijn (Chapter 9), as well as many others in this book, have noted, fair trade has made important strides toward decolonization, but much of this has come about as a result of the struggle of farmers and workers themselves. They have demanded and attained a greater voice in Fairtrade International and, in the case of SPP, created their own labelling organization where they are the central protagonists. Moving forward, fair trade must continue in this direction. This involves reaffirming and strengthening the commitment to those aspects of fair trade that producers say are among the most important to them, such as higher and fairer prices, despite pressure from corporations and international organizations to weaken or abandon these commitments for more market-friendly models.

Decolonization also entails centring fair trade around the priorities of producers and their vision of dignity, love, trust, respect and equality. This, as political economy professor Elizabeth Bennett (2021) argues, not only makes fair trade more effective but should be a key objective "in and of itself," as well as mechanism for "modelling the world we want to see." To Melo Maya, a decolonized vision of fair trade "is possible, but only if we trade the Global North's mantra of efficiency and productivity for that of balance and respect for people and our planet."

2. THE RIGHT KIND OF BUSINESS

Being a fully committed business with fair trade and sustainability at the core of everything you do is not easy. Whereas competitors can look for cost savings, fair trade sourcing, sustainable packaging, purchasing carbon offsets and paying employees well often keep companies who are "doing it right" locked into higher costs. As many writers discussed throughout the book, there are numerous challenges to being 100 percent dedicated, especially while other companies out there might sell non-fair trade products to help prop up their bottom lines. The fair trade movement and the businesses within it, however, are playing the long game. They are investing in people and planet, not just profit. They think critically about everything they do and about how they can be better and do more. They do this knowing that profits might be thinner and business might be more difficult, but they're committed. They're committed to who they are, what they do and the people they work with and serve. They're committed to engaging their customers, to help them to understand why their product might cost just a little bit more. They're committed to building something bigger than themselves and their own business. They're committed to being part of the solution and to changing how things work.

As we heard from the folks at ORGANICA and Just Us! (Chapter 7), La Siembra (Chapter 12), Equifruit (Chapter 10), and others, while it's not always easy, real change is possible. As the world continues to change, as consumers change and become more aware of what they buy, as our world becomes increasingly interconnected, as we have access to information like never before, there are no longer enough excuses for inaction, at least none that can be justified. Fair traders have lived their values for years, and consumers are taking notice. Now is the time for the businesses with community at their core to emerge and flourish!

3. THE ENVIRONMENT AND CLIMATE CHANGE

Climate change, environmental degradation and biodiversity loss are critical challenges facing the world. Everything we do has an impact on the planet, and producing goods that are often transported around the globe, even if fair trade, is no exception. Fair trade standards support sustainable environmental practices by rewarding initiatives such as integrated farm management that minimizes pollutants, pesticides and herbicides; organic farming techniques; bans on dangerous pesticides; and the general safeguarding of natural resources. But do these standards go far enough?

Do fair trade businesses do enough to offset their impacts? Is there more that producers can do to offset the impacts of growing, processing and bringing products to market?

While baseline environmental standards within fair trade standards are good, it is time that all businesses, fair trade or not, adopt them as a baseline. Fair traders can then lead the way beyond the baseline, as Monika Firl (Chapter 5) shows us. Cooperative Coffees, the importing company she works for, has put in place a small premium on every pound that is purchased by their roaster-members. This premium then goes into a fund that helps support Cooperative Coffees' producer partners with climate change–related adaption and mitigation projects. This has led to a focus on agroforestry and soil and plant health as mechanisms to protect against a changing climate and methods to sequester carbon more efficiently. More companies can and should do this.

Just Us! Coffee Roasters in Nova Scotia brought in a shipment of green coffee beans by sail in 2019, experimenting with very low-carbon coffee, while other Canadian roasters have made technical improvements to their roasteries, introduced innovative packaging and bought carbon offsets to balance out their emissions. In 2015, Fairtrade International launched Fairtrade climate credits, to help incentivize farmers and co-ops to develop carbon offset projects, such as tree planting, with Fairtrade standards, including the minimum price, social premium, knowledge sharing and real ownership by the communities involved.

Can the fair trade movement do more? Of course. Advocates can plan zero waste events, businesses can encourage their employees to cycle to work, and most importantly, the movement as a whole can both live their values and push for improved policies and legislation at the institutional and government levels, as we're all in this together.

4. FAIR TRADE STANDARDS AND LABELS

There is considerable downward pressure to make things easier, to simply slap a label on something, call it fair trade and not actually change any-thing substantive. And while it would be great to see a fair trade mark on everything that we buy, it doesn't mean anything if things don't change along the way; that is, after all, the whole point. The fair trade movement has always been filled with contradictions and trade-offs, but it has been its most successful when it stuck to its guns and demanded more. While it might be difficult, we must not sacrifice long-term change for short-term gain. Fair trade standards must remain rigorous and should focus on constant improvements. Most importantly, producers must remain front and centre, as at the end of the day, they are who this movement is meant to be about.

5. FAIR TRADE ADVOCACY: CHANGING TRADE

Changing trade policy has become an increasingly important goal to fair trade. In the post-war era, this was already central to what was considered "fair trade" — demanding higher prices for commodities through regulation, codes of conduct for corporations, forgiveness of unfair debt and facilitated access to Northern markets — but it became less popular in the 1990s and 2000s as fair traders focused energies on expanding ethical markets (Fridell 2014). Today, there is growing recognition that fair trade's immediate and practical goals must be matched by broader action on the part of governments and that fair traders have a key role to play in getting their values inserted into existing trade agreements, emerging ones and new models that have not yet been developed.

In terms of existing agreements, governments around the world have shown growing support for new chapters in trade agreements that at least nominally support labour rights, gender equity and the environment. Unfortunately, most lack genuine enforceability and adopt a narrow lens on the issue at hand. As Laura Macdonald and Nadia Ibrahim observe in Chapter 4, many new gender chapters focus on market opportunities for relatively elite women while ignoring the ways in which trade liberalization has contributed to low-wage work for women and added to their unequal work burden. Fair traders need to push back and demand more extensive policies that support care work and human rights while also looking inward at their own projects, which have neglected the importance of gender equity for too long.

What else should concern fair traders? It is not only what needs to be added to trade agreements but also what needs to be removed. As Sujata Dey argues (in Chapter 18), trade agreements contain monopoly protections and corporate investment rights that have little to do with "freeing" trade. In place of this special treatment, new international agreements are required that do not extend the power of the already-powerful but rather impose new rules and expectations on them to "end corporate impunity."

Outside of bilateral and multilateral trade agreements, fair traders have already taken a lead role in emerging global supply chain legislation around modern slavery, child labour and human rights. Fair traders need to continue to make sure that fair trade values are part of the evolution of these agreements, making sure in particular, as Elena Lunder and Sergi Corbalán argue in Chapter 16, that the responsibility and costs of compliance are not passed along to "the weakest parts of the value chain," as has so often been the case.

Finally, many of the guiding principles of fair trade, emerging out of decades of dialogue between producers, workers, consumers, businesses, NGOs and fair trade organizations can be used not only to influence existing agreements but also to inspire the creation of entirely new ones. Here Gavin Fridell and Kate Ervine (in Chapter 19), building on work by the FTAO, encourage us to envision voluntary partnership agreements that avoid the paternalist impositions of the past and deal with one of the most pressing issues of our time, climate change, while putting the agency and needs of smallholder farmers and workers first.

6. THEORY OF CHANGE

The Fair Trade Handbook is just one piece in the puzzle of bringing about fundamental and longstanding social change that helps to create a better world. That better world would seriously address and work to eradicate the causes of poverty, environmental degradation and human rights abuses. A theory of change sets long-term goals, does a 360-degree assessment of current conditions and maps out a plan and all the processes necessary to bring about the desired change. *The Fair Trade Handbook* offers historical background, describes the impact of past mistakes and crimes, looks at fair trade as it now stands, offers critiques and suggestions for improvement of the current fair trade model and thought process, tells stories that make fair trade something worth working toward and celebrates some of the people and programs active today in the Global South and North in the fair trade movement.

A social movement is an organized effort by a large and diverse group to achieve a particular purpose. It is an opportunity for organizations, businesses, governments, institutions and others to join together to push an agenda in which all can find something to agree on and to make happen. But it's not easy. Getting different sectors of our society to work together despite their differing mindsets and motivations is a challenge. Getting them to see the world and its challenges the same way is even tougher. A colleague likened people in social movements to "the sweaters" and people in government and business to "the suits." She said that it's a cultural leap to bring these two opposites together. Another colleague suggested canvassing various philanthropic, charitable, not-for-profit and aid organizations to see what a "theory of change" meant to them. After all, if you are trying to create a better world, you must have a starting point, an end in mind and a process to get you from one to the other. What was heard back from those surveyed was that some hadn't heard the phrase "theory of change"; some said it took too much navel-gazing to go through the process; some sent me short statements that had been adopted by their organizations and then seldom shared, revised or studied. Finally, a few lengthy and detailed environmental scans and theories of change arrived and really spoke to the issues at hand.

Fair trade principles can be templates for equitable, participatory and sustainable development if matched up against and folded into the kinds of programs that NGOs, development banks, government foreign affairs departments and others pursue. As you read the chapters in this book and see the issues that face our world, "solutions" will hopefully become evident: paying people a fair wage or return on their product, seeing to their health and safety, guarding women and children against oppression and exploitation, helping producers take their product to the world market, remembering the natural world as we develop our economies and more. Think about how you can create a theory of change in your own milieu and how you and yours can be part of this social movement.

We are in it for the long haul. We know what the issues are and we are working at them. This is so important that government, institutions, business, NGOs, labour, academia, and active citizens can and should work at it together. Reading *The Fair Trade Handbook*, of course, is not enough. Hoping that "things get better" is not an option. Saying all the right things but continuing as we have always done endangers people and planet. Taking positive, concrete action is the answer. Personally, you can set yourself a goal of learning more, spreading the word and of course practising what you advocate by purchasing fair trade products for yourself and in your workplace, your place of learning, your faith group, as gifts during the year and more. You can also join with others to encourage organizations, governments, business and others to support fair trade businesses and fair trade policies and practices on a larger scale, from the local to the global. Start now!

Recommended Resources

Bennett, Elizabeth, 2020. "The Global Fair Trade Movement: For Whom, By Whom, How, and What Next." In Michael Bell, Michael Carolan, Julie Keller and Katharine Legun (eds.) *The Cambridge Handbook of Environmental Sociology*. Cambridge: Cambridge University Press.

Byrne, Stacey, and Errol Sharpe. 2014. *In Pursuit of Justice: Just Us! Coffee Roasters Co-op and the Fair Trade Movement*. Black Point Nova Scotia, Fernwood Publishing.

Cope, Zak. 2019. *The Wealth of (Some) Nations: Imperialism and the Mechanics of Value Transfer*. London: Pluto Press.

Fridell, Gavin. 2014. *Coffee*. Cambridge, England: Polity Press.

Raynolds, Laura T., and Elizabeth A. Bennett (eds.). 2015. *Handbook of Research on Fair Trade*. Cheltenham, UK: Edward Elgar Publishers.

Acronyms

ALBA	Alianza Bolivariana para los Pueblos de Nuestra América/ Bolivarian Alliance for the Peoples of Our America
ATOs	alternative trade organizations
CAFTA-DR	Dominican Republic-Central America Free Trade Agreement
CCFTA	Canada-Chile Free Trade Agreement
CETA	Canada-European Union Comprehensive Economic and Trade Agreement
CIFTA	Canada-Israel Free Trade Agreement
CLAC	Coordinadora Latinoamericana y del Caribe de Pequeños Productores de Comercio Justo/Latin American and Caribbean Network of Fair Trade Small Producers and Workers
CJM	Comerico Justo Mexico
COMSA	Café Orgánico Marcala (Honduras)
CFTN	Canadian Fair Trade Network
CUSMA	Canada-United States-Mexico Agreement
EFTA	European Fair Trade Association
EU	European Union
FLEGT	Forest Law Enforcement, Governance and Trade Action Plan (EU)
FLO	Fairtrade International, or Fairtrade Labelling Organizations International
FTA	free trade agreement
FTAO	Fair Trade Advocacy Office
FTF	Fair Trade Federation
GBA+	Gender Based Analysis Plus
GMOs	genetically modified organisms
GSP	Generalized Systems of Preferences
HRDD	human rights due diligence

IMF	International Monetary Fund
ISO	International Organization for Standardization
ICA	International Coffee Agreement
ICO	International Coffee Organization
IGTN	International Gender and Trade Network
IISD	International Institute for Sustainable Development
ILO	International Labour Organization
ISDS	Investor State Dispute Settlement Provisions
ITC	International Trade Centre
MNCS	multinational corporations
NAP	National Action Plan
NGOS	non-governmental organization
ODA	Official Development Assistance
SDGS	Sustainable Development Goals
SME	small- and medium-sized enterprise
SPO	small-scale producer organization
SPS	Símbolo de Pequeños Productores/Small Producers Symbol
TNCS	transnational corporations
TPP11	Comprehensive and Progressive Agreement for a Trans-Pacific Partnership
UCIRI	Unión de Comunidades Indígenas de la Región del Istmo/Union of Indigenous Communities of the Isthmus Region
UN	United Nations
UNCTAD	UN Conference on Trade and Development
UNFCCC	UN Framework Convention on Climate Change
UNGP	UN Guiding Principles on Business and Human Rights
VAP	voluntary partnership agreement
WFTO	World Fair Trade Organization
WTO	World Trade Organization

References

Alberti, Francesco. 2020. "Asean Trade Measures and COVID-19." *Asean Post*, July 18. <theaseanpost.com/article/asean-trade-measures-and-covid-19>.

Amnesty International. 2017. *Federal Government Failing First Nations on Drinking Water Promise: Report.* February 09. <https://www.amnesty.ca/news/federal-government-failing-first-nations-drinking-water-promise-report>.

Anner, Mark. 2019. "Squeezing Workers' Rights in Global Supply Chains: Purchasing Practices in the Bangladesh Garment Export Sector in Comparative Perspective." *Review of International Political Economy*, 27 2.

___. 2020. "Abandoned? The Impact of COVID-19 on Workers and Businesses at the Bottom of Global Garment Supply Chains." Penn State Center for Global Workers' Rights, March.

Augustin, Ed. 2020. "Cuba Has Sent Over 2,000 Doctors and Nurses Overseas to Fight COVID-19." *The Nation*, May 22. <thenation.com/article/world/cuba-doctors-covid-19/>.

Barlow, Maude. 2015. *Why Canada Is One of the Most Sued Countries in the World.* Council of Canadians, October 23. <canadians.org/analysis/why-canada-one-most-sued-countries-world>.

___. 2019. *What Trade Would Look Like with a Different Set of Values.* Council of Canadians. <canadians.org/analysis/what-would-trade-look-different-set-values>.

Barlow, Maude, and Sujata Dey. 2015. "CETA's Promise of 80,000 Jobs Doesn't Add Up." *Huffington Post*, May 29. <huffingtonpost.ca/maude-barlow/free-trade-agreement_b_7462578.html>.

Benedetteli, Massimo. 2020. *Could COVID-19 Emergency Measures Give Rise to Investment Claims? First Reflections from Italy.* Global Arbitration Review. March 26. <globalarbitrationreview.com/article/1222354/could-covid-19-emergency-measures-give-rise-to-investment-claims-first-reflections-from-italy>.

Bennett, Elizabeth. 2021. "Producer Agency in Certification Schemes: Challenges and Opportunities." International Institute for Environment and Development, Webinar, January 20. <https://www.iied.org/producer-agency-certification-schemes-challenges-opportunities>.

Berger, Axel. 2015. *Financing Global Development: Can Foreign Direct Investments be Increased through International Investment Agreements?* German Development Institute, September. Bonn, Germany. <die-gdi.de/uploads/media/BP_9.2015.pdf>.

Bernstein, H. 2000. "Colonialism, Capitalism, Development." In T. Allen and A.

Thomas (eds.), *Poverty and Development into the 21st Century*. Oxford: Oxford University Press.

Bhagwati, Jagdish. 2008. *Termites in the Trading System: How Preferential Agreements Undermine Free Trade*. Oxford: Oxford University Press.

Bissio, Roberto. 2017. *Is 'Gender' a Trojan Horse to Introduce New Issues at WTO?* Third World Network. <https://dawnnet.org/2017/12/is-gender-a-trojan-horse-to-introduce-new-issues-at-wto/>.

Björnsson, Olaf. 2020. *Toxic Tech: Occupational Poisoning in ICT Manufacturing*. Swedwatch, June 23 <https://swedwatch.org/wp-content/uploads/2021/01/98fi lipinerna20201215.pdf>.

Blackburn, Robin. 2011. *The American Crucible: Slavery, Emancipation and Human Rights*. London: Verso.

Bollyky, Thomas J., and Chad P. Bown. 2020. "The Tragedy of Vaccine Nationalism: Only Cooperation Can End the Pandemic." *Foreign Affairs*, September/October. <foreignaffairs.com/articles/united-states/2020-07-27/vaccine-nationalism-pandemic>.

Brack, Duncan. 2019. *Towards Sustainable Cocoa Supply Chains: Regulatory Options for the EU*. Fern, Tropenbos International, Fair Trade Advocacy Offices, June. <fern.org/news-resources/towards-sustainable-cocoa-supply-chains-regulatory-options-for-the-eu-1978/>.

Bunn, Christian, Peter Laderach, Juan Guillermo Pérez Jimenez, Christophe Montagnon, and Timothy Schilling. 2015. "Multiclass Classification of Agro-Ecological Zones for Arabica Coffee: An Improved Understanding of the Impacts of Climate Change." October, 27. *PLOS ONE*. <https://journals.plos.org/plosone/article/related?id=10.1371/journal.pone.0140490>.

BHRRC (Business and Human Rights Resource Center). 2019. *Over 100 Civil Society Organisations Call for EU Human Rights and Environmental Due Diligence Legislation*. December 2 <https://www.business-humanrights.org/en/latest-news/over-100-civil-society-organisations-call-for-eu-human-rights-and-environmental-due-diligence-legislation/>.

____. 2020. *Malaysia: Top Glove Denies Migrant Workers Producing ppe Are Exposed to Abusive Labour Practices & covid-19 Risk; Incl. Responses from Auditing Firms*. June 28 https://www.business-humanrights.org/en/latest-news/malaysia-top-glove-denies-migrant-workers-producing-ppe-are-exposed-to-abusive-labour-practices-covid-19-risk-incl-responses-from-auditing-firms/>.

Camargos, D. 2019. "Slave Labor Found at Second Starbucks-Certified Brazilian Coffee Farm." *Mongabay*, May 3. <https://news.mongabay.com/2019/05/slave-labor-found-at-second-starbucks-certified-brazilian-coffee-farm/>.

CARE International. 2017. *Made by Women: Dignified Work in Asia Impact Report 2017*. <https://www.care.at/wp-content/uploads/2017/12/Made-by-Women_Dignified-Work-in-Asia-Impact-Report-2017.pdf>.

Clark, Simon, and Heather Walsh. 2011. "Fair Trade Proving Anything But in Growing $6 Billion Market." *Bloomberg*, December 23. <bloomberg.com/news/articles/2011-12-23/fair-trade-proving-anything-but-to-farmers-with-6-billion-sales-at-stake>.

Clean Clothes Campaign. 2020. *Reality Check for the Bangladesh Garment Industry: What Needs to Be Addressed?* May 2. <https://cleanclothes.org/news/2020/reality-check-for-the-bangladesh-garment-industry-what-needs-to-be-addressed#:~:text=Clean%20Clothes%20Campaign%20believes%20a,in%20absence%20of%20worker%20voices.&text=Just%20over%20one%20year%20ago,protest%20their%20abominably%20low%20wages>.

Climate Institute. 2016. *A Brewing Storm: The Climate Change Risks to Coffee.* September. <https://files.fairtrade.net/publications/2016_TCI_ABrewingStorm.pdf>.

Climate Transparency. 2020. *The Climate Transparency Report.* Berlin, Germany <www.climate-transparency.org>.

Cockayne James. 2021. *Synopsis, Developing Freedom: The Sustainable Development Case for Ending Modern Slavery, Forced Labour and Human Trafficking.* New York: United Nations University.

Cooperative Coffees (Co-op Coffees). N.d. "About." <https://coopcoffees.coop/about/>.

Cope, Zak. 2019. *The Wealth of (Some) Nations: Imperialism and the Mechanics of Value Transfer.* London: Pluto Press.

Council of Canadians and Foodwatch. 2020. *Canada Using CETA to Attack Food Safety Rules, New Documents Reveal.* February 12. <canadians.org/ceta-EU-food-safety>.

Cranston, Chloe, Rocío Ramos, et al. 2020. *What If? Case Studies of Human Rights Abuses and Environmental Harm Linked to EU Companies, and How EU Due Diligence Laws Could Help Protect People and the Planet.* European Coalition for Corporate Justice (ECCJ), September 11. <https://corporatejustice.org/eccj-publications/16830-what-if-case-studies-of-human-rights-abuses-and-environmental-harm-linked-to-eu-companies-and-how-eu-due-diligence-laws-could-help-protect-people-and-the-planet>.

De Schutter Oliver. 2020. *Towards Mandatory Due Diligence in Global Supply Chains.* Prepared by Prof. Olivier De Schutter at the Request of the International Trade Union Confederation.<https://www.ituc-csi.org/IMG/pdf/de_schutte_mandatory_due_diligence.pdf>.

Dey, Sujata. 2019. "Agriculture." *Le libre-échange aujourd'hui: Bilan des accords de libre-échange soutenus par le Canada.* Pointe Calumet: M Éditeur.

Duggan, Kyle. 2018. "Drug Patent Extensions under CETA Could Cost Feds $270M a Year: pbo." *Ipolitics,* April 16. <ipolitics.ca/2018/04/26/drug-patent-extensions-under-ceta-could-cost-feds-270m-a-year-pbo/>.

Ecolabel Index. <http://www.ecolabelindex.com/>.

Ethical Trading Initiative. 2017. *The Joint Ethical Trading Initiative's Guide to Buying Responsibly.* <https://www.ethicaltrade.org/sites/default/files/shared_resources/guide_to_buying_responsibly.pdf>.

Fairtrade Canada. 2021. "What Is Fairtrade?" <https://fairtrade.ca/what-is-fairtrade/>.

Fairtrade International. "Gender Equality." <https://www.fairtrade.net/issue/gender-equality>.

___. 2015. "Equal Harvest: Removing the Barriers to Women's Participation in Smallholder Agriculture." March. <https://www.fairtrade.org.uk/wp-content/

uploads/legacy/doc/Equal%20Harvest%20Full%20Report%20v2.pdf>.

___. 2019. *Choosing a Fairer Future Through Trade: Annual Report 2018–2019.* Bonn: Fairtrade International.

___. 2021. "Our General Assembly and Board." <https://www.fairtrade.net/about/ga-and-board>.

Fairtrade Foundation. 2015. *Delivering the Sustainable Development Goals Through Trade — A Five-Point Agenda for Policy Coherence.* London: Fairtrade Foundation. <https://www.fairtrade.org.uk/wp-content/uploads/2020/07/Delivering-the-SDGs-through-Trade_Five-Point-Agenda_FINAL.pdf>.

Fairtrade Foundation and Mondelez International. 2018. *Fairtrade and Cocoa Life: Annual Partnership Statement 2017–18.* London: Fairtrade Foundation. <fairtrade.org.uk/wp-content/uploads/legacy/doc/Mondelez_Annual_Partnership_Statement_2.pdf>.

Food and Agriculture Organization of the United Nations. N.d. "India at a Glance." <http://www.fao.org/india/fao-in-india/india-at-a-glance/en/>.

Fridell, Gavin. 2014. *Coffee.* Cambridge, UK: Polity Press.

Friends of the Earth International. N.d. *The UN Treaty on Transnational Corporations and Human Rights.* <https://www.foei.org/un-treaty-tncs-human-rights>.

Global Labor Justice. 2018. *Gender Based Violence in the gap Garment Supply Chain and Gender Based Violence in the H&M Garment Supply Chain.* Reports to the ILO. Washington, DC: Global Labor Justice.

Hickel, Jason. 2017. *The Divide: A Brief Guide to Global Inequality and Its Solutions.* London: Heinemann.

Hudson, M., I. Hudson, and M. Fridell. 2013. *Fair Trade, Sustainability, and Social Change.* New York: Palgrave Macmillan.

Husser, Amy. 2018. "Will USMCA Affect Canada's Dug Prices? Depends on What Happens Next, Experts Say." CBC Online, October 2. <cbc.ca/news/health/usmca-pharma-drugs-prices-cost-1.4846421>.

Institute for Policy Studies. 2020. *US Billionaire Wealth Surges to $584 Billion, or 20 Percent, Since the Beginning of the Pandemic.* June 18. <ips-dc.org/us-billionaire-wealth-584-billion-20-percent-pandemic/>.

International Fair Trade Charter. 2018. September. <https://ce325540-bc7d-484f-b04a-a5cfded0ef09.filesusr.com/ugd/291e20_d0760267b37a41328b80e4df127f85cb.pdf>.

Investor Alliance for Human Rights. 2020. *Investors with US$5 Trillion Call on Governments to Institute Mandatory Human Rights Due Diligence Measures for Companies.* April 21. <https://investorsforhumanrights.org/news/investor-case-for-mhrdd>.

Ionova, Ana. 2017. "Chocolate Giants Are Moving Away from Fairtrade Labelling." *Independent,* September 4. <independent.co.uk/news/business/news/chocolate-fairtrade-labels-mondelez-cadbury-toblerone-unilever-tea-liptons-pg-tips-a7928421.html>.

Jaffee, D. 2010. "Fair Trade Standards, Corporate Participation, and Social Movement Responses in the United States." *Journal of Business Ethics,* 92.

Kennedy, Jonathan, and Lawrence King. 2014. "The Political Economy of Farmers'

Suicides in India: Indebted Cash-Crop Farmers with Marginal Landholdings Explain State-Level Variation in Suicide Rates." *Globalization and Health*, 10, 1. <DOI: 10.1186/1744-8603-10-16>.

Lekakis, E.J. 2012. "Will the Fair Trade Revolution Be Marketised? Commodification, Decommodification and the Political Intensity of Consumer Politics." *Culture & Organization,* 18, 5.

Lynch, Colum. 2020. "'America First' Versus 'The People's Vaccine.'" *Foreign Policy,* July 6. <foreignpolicy.com/2020/07/06/coronavirus-vaccine-nationalism-america-first-covax/>.

Macchi, Ciara, and Claire Bright. 2019. "Hardening Soft Law: The Implementation of Human Rights Due Diligence Requirements in Domestic Legislation." In Buscemi Martina, Lazzerini Nicole, Magi Laura, and Russo Deborah (eds.), *Legal sources in Business and Human Rights: Evolving Dynamics in International And European Law.* Leiden, Boston: Brill Nijhoff.

Macdonald, Laura, and Nadia Ibrahim. 2019. "Canada's Feminist Trade Policy: An Alternative to Austerity Trade Politics?" *Austerity and Its Alternatives,* February. <https://altausterity.mcmaster.ca/documents/laura-berlin-2019-to-post.pdf>.

McCall, Rosie. 2020. "Big Pharma Companies Earn More Profits than Most Other Industries, Study Suggests." *Newsweek,* March 4. <newsweek.com/big-pharma-companies-profits-industries-study-1490407>.

McLaughlin, David. 2018. "What the UN Panel's Special Climate Change Report Means for Canada." *International Institute for Sustainable Development* (IISD), October 19. <https://www.iisd.org/articles/ipcc-canada>.

Nadeau, Jean-François. 2020. "La main invisible." *Le Devoir,* March 16. <ledevoir.com/opinion/chroniques/575011/la-main-invisible>.

Nelson, Valerie, Olga Martin-Ortega and Michael Flint. 2020. *Making Human Rights Due Diligence Frameworks Work for Small Farmers and Workers.* University of Greenwich Report Commissioned by the Fair Trade Advocacy Office and Brot für die Welt. Chatham: UK.

Nieburg, Oliver. 2019. "What Next for Fair Trade after Confidence Crisis?" *Food Navigator,* December 11. <https://www.foodnavigator.com/Article/2019/12/11/What-next-for-fair-trade-food-and-drink>.

Nikiforuk, Andrew. 2020. "Ten Thoughts on the Power of Pandemics." *The Tyee,* March 17. <thetyee.ca/Analysis/2020/03/17/Ten-Ways-Pandemics-Change-Humanity/>.

Office of the United Nations High Commissioner for Human Rights. N.d. *State National Action Plans on Business and Human Rights.* <https://www.ohchr.org/en/issues/business/pages/nationalactionplans.aspx>.

Olivet, Cecilia, and Bettina Müller. 2020. *Juggling Crises: Latin America's Battle with COVID-19 Hampered by Investment Arbitration Cases.* The Transnational Institute, August 25. <longreads.tni.org/jugglingcrises>.

"Open Letter to Governments on isds and covid-19." Seattle to Brussels Network. <http://s2bnetwork.org/sign-the-pen-letter-to-governments-on-isds-and-covid-19/>.

Oxfam International. 2021. *The Inequality Virus.* January 25. <www.oxfam.org/en/research/inequality-virus>.

Patnaik, Utsa. 2006. "The Free Lunch: Transfers from the Tropical Colonies and Their Role in Capital Formation in Britain during the Industrial Revolution." In K.S. Jomo (ed.), *Globalization Under Hegemony: The Changing World Economy*. Oxford: Oxford University Press.

Piketty, T. 2020. *Capital and Ideology*. Harvard, MA: Belknap Press.

Rogelj, J., D. Shindell, K. Jiang, S. Fifita, P. Forster, et al. 2018. "Mitigation Pathways Compatible with 1.5°C in the Context of Sustainable Development." In V. Masson-Delmotte, P. Zhai, H.-O. Pörtner, D. Roberts, J. Skea, et al. (eds.), *Global Warming of 1.5°C. An IPCC Special Report on the Impacts of Global Warming of 1.5°C Above Pre-Industrial Levels and Related Global Greenhouse Gas Emission Pathways, in the Context of Strengthening the Global Response to the Threat of Climate Change, Sustainable Development, and Efforts to Eradicate Poverty*. <https://www.ipcc.ch/report/sr15/mitigation-pathways-compatible-with-1-5c-in-the-context-of-sustainable-4-development/>.

Roozen, Nico. 2017. "Blog: Ethical Branding — Overpromise and Underdeliver?" *Solidaridad*, April 20. <solidaridadnetwork.org/news/blog-ethical-branding-overpromise-and-underdeliver>.

Roozen, Nico, and Francisco van der Hoff. 2001. *La aventura del comerce equitable*. Paris: J.C. Lattès.

Ruskin, J., and C. Wilmer. 1986 [1860]. *Unto This Last and Other Writings*. New York: Penguin Classics.

Rutta, Rebecca, Rodd Myers, Sabaheta Ramcilovic-Suominen, and Constance McDermott. 2018. "FLEGT: Another 'Forestry Fad'?" *Environmental Science and Policy, 89*.

Sinclair, Scott. 2018. *Canada's Track Record Under NAFTA's Chapter 11*. Canadian Centre for Policy Alternatives. Ottawa, January. <policyalternatives.ca/sites/default/files/uploads/publications/National%20Office/2018/01/NAFTA%20Dispute%20Table%20Report%202018.pdf>.

Sinclair, Scott, and Stuart Trew. 2019. *Taking Stock of CETA*. Canadian Centre for Policy Alternatives. October 1. <policyalternatives.ca/publications/reports/taking-stock-ceta>.

Smit, Lise, et al. 2020. *Study on Due Diligence Requirements Through the Supply Chain*. February. <https://op.europa.eu/en/publication-detail/-/publication/8ba0a8fd-4c83-11ea-b8b7-01aa75ed71a1/language-en>.

Spinney, Laura. 2020. "Is Factory Farming to Blame for Coronavirus?" *Guardian*, March 28. <theguardian.com/world/2020/mar/28/is-factory-farming-to-blame-for-coronavirus>.

Stafford-Smith, M., D. Griggs, O. Gaffney, et al. 2017. "Integration: The Key to Implementing the Sustainable Development Goals." *Sustainability Science*, 12. <https://doi.org/10.1007/s11625-016-0383-3>.

Starbucks. 2016. "C.A.F.E. Practices — Generic Scorecard." <https://cdn.scsglobalservices.com/files/program_documents/cafe_scr_genericv3.4_011516.pdf>.

___. 2020. "C.A.F.E. Practices — Terms & Conditions — v4.0." <https://cdn.scsglobalservices.com/files/program_documents/C.A.F.E.%20Practices%20Terms%20and%20Conditions_v4.0_ENG_100220.pdf>.

Stephens, Beth. 2014. "The Curious History of the Alien Tort Statute." *Notre Dame Law Review,* 89.

TaxCoop. 2020. "TaxCoop — Top 5 Richest Canadian Billionaires During the Canadian COVID-19 Lockdown." May 25. <newswire.ca/news-releases/taxcoop-top-5-richest-canadian-billionaires-during-the-canadian-covid-19-lockdown-849047486.html>.

Taylor, B. Mark. 2020. "Litigating Sustainability — Towards a Taxonomy of Counter-Corporate Litigation." University of Oslo Faculty of Law Research Paper, No. 2020-08.

Taylor, Matthew, and Jonathan Watts. 2019. "Revealed: The 20 Firms Behind a Third of All Carbon Emissions." *Guardian,* October 9. <theguardian.com/environment/2019/oct/09/revealed-20-firms-third-carbon-emissions>.

Team Green Analytics (Green Analytics Corp. & Ontario Centre for Climate Impacts and Adaptation Resources). 2015. *The Economic Impacts of the Weather Effects of Climate Change on Communities. Final Report.* May 8. Ontario: Team Green Analytics.

United Nations. N.d. "The 17 Goals." <https://sdgs.un.org/goals>.

United Nations Convention on Biological Diversity. N.d. *Biodiversity & Climate Change. Key Messages from the Recent Reports and Assessments.* <https://spark.adobe.com/page/zp9cpWoK9eNBu/>.

United Nations Department of Economic and Social Affairs. N.d. "Indigenous Peoples: Climate Change, The Effects of Climate Change on Indigenous Peoples." <https://www.un.org/development/desa/indigenouspeoples/climate-change.html#:~:text=Indigenous%20peoples%20are%20among%20the,the%20environment%20and%20its%20resources>.

UNCTAD (United Nations Conference on Trade and Development). 2017. *Trade and Gender Toolbox.* <https://unctad.org/en/PublicationsLibrary/ditc2017d1_en.pdf>.

___. 2018. "Investor-State Dispute Settlement: Review of Developments in 2017." IIA Issues Note: International Investment Agreements (2).

___. 2020. "UNCTAD ISDS Navigator Update: Investment Treaty Disputes Hit 1,000 Mark." April 7. <investmentpolicy.unctad.org/news/hub/1644/20200407-unctad-isds-navigator-update-investment-treaty-disputes-hit-1-000-mark>.

United Nations Department of Economic and Social Affairs. 2019. *Safe Drinking Water, Sanitation, Are 'Basic Human Rights': New UN Water Development Report.* March 19. <https://www.un.org/development/desa/en/news/sustainable/new-un-water-development-report.html>.

Vanpeperstraete, Ben. 2021. "Towards an EU Import Ban on Forced Labour and Modern Slavery: Discussion Paper Commissioned by the Greens/efa Group in the European Parliament." February. <https://www.annacavazzini.eu/wp-content/uploads/Towards_an_EU_import_ban_on_forced_labour_and_modern_slavery_February.pdf>.

Vaughan-Whitehead, Daniel, and Luis Pinedo Caro. 2017. "Purchasing Practices and Working Conditions in Global Supply Chains: Global Survey Results." International Labour Organisation INWORK Policy Brief No. 10.

Vaillaincourt, Claude. 2019. *Le libre-échange aujourd'hui : Bilan des accords de libre-échange soutenus par le Canada.* Pointe Calumet: M Éditeur.

Van Harten, Gus. 2015. *An ISDS Carve-Out to Support Action on Climate Change.* Council of Canadians. Ottawa.

___. 2016. *Investment Treaties and the Internal Vetting of Regulatory Proposals: A Case Study from Canada.* Osgoode Legal Research Series. <digitalcommons.osgoode.yorku.ca/olsrps/151/>.

Westcott, Todd. 2018. *IPCC Report Shows World, Canada, Must Do More to Mitigate Climate Change.* Water Canada, October 10. <https://www.watercanada.net/ipcc-report-shows-world-canada-must-do-more-to-mitigate-climate-change/>.

Wetzels, Hans. 2019. "Countries Propose Treaty to End Corporate Impunity." United Nations African Renewal, April 9. <un.org/africarenewal/magazine/april-2019-july-2019/countries-propose-treaty-end-corporate-impunity>.

World Bank. N.d. "Data. CO2 Emissions (metric tons per capita)." <https://data.worldbank.org/indicator/EN.ATM.CO2E.PC>.

Index